VERONICA LAKE
VERONICA: THE AUTOBIOGRAPHY OF VERONICA LAKE

CONSTANCE Frances Marie Ockelman (Veronica Lake) was born in Brooklyn on November 14, 1922. Her father died when she was 10 years old.

After being expelled from a Catholic boarding school in Montreal, Veronica participated in beauty pageants in her teens. In 1938 she moved with her mother and step-father to Beverly Hills, and appeared as an extra in several films before her break-out role in *I Wanted Wings* (1940). Numerous starring roles followed, trading in part on Veronica's legendary and much-imitated 'peek-a-book' hair-style. These films included *Sullivan's Travels* (1941) and *The Blue Dahlia* (1946).

In the 1950's, following bankruptcy and her third divorce, Veronica moved to New York City, subsequently appearing mostly in live theatre in the USA and England. Her memoir *Veronica* was first published in 1969.

Other than travelling theatrical engagements, Veronica spent most of her final years living in Miami. She died, aged 50, in 1973, leaving two adult daughters and a son.

VERONICA LAKE

(WITH DONALD BAIN)

VERONICA
THE AUTOBIOGRAPHY OF
VERONICA LAKE

With an introduction by
Eddie Muller

DEAN STREET PRESS

Published by Dean Street Press 2020

Copyright © 1969 Veronica Lake

Introduction © 2020 Eddie Muller

All Rights Reserved

Published by licence, issued under the UK Orphan Works
Licensing Scheme.

First published in 1969 by W.H. Allen (UK), and 1970 by
Citadel Press (US)

Cover by DSP

ISBN 978 1 913054 73 1

www.deanstreetpress.co.uk

To the gleam in the eye of my friend and editor,
Samuel H. Post

AND

Thank goodness for Courtney Wright, my dear
friend in New York

INTRODUCTION

VERONICA Lake, movie star, was a tiny but luminous beacon of sexiness and sass who shined bright and cool during the dark days of World War II. Barely out of her teens, she became an icon of mid-20th century America. Women emulated her spunk and style and that famous come-hither cascade of blonde luster. Men fantasized about her. The movie business exploited her. She lived high, metaphorically and literally, working and cavorting with the most beautiful and talented people in the world.

Constance "Connie" Ockleman, working stiff, was a gal with no great aspirations, no grand illusions. She lived hand-to-mouth, never sure of her future, the wolf always at the door. She was regular folk, both a clock-puncher and a vagabond, never above an honest day's labor. She was a struggling single mother and, by her own admission, not very good at it. She liked to laugh, loved a party, and had a wicked sense of humor. She could fly a plane, mix a cocktail, and knock you on your ass with a short right cross.

That they're the same woman, co-existing in a single face and body, makes for a remarkable, enthralling story. What a gift to hear it from Connie/Veronica in her own words, ones that are sharp, funny, sensitive, honest, and heartbreaking. She tells her story with an easy eloquence that, at times, is as breathtaking in its self-awareness as it's startling in its ambivalence.

I knew the image of Veronica Lake before I ever appreciated the actress who embodied it. She was parodied in comic books and TV shows for years after her glorious star had dimmed. Such was the shimmering afterglow left by this diminutive damsel. She may have been barely five-feet tall, but she photographed big enough to fill anyone's imagination. Let's be honest—Veronica Lake was doing Lauren Bacall before Betty Joan Perske had even screen-tested for *To Have and Have Not*. The insouciance, the take-it-or-leave-it flirtatiousness, the "Watch it, buster!" self-reliance—Veronica Lake always had it, in spades.

But, like so many actresses in Hollywood, she got labeled by the guys who run the show: temptress, siren, vixen, femme fatale

. . . these tags are still affixed to her, to this day, even though she rarely played the part onscreen. Watching Lake now, in films like *Sullivan's Travels*, *The Glass Key*, and *This Gun for Hire*, it's her feisty spirit, more than her physical allure, that's the main attraction. Men may have seen her as a sex kitten, but women—then and now—see her as a cat who could take care of herself. This was no doubt a huge part of her appeal during wartime, as it is now for retro-savvy women who religiously watch Turner Classic Movies.

Yet in her prime, the doubters could be cruel. Raymond Chandler should have been ashamed for his schoolboy jibe, calling the star of his only original screenplay, *The Blue Dahlia*, "Moronica Lake." And when I once asked André de Toth for insight into his relationship with Lake, he merely spoke of her as a "fallen angel" whom he'd tried and failed to "save." Reading Lake's own account of their marriage puts a decidedly different spin on things. De Toth's protection of her was, of course, a form of possession. And one thing Ms. Lake makes clear in her memoir is that she was a naturally rebellious sort who had no intention of being possessed.

In fact, the Hollywood performer Lake most reminds me of—and this came as an amusing realization given their colossal physical dissimilarity—is Sterling Hayden, another reluctant star and natural-born rebel who turned his back on Hollywood, swapping fame for life as a nomadic free spirit.

Part of Veronica's rebellion, like Hayden's, was a fondness for drink and, presumably, drugs—a predilection she discusses openly, if delicately. In the 1949 film *Slattery's Hurricane*, André de Toth cast his then-wife in the role of an addict, with veiled allusions to heroin use. He told me her casting was intended as "shock therapy." Her reputation for being difficult on sets—and inebriated off them—cost her dearly. She was going to be cast in the cult classic *Gun Crazy* (a role that made Peggy Cummins a legend), but the producers were warned to steer clear of her.

Some readers, mining these pages for sordid details, may find Lake's discussion of her vices a bit coy. I don't. It's her story, she's telling it, and she should be allowed whatever measure of restraint and dignity she desires. I'll point out instead that while the public has granted Sterling Hayden, a legendary boozer and hash-head, a legacy as a heroic, larger-than-life iconoclast, it has branded Lake's life after Hollywood a steady downward spiral of abasement, worthy only of pity. Blame a cultural double standard that applauds reckless rebellion in men but shames it in women.

Having myself collaborated on a similar movie star autobiography, *Tab Hunter Confidential: The Making of a Movie Star*, I appreciate Donald Bain's contribution to this book. I have no idea how he came to be the sounding board, organizer, and editor of Ms. Lake's saga, but we can all be grateful he was Johnny-on-the-Spot, the right person at the right time. He does a commendable job respecting the balance between the woman's two selves, letting Connie come through Veronica's guise, bright and clear. It speaks to a bond of trust they shared, the most critical factor in a project such as this. Being the caretaker of a person's life story is a weighty responsibility. My heart broke a little—from sadness, not surprise—when I learned that after her death, Donald Bain also assumed responsibility for Veronica Lake's cremated remains. No one else came forward.

This is a courageous, beautiful book. I don't feel it is sad, although some surely will. Many people believe a life well lived is supposed to culminate in material wealth and an expansive family. Not renegades—for them, living on their own terms is both the adventure and the reward, whatever pain or glory results. That's why I can't see her tale as a tragedy, despite its premature ending. Once you know the whole story, maybe you too will find Connie Ockleman as memorable as her cinematic chimera, Veronica Lake.

Eddie Muller

1

VERONICA Lake is a Hollywood creation. Hollywood is good at doing that sort of thing. Its proficiency at transforming little Connie Ockleman of Brooklyn into sultry, sensuous Veronica Lake was proved by the success of the venture. And the subject, me, was willing and in some small ways able.

I don't mean to imply that Veronica Lake is pure past tense. I still sign my checks Veronica Lake. My telephone is listed under that name. And, in general, I *am still* Veronica Lake.

But it would be spurious to write this book from Veronica's point of view. Constance Ockleman has been the veracious liver of the life, and she's the proper person to tell the story.

l was sixteen when I first saw Hollywood. My first stepfather, mother, cousin Helen and I made the automobile trip from Florida in the summer of 1938. The car was a Chrysler Airflow and I remember the all night drive across the final stretch of desert and crossing the California state line early the next morning. It was the Fourth of July, a significant date in American history and certainly in my life.

Hollywood had, quite naturally, captured my imagination as it had that of most other young girls. It had exerted its powerful and mysterious magnetism in darkened theatres where shadowy images flickered on large screens and dashing gentlemen spoke to frail, beautiful women, their words in surprising syncopation with their lips. Romance prevailed at all times. I'd sit there, popcorn, purchased with money saved by walking instead of riding clutched tightly on my lap, and be swept away, far away with whatever particular hero happened to reign that Saturday. What splendor fifty cents could buy. What virile men and what fortunate women to be with those men.

Of course, it isn't that way today, with shared knowledge that the leading male box office idol is really homosexual, and the top siren of the screen is asexual and smokes pot—alone.

But Hollywood promised something to everyone. As with aviation, 1938 pointed to bigger and better things; jets to replace

Ford Tri-Motors and new stars to replace old. And where did new stars come from? Heaven, maybe, or some place equally as vague.

And there I was in 1938. I was in Hollywood. And strangely enough, it didn't seem any different from any other place I'd seen. We drove through streets, each looking out his or her window for movie stars or gold pavements or anything to fulfill the promise. And it looked the same as Florida, or Brooklyn, or even Saranac or Placid in summer, with only minor variations not worth mentioning.

Why the hell I expected it to look any different is something else again. I find myself being drawn into a shell of feigned sophistication as I think of my autobiography. How nice to present a devil-may-care attitude when reaching back into your own private past, a past with no one really to refute what you say about your inner feelings. It's a strong temptation to lie, or at least embellish, which is probably why any autobiography is usually less true than biographies written by the impartial bystander.

But I won't succumb at this early stage to such an impulse. Veronica Lake might. Not Constance Ockleman.

I certainly wasn't blasé when I saw my first real live star. We'd driven around for over an hour when hunger dictated the next move. We found a drive-in restaurant, pulled in and happily ordered hamburgers and Cokes. We'd almost finished eating when another car pulled in alongside ours. I looked over and there behind the wheel sat Ann Shirley. I over-reacted, of course. What would you expect of a fifteen-year-old girl?

"There's Ann Shirley," I babbled.

"Where?" My mother also over-reacted, which was not at all unusual. I didn't realize it fully then, but there was little doubt my mother was banking on a film career for her only child. Maybe Ann Shirley could help things along.

"Next to us." I'd fallen into a whisper for fear she'd overhear.

"Why don't you go over and say hello, Connie?" my mother suggested with a smile to breed confidence.

"Oh no, Mommy." She insisted I call her Mommy.

I couldn't. I just sat there gaping through the window, turning away now and then to avoid being caught. I was actually relieved Miss Shirley finished her hamburger, the same kind we enjoyed, paid the girl the same amount of money it would cost us, and drove away. I sighed a long sigh of satisfaction at having seen a movie star.

My mother's sigh was equally as long, but indicated a different emotion.

At that point I was ready to head back home to friends and familiar surroundings. The trip, now that I'd seen a Hollywood personality, was over for me. There didn't seem any sense in staying longer.

But Hollywood was home now. Our new home. And it was to be my home until 1952.

We moved into a small rented bungalow on Oakhurst Drive, Beverly. It wasn't twenty-four hours before I'd forgotten about being in Hollywood and about movie stars and other star-spangled dreams. It was just a matter of settling into a new neighborhood, searching out new friends, finding one's way after losing the security of ways already explored and charted.

Thank goodness for Helen Nelson, my cousin. We were more chums than blood relations, and we soon set out to establish rapport with Los Angeles. It was easier together, as is usually the case. We did sixteen-year-old things, ordinary things, and found sixteen-year-old enjoyment from them. There wasn't the smog then, and we'd walk along together in the warm California sun enjoying whistles and comments from drugstore cowboys and new street names and giggle-giggle at almost everything. I had a full figure at sixteen, with surprisingly full breasts, a fact that many people assume was *never* the case with me. Why people think short girls must also be flat-chested is beyond me. I jutted out in front pretty good and was aware enough at that age to be able to walk certain ways to give me some jiggle and jounce. I knew the boys enjoyed that sort of thing, and I enjoyed their enjoyment.

Sometimes, when we wanted to discourage a boy from continuing his awkward advances, we'd set him up a little by encouraging him along. Then I'd say something to Helen like, "Have you ever heard anything so childish?" Or, "How do you like *that*?" with emphatic rising inflection at the end.

Adapting to the new situation really didn't prove as trying an experience as it might have been. Change had been a fairly constant part of my life.

I was born in Brooklyn, spent my pre-school years in Florida, my grade-school years in Brooklyn, and my high school years in Florida and Montreal. No, my roots weren't as deep as they might have been under other family circumstances. I'd even taken on a new name. Constance Ockleman became Constance Keane with my father's death in February 1932, and my mother's remarriage a year later to Anthony Keane, a staff artist with the *New York Herald Tribune*. I liked my stepfather, although I didn't know him very well and he in no way served to replace my real father. Little girls like their daddy, and I adored mine. But Anthony Keane was nice, an outgoing man with certain warmth and the ability to make you feel comfortable when he was with you. My mother knew him before my father died, and I suppose loved him, at least enough to marry him.

I'm quite certain in retrospect that part of my ready acceptance of this new father was the fact he wasn't a well man. His frailty brought me closer to him. I'd always been attracted to the sick or unattractive, and still am. I don't mean to have you presume me a patron saint of the unfortunate. Far from it. In many cases people drawn to less fortunate people are somewhat perverted, or, at best, are playing out and satisfying certain self-serving interests and needs. It's good these people exist, no matter what the motivation. They do help their fellow men, and you can't fault that. I'm not looking for faults in my own make-up, either. I've got enough without looking for them. It just seems honest to admit to the possibility of less than philanthropic inducement for my actions.

I spent most of my first year in Hollywood killing time. Sure, I thought of becoming an actress from time to time. But it was daydreamed in passing; there was no compulsion, no inner drive that lent urgency to the notion. It was still little-girl romanticizing without basis or, most important, without a potential resolution of the dream. I'd talk big sometimes but it was just talk. Like when I announced to Helen as we passed Grauman's Chinese Theatre, "Someday my hand print will be there," pointing at the famous cement. I was asked to join the concrete hands of Grauman's after

I became a star and turned it down. No special reason. I just didn't feel like it.

I was enrolled by my mother at the Bliss Hayden School of Acting on Wilshire Boulevard. I'd met some girls who were working as extras in films and again, without the proverbial stars in my eyes, entered the school because it was something to do.

(I apologize here for taking time to again stress my attitudes towards a career in motion pictures. So many girls enter acting classes convinced they will become stars. They must become stars and seldom do. I began lessons convinced I would not become a movie star. Or, to soften my vehemence, quite sure it could not happen until I was at least fifty years old.)

Studying at the Bliss Hayden School was fun, although hardly stimulating. We would put together scenes from various plays, each with a broad range of parts that would not prove too discouraging for us. There was no sense in losing paying pupils.

I remember starring in many of these intra-squad productions and giving my all with such lines as:

"Good morning, mothaaaaaa."

"Dinaaaaaa is served."

Or even,

"Tennis anyone?????"

We also indulged in the inevitable exercises of walking into a room with a heavy book balanced precariously on your head, walking down steps with chin held high, and talking in time with a metronome, the latter a funny feat but one I've always been suspicious of in terms of furthering an acting career.

But it was all enjoyable, and since that's the only reason I ever showed up at all, I can't complain.

I did make a lot of friends at Bliss Hayden, many of them girls working around town as extras. And one of them, Gwen Horn, was directly responsible for my ever appearing in a film in the first place.

Gwen had been notified of a casting call for *Sorority House*, a feature with James Ellison, Barbara Read, Adele Pearce and none other than Ann Shirley.

It would be flattering to Gwen and very showbiz to say she convinced me to answer the call with her because she'd seen some hidden acting ability gone unnoticed by the Bliss Hayden instructors. But that isn't the way it happened.

"Connie, I've got to make this call at RKO for *Sorority House*. Come on with me and keep me company."

"Sure Gwen, I'd be happy to."

That's what happened. I went with Gwen and they gave both of us parts.

You don't have to act very much to be an extra in films. Casting directors choose extras simply because they look like the kind of people you'd expect to see in a given scene. In fact, directors will occasionally get damned mad at an extra who does act, and is caught at it. In a way, extras are supposed to be the only real people in a movie. It's just plain old you there on the screen, not trying to emote in any way but just *there* on the street while the good guy kills the bad guy, or *there* in the audience as the singer sings his heart out in lip sync.

I stood completely in awe of John Farrow, the film's director. He was not only a fine director but was a fine man. He'd been knighted by the Catholic Church for writing *Father Damien and the Leper*. You remember the Father Damien story, don't you? He was the Belgian missionary to the lepers of Molokai.

Well, John Farrow was obviously a very good Catholic. And it impressed me. I was a Catholic also, but one of the growing number who even then began a gradual slide away from the church's dogma. I'd already begun my religious decline, but you don't easily shake the Roman Catholic Church. I was sufficiently saturated still to respond automatically to a "good Catholic," and John Farrow fell into that category.

I was also impressed with Ann Shirley. I wanted so much to tell her about the drive-in but never really found the nerve.

I did talk to her on my last day of shooting.

"I never thought I'd be in a film with you, Miss Shirley," I told her, or something equally insipid.

"I hope you're in many more," she answered.

I doubted if I would be. But the thought did have its appeal. I was learning more just standing around watching the professionals work than I'd learned in all the academic exercises at Bliss

Hayden. But that's usual in any field, and I cannot refute the benefits I received from classroom training. Mr. Hayden himself was very encouraging to all the students, and he did help me build some smattering of confidence.

I've thought many times how nice it would have been to have enjoyed more formal training. Schooling of any kind enables you to become so sure of the basic skills and tools of your trade that you don't have to waste precious energy thinking about them. You're free to use them naturally in developing whatever it is you're doing. Fortunately, I was blessed with some unexplainable intuition about performing. That isn't an egotistical statement. It doesn't mean I was born a gifted actress. There were occasional critics who thought I was slightly gifted, at least in those specific roles they reviewed. Bless those few.

But I did have a certain natural feel at times for what to do in a given situation. And having that went a long way in making up deficiencies in academic training.

I also talked with John Farrow during that day. The scenes in which I appeared were completed, and I drew a deep breath before approaching him. Actually, I was about to indulge in a sophomoric stunt to indicate to him my esteem for his religious strength.

I'd decided to wait until my involvement in the film was completely finished. I didn't want to do anything that might be constructed as currying favor with the director. The last thing I wanted was to be known as a young, ass-kissing extra looking for bigger and better parts. That's a pretty silly attitude when you think about it. It was totally accepted for a young girl to offer herself to anyone of importance in return for a break in films. My little token offering was straight out of *Snow White*.

My gift to John Farrow was, in fact, a gift to me from an aunt on the Keane side who was a nun. She was constantly sending me religious articles that had been blessed by the Pope. Whether she did this believing me to have deep love for the church, or because she was given divine inspiration into my falling from grace, is unknown to me to this day. The important thing is she *did* send me these gifts quite regularly. And as disillusioned as I was with things religious, I wasn't sure enough to come out with a final condemnation.

I suppose I was trying to copper my chances with heaven and hell, a cowardly approach but practical, you'll admit.

"Mr. Farrow," I said with as much spunk as I could muster at the time, "I'm Catholic, too . . . like you . . . and I'd like you to have this, if you don't mind."

He was surprised. I think he wanted to laugh, or didn't want to but couldn't help himself. Maybe it was the southern accent into which I'd slipped. Maybe it was my size, two inches over five feet and about 95 pounds.

His control was admirable. He stood with the medal and chain in his hand and thought of what to say.

"That's very thoughtful, Connie. Thank you."

"And thank you for having me in your film."

I quickly walked away and cried when I reached the outside air. What a dumb stunt, I told myself. But I was also pleased. In a word, I was confused, natural enough for a sixteen-year-old girl. The fact that I'm still confused about most things is less understandable.

2

THE NEXT bit part was in an RKO three-reeler with Leon Erroll. It was called *The Wrong Room* and in it I played Leon's child bride. All I had to do was faint every time he entered the room. Strangely enough, I wore a dress in the film that had been designed for Ann Shirley.

I've never seen *The Wrong Room* and would love to. I've often thought of calling one of the Miami TV stations that programs a show called "Funny Flickers" and ask them if they could find a print. It was straight slapstick and seeing it would bring back many fond memories for me.

And then on to Metro as a run-of-the-picture bit player in the Eddie Cantor film, *Forty Little Mothers*. And here begins the incredible, stranger-than-fiction saga of that world famous peek-a-boo, striptease, sheepdog, bad-girl hair style known the world over as Veronica Lake's stock-in-trade.

But it really wasn't Veronica Lake who introduced that hair style to the movie-going public. It was Constance Keane, and she did it at the suggestion of Busby Berkeley.

We did some scenes in *Forty Little Mothers* in which I engaged in some moderate physical activity. My hair is fine, naturally blonde and damned hard to manage. I spent my whole life trying to keep it from falling in my eyes. It's annoying to walk around half blind. And dangerous.

It fell over my one eye during the filming of the Cantor film, and I was very upset about the whole thing. So was Cantor.

But Berkeley, the director, wasn't.

"If I were you, Eddie, I'd let it fall," he suggested to Cantor.

"She looks like some damned sheepdog, Buzz. It's a mess." I agreed silently with the star.

But Berkeley wasn't to be put off.

"I still say let it fall. It distinguishes her from the rest."

Eddie Cantor, the film's star, respected Buzz Berkeley and allowed me to function with one eye.

So *Forty Little Mothers* presented "the" hair style of the century. The only problem was that no one noticed. I did, of course, but from a negative sense of ego. Yes, it did distinguish me from the other female extras. But it seemed an unfortunate way to gain notoriety.

It was forgotten, my hair went back up behind my ears at all times, and I continued killing time in Hollywood.

I've always loved to walk. And I took many long walks that year, sometimes at the shore where I'd breathe deeply to fill myself with the smell and sense of the sea. There were walks through nearby mountains and valleys, the fresh air clean and cool with its special promise of good things to come. Not good things of a practical nature. Just good, never-to-be-explained goodness that seems so difficult to find these peculiar days.

I'd also walk through the lots of the studios, stopping now and then to watch an exterior scene being photographed: a western chase with the stunt men risking their necks in performing the impossible while the stars, presumed in the saddle by their publics, lounged comfortably and safely under a tree; love scenes under evening southern skies (filtered in daylight) and very weepy willow trees, each nailed to a box that was held in place with taut guide wires; gallant men braving wind and rain driven by giant electric fans blowing water from garden hoses; ships being destroyed at sea, the sea nothing more than an oversized swimming-pool, the ships miniatures propelled by rods under the water. It was interesting, but also disillusioning. I remember having the same feeling of disenchantment when I attended my first radio show. When you sit at home in front of a radio, at least in the days when drama and comedy held court and all this horrible rock and roll and hysterical disc jockey dribble was nothing more than an undiscovered dream of today's promoters, you could be swept as far as your imagination could carry you. You never once wondered how the scenes, each so vivid in its imagery as it assaulted your ears and mind, were actually created. It made no difference. You believed.

And then you attend the live broadcast and see the bored actors and actresses waiting their turn at the mike, crumpled scripts in hand, sound effects man ready for cues to shake the sheet metal for thunder and wrinkle the Cellophane for fire and clump the wooden pegs on the table for marching feet.

I felt a little cheated watching movies being made in bits and pieces, never what they really seemed to be, a technician's medium.

I did feel "in" being granted access to studio lots. I was a working extra, and that entitled you to be there. And if I hadn't been there that certain day in the spring of 1939, there might never have been a Veronica Lake. I might still be Constance Keane, or Ockleman, or whatever.

On that day I was strolling past the offices of some of Metro's directors. One of them, Freddie Wilcox, poked his head out of his door and stopped me.

"Hey, kid."

I was always good at double takes.

"Me?"

"Yes. I'm Freddie Wilcox."

What do you say?

"Oh."

"I'm a director here at Metro."

"I know. I mean, I've heard of you. You're a director . . . a good one too, I know."

"Thanks."

At this point I was probably doing some ridiculous pigeon-foot-in-the-sand routine.

"What's your name?" Wilcox asked.

"Connie. Connie Keane."

"You an extra?"

"Yes."

"What've you been doing?"

"I'm an extra . . . Oh, what films you mean . . . Well, *Sorority House, Forty Little Mothers, All Women Have* . . ." He cut me off.

"You know what?"

"What?"

"You look very interesting. I mean that. You look like a very interesting type."

Now I was wary. At this point in my life I was convinced every male in the movie business was on the make. Now that I think of it, all men are on the make. But Hollywood gives a young girl the aura of one giant, self-contained orgy farm, its inhabitants dedicated to crawling into every pair of pants they can find. And you become egotistical enough to think you're the prime pair of pants. You don't believe anyone. You don't trust a soul. You say to yourself over and over you won't sacrifice your precious virginity for the sake of a career like so many before you. It's all pretty stupid, of course, and naïve. But at seventeen you've got the right to think this way.

I think I snarled at Freddie Wilcox. And covered my breasts with crossed arms.

"In fact," he continued, "the first thing that crossed my mind when I saw you walk past was that there goes a star."

Come on, fella.

But then he smiled.

"I'm legitimate, sweetie. Believe me."

He began to look less menacing. I smiled. He smiled again.

"How about my setting up a screen test for you? Can you act as good as you look?"

"Oh, I'm a good actress. I really am."

He bristled a little at my cockiness. But the smile replaced the slight wince.

"Call me next week, Connie, and we'll set up a test." With that he turned and went back into his office. I continued my walk and had the strangest feeling of both elation and depression.

"So what?" I said to myself. "Who wants to be a movie star anyway?"

I decided I did.

3

BLASÉ little Connie Ockleman had succumbed. The stardust had penetrated my pores and I was ready for the fling. I did automatically adopt a pessimistic shell as protection against possible failure. Secretly, I advanced the whole situation to unlimited success for myself. But on the outside, I laughed it off and joked about the whole affair.

Mentioning the Freddie Wilcox thing to my mother was a mistake. She immediately leaped into things as the star-maker, telling me every minute what to do and how to act with him and on and on until I was ready to scream.

I called Freddie Wilcox and he arranged the test. I could feel the tension progressively building every day leading up to the big moment. It would come at strange times, like when I was brushing my teeth or reading a book or talking to a girl friend on the phone. It would catch me in the pit of my stomach and hang on until some thought or action replaced it.

By three days before the test I was a wreck. I told myself over and over it was silly to be so nervous, especially about a screen test. I didn't want to be an actress, I reminded myself. And then myself reminded me that I did want to be an actress.

The test was to be on a Thursday. That Tuesday, my stepfather suffered a complete collapse of the left lung. He was in serious condition. I watched him twist up in the agony of not being able to breathe and watched my mother reach and maintain a peak of hysteria. The doctor sent her next door and had her put under heavy sedation. Her dramatics weren't helping anyone, especially my stepfather. He wouldn't let my mother near him. I stayed close and he seemed to like that. The amazing thing was that Freddie Wilcox heard about the condition at home and arranged for around-the-clock nurses for my stepdad. It was an incredible show of generosity and I've always been grateful. And Freddie had a chauffeur-driven limousine take me for a ride in the country the morning of the test to help me relax. Quite a guy.

I enjoyed helping my stepfather. He would allow only me to help him to the bathroom. He was an Irishman with old country Irish pride. It pained him to be so helpless in front of me, but it pained him more to accept the help of my mother or the nurses. He'd lean on me to the bathroom and sometimes I would even have to hold his penis for him while he went.

My mother seemed to resent this close relationship I enjoyed with my stepfather. His sickness and my help drew us closer together, my mother's resentment only further cementing the bond.

He did eventually get better. The two of us went to The Brown Derby restaurant to celebrate his recovery. We got bombed together on Zombies, and when I mentioned helping him in the bathroom, he blushed almost purple. He didn't remember.

My mother snapped out of her dramatic hysteria when it came time for me to go to the screen test. She smeared me with make-up despite my protests.

"They'll have a make-up man, Mommy," I pleaded. She put on a hurt look designed to make me feel the complete and total ingrate.

"You're here, aren't you, Connie? You're here because I cared and always knew how to make you look your best."

"Yes Mommy." I could barely keep my eyes open with the heavy, weight-like false eyelashes she attached as the final touch. The rest of my face was smeared with gop and goo.

She put on the final touches of my make-up and stood back to admire her work.

"There. You look just like a movie star."

"Thank you, Mommy."

"Now do your best, Connie. And don't worry about your father. He'll do fine."

"Yes, Mommy."

We stood silently apart in the small living-room. I thought of my stepfather and suddenly felt very ashamed, just as today when I pray to a god I know doesn't exist. There I stood, looking like an end-of-the-road whore waiting to go through some silly antics known as a screen test. And with him dying.

"Smile, Connie. Smile big. They like big smiles."

"Yes, Mommy."

I don't think there was anyone present at that test who didn't want to crawl under the nearest false grass mat. I did the test with a piano player named Franz something or other. He was an excellent piano player and a very good actor. And I was terrible. Freddie Wilcox tried so hard to get something out of me but nothing I did made any sense at all. Finally, with great shaking of his head, he walked out muttering, "No, no, no, no, no."

"I'm sorry," I said to the cameraman.

"Forty years from now who'll know?" He laughed and capped his lens.

My self-imposed shell of pessimism hadn't worked at all. I was shattered, dismal and humiliated. I could picture Freddie Wilcox sitting at some bar telling his friends about this little blonde broad who was the worst actress he'd ever worked with. Or sitting alone getting drunk and questioning his ability to recognize talent when he saw it.

My mother was waiting at the door when I came home.

"Was it good?" she asked.

"How's Dad, Mommy?"

"Fine. How was the test?"

"It was fine, Mommy. They say I did very good."

"That's good, Connie. That's good."

And then the tears came. They've always come easily for me.

"Why are you crying, Connie?"

"Just because I'm happy, Mommy. Just because I'm so happy."

4

I DID a few more bit parts for Metro, acquired an agent, the William Morris Agency, and pursued once again the business of hanging around Hollywood. The screen test, reluctantly delivered to William Morris, had completely deflated any ego I may have possessed. But simply having an agent, a fact worn as a badge by everyone in Hollywood, did something for my confidence. It really wasn't confidence that I'd succeed in motion pictures. It was more like confidence that I wouldn't be hit by a car in the next six months.

My stepfather wasn't doing very well. I resigned myself to losing another father, but never thought much beyond that. There would always be my mother, a fact of life I viewed with mixed feelings. I found myself thinking only of finding freedom. It wasn't a matter of loving or hating my parents. That's probably why a lot of kids leave home, but with me it was simply the need to be my own person all the way, to think my own way and do my own thing.

Naturally, such expression of my inner thoughts was met with raised eyebrows for openers, and direct and vehement accusations as a follow-up. How ungrateful I must be to leave those who love me most. What did I want, to run free and get in trouble and make a moral mess of myself?

No, I'd answer in silence. *No*. I wanted only peace and quiet. I wanted to progress at my own pace and level without a push or shove in pursuit of the goals. I wanted a lot of things I probably didn't deserve, but I wanted them none the less. And I found as years went by that peace, inner and outer peace, was the only goal worth going after.

I found myself going on more and more auditions now that I had an agent working for me. But let me state right here and now that the Agency might be red-hot for some people, but I was never satisfied with what they did for me. I can hear all the black suit, white-on-white agents moaning now. Only Johnny Hyde seemed interested in *me* and what was good for *me*.

"Ungrateful little bitch," they'll mutter. "Every dame who makes it blasts their agent *after* they've made it."

That's probably very true.

Making the rounds as an aspiring actress can create a vast and varied number of impressions, both sad and funny. Naturally, there are too many men who view the whole casting interview as license for sex. You know, the old couch casting routine. And if you'd like to credit them with a certain amount of common sense, they were right in feeling this way. Getting into the movies was a big deal for girls those days. It still is, I suppose, but with morals and sexual attitudes looser and freer, putting out for a role doesn't seem so special any more. It isn't as much of an excuse as in the Forties.

But many producers know the girls who come through their office doors desperately want a part. In many cases, it's a matter of pride; what to write their parents or boy friends back in Waterloo or Louisville or Amarillo about Hollywood and how it's being so good to them. They have to succeed because they were told they wouldn't when they pulled up their roots and headed west.

The town was crawling with out-of-town girls who were there trying to prove something to someone back home. And the longer they went without even a crowd scene in a Grade B thriller, the more desperate they became. And producers sense this.

Producers also know Hollywood is synonymous with sex in many people's minds. For some reason, what's wrong some place else is accepted if it happens in Hollywood. Many producers strike accordingly.

But now I'll contradict myself and say there are probably more good guys than bad. Most producers at the major and important small studios are straight and stick to business.

It's the smaller operator who figures he's not going to make money in films so he might as well make as many girls as possible.

I remember meeting one of these small-time movie moguls, a greasy fellow with bad breath and dandruff. I met him at a small Italian restaurant and he went into raves over my looks, figure, smile and personality. I sensed he was a phoney, but figured it couldn't hurt to at least follow up on his offer of a small part in a low-budget film he was currently filming.

He had a small building on Wilshire, and I showed up at the appointed time. His office was grubby and looked very temporary. He greeted me himself and we talked a few minutes about his film.

"How much are you paying?" I asked.

"If you do a good job, fifty bucks a day. And I can keep you working steady."

"Can I see a script?"

"Script?" He went into gales of dirty laughter and finally sat back against the wall.

"There's no script, baby. No need for a script. This script was written by the cave men. Come on, I'll show you."

He led me into a room behind his office. There, under a battery of lights, were two girls and a hairy man. They were naked and were entwined together on a mattress on the floor.

I was shocked. The three bodies were in violent motion and the camera rolled on capturing every one of their actions.

"Oh, no," I said and turned away. "I'm not a girl for you."

My producer friend grabbed me by the arm and held tight.

"Hey, baby. Don't tell me you haven't made that scene before, only for some big shot type who only promised you something some day. I've got cash on the line and all you gotta do is lay back and enjoy it."

His bad breath almost overcame me.

"No," I said loudly and shook away from his grip.

He followed me back through the door and into his office. His face turned very hard and cruel, and he shoved his index finger hard against my shoulder.

"Listen, baby, you walk outta here and you go talkin' about this and I'm in big trouble. But you're in bigger trouble, baby, 'cause I'll find you again and tear your crotch out."

Oh, did I run. I ran and ran until I thought my lungs and heart would burst. Later, I did mention the incident to a few of my friends and was absolutely floored to find that some of them paid their rent many months by appearing in pornographic films.

"Sure, I know the guy you're talking about," one of them told me. "He's one of the nicest guys in that business."

The bad ones must be beautiful.

I had only one other incident where the producer involved came up with too strong a pitch for my blood. I had an appointment with this gentleman one late afternoon in the winter. His name shall go without mention for two reasons: it would be terribly embarrassing for him, enough so that he'd undoubtedly sue me for everything I haven't got; and we've become very good friends since the day in question. I'm very fond of him and can only explain away his actions that afternoon by saying he was trying, and that's man's natural inclination. It's just that most men are more subtle.

His secretary ushered me into his office. I smiled broadly at him and took the chair he indicated in front of his desk. It was an elegant room, richly panelled in dark wood and made to look huge by the sea of green carpeting, at least two inches thick, that seemed to stretch everywhere.

I was no sooner seated when I saw him reach under his desk. And then I heard the syncopated "click" from every door in the room.

"What's that?" I asked in a slight panic.

"Nothing, Miss Keane. Nothing at all. Just to insure a fair hearing for you. For privacy."

A thoughtful man, I decided. And then I decided maybe he wasn't that at all. Rape had crossed my mind before in producer's offices, and his security system I'd just seen in action would make escape very difficult.

"You look nervous, Miss Keane. Anything troubling you?"

"Oh no, not a thing. What film are you casting for, sir?"

"Well, let's not rush into that right now. Drink?"

"No. No thank you."

"Mind if I have one?"

"No."

I watched him pour his drink, watched him drink his drink, and watched him pour another. I was getting a little mad now. After all, even an out-of-work actress can consider her time precious. And I was sure my only reason for being there was to receive the standard male proposition. Would I go to bed with him?

"I don't have a lot of time," I said with as much indignation as possible. "Could we talk about the movie?"

The producer sat back in his large, over-stuffed chair and sighed.

"Miss Keane, before we talk of your being in my films, there are some other urgent matters to be discussed."

I didn't really see him reach down to unzipper his pants, but the next thing I knew he'd stood up and laid his penis on the desk. He stood there, a large smile on his face and his half-erect penis lying there like a sausage on display in the local supermarket.

"Never seen one before, Miss Keane? Most natural thing in the world. Fun, that's what we need more of. Let's have fun and then we'll talk about silly things like making movies."

I suppose there's no way to describe my thoughts at that time. They bombarded me in a one- or two-second period of time and I'm sure they ranged from horror to interest to humor.

But I do remember jumping up, grabbing a dictionary from the edge of his desk and throwing it at the half-cocked male member he'd so proudly placed on display for me. My aim was true and the book hit its mark.

He screamed a blood-curdling scream as he pulled back in pain. "God damn it," he yelled, "you little bitch."

I didn't apologize. I just made for the door and started banging. I reached down and tried the knob. To my surprise, it was open. Maybe he had those clicks sound just for psychological effect, like holding up a bank with a water pistol. The last thing I recall as I ran past his smiling, knowing secretary (knowing what her boss was after but not knowing I'd injured his primary weapon) was the producer wailing, "Jesus Christ!" as he inspected the damage. He was really pretty lucky when you think about it. It was a thin little dictionary I'd thrown. Think if it had been the Random House Dictionary.

Later, after we'd become friends, I asked him if he'd called his secretary in to help inspect the damage.

"No, but she came running in when she heard me moaning and started laughing like hell at me. I guess I was a pretty funny visual standing there holding the thing in my hand like that."

But all in all, making the rounds proved pretty tame. And there's no sense in making up stories for the sake of this book. Veronica Lake might do that. But not Constance Ockleman.

5

I DIDN'T know who was sending the flowers to my home. The first ones arrived in March of 1940. They came while I was out on a casting call. Naturally, my mother had a few questions when I got home. And she didn't even try to be subtle.

"Who sent you these flowers, Connie?" were her first words as I walked in the door. They were beautiful. A plash of spring color.

"I don't know, Mommy."

"What do you mean you don't know?"

"Mommy, I don't know. I really don't know. Isn't there a card?"

"No. No card. Nothing."

"They're beautiful, aren't they, Mommy?"

"That doesn't matter. Who have you been seeing behind my back?"

"No one."

It was true. I hadn't had a date, a real date, since we arrived in Hollywood. Sure, there were the Coke dates with local boys and a few beach parties but nothing to warrant flowers.

My mother sneered.

And I didn't care. Strange flowers from a secret admirer was slightly thrilling at first. But the thrill was gone, as the song says, and I didn't care if the flowers burned or shrivelled up or were sent back. I just didn't care after my mother's suspicions.

"I'm going to lie down."

"What happened today, Connie. Who did you see?"

"Just a couple of producers. Nothing really."

"Did you call that Mr. Wilcox again?"

"No."

"I hope you're not losing interest. I've worked so hard to get you to this point and . . ."

Did I shut her words out of my mind or walk away or yell? I don't remember. It happened too many times to try and recall the specifics. I do remember taking the flowers to my room and holding them as I lay across my bed crying. I never even put them in water. They just died the next day and went into the garbage.

I didn't bother making the rounds the next day and was at home when the second flowers arrived. This time they were chrysanthemums, big and alive and vivid with color.

And so it went on. Day after day flowers would arrive without benefit of card or message. It became almost comic, a regular supply of fresh flowers from a madman.

But then a month later the telephone rang. I answered and heard this smooth, masculine voice ask, "Is this Connie?"

Since I was, I affirmed.

"I'm John Detlie, Connie. I'm an art director at Metro. We've never met but I've seen you around the studio and got your phone number from a gal there."

"Oh, well that's nice."

"I was wondering if we could have lunch or dinner."

"I suppose so. But I'd like to know who you are before I accept a date with you. You understand that, don't you?"

There was a long silence.

"But I'd like to have lunch with you," I hastily threw in to break the awkward void.

"You do know me a little bit, Connie. I suppose you've been receiving my flowers."

It had never dawned on me to connect the caller with the flowers. Of course.

"I've loved them, Mr. Detlie."

"John."

"John."

We did have lunch a few days later at The Brown Derby; John Detlie, me and my mother. She insisted on coming along but John made it seem he had wanted her to join us. That impressed her. She liked what she felt was an old-fashioned sense of morality and courtship. His flowers to me were now appreciated.

I was impressed with this thirty-three-year-old man. He seemed old, wise and travelled to a seventeen-year-old girl. But I decided he had a youthful laugh and outlook and his age could be discounted. My mother seemed to like John. As long as we could all get together, that would be fine with Momma.

We chatted about movies, my goals which my mother greatly blew up out of reality, and John's career. He'd graduated from two universities, had been Phi Beta Kappa at one of them and held architecture as his primary love in life. But films were a lucrative career for a talented art director and set designer, and John seemed quite happy with what he was doing.

After that first lunch, John became an energetic suitor for my affections. And I was completely willing to be pursued by such a handsome, mature, successful and talented man. I was probably falling in love with John Detlie, at least love within the capability of my age and reason.

Whatever it was, it did something positive to my life.

It opened visions of a new world for me, a free world with John Detlie as my knight of liberation.

It also brought me luck of a sort.

Arthur Hornblow, Jr., one of the most respected and active producers of the period, was about to produce one of the big films of the year, *I Wanted Wings*. It was to be a salute to our nation's aviators, and Hornblow had already signed Ray Milland, Brian Donlevy, William Holden, Wayne Morris and Constance Moore to star in the film. It was adapted for the screen by Richard Maibaum from the book by Lieutenant Beirne Lay, Jr.

With all that powerful male box-office lure, Hornblow felt he could take a chance with a newcomer in the role of Sally Vaughn, an out-and-out and unsympathetic siren nightclub singer.

My agent at William Morris took my Metro screen test to Hornblow and asked him to screen it and consider me for the part. Hornblow declined, certainly with justification when you consider the fact that my agent told him the test was lousy but he should look anyway. If my own agent didn't think I was good, why should Hornblow waste his time looking at me?

But Arthur Hornblow, Jr. had a secretary, Isabel, who pulled a lot of weight with the big man. She persuaded him to look at the test. He did, hated it as much as I did, but decided for reasons of his own to give me another test at Paramount.

I was more frightened at the Paramount test than I'd ever been for the Metro test. And again, that damned hair drove me crazy.

We did a scene in which I was supposed to be tipsy at a table in a small nightclub. Things were going nicely until I leaned my elbows on the edge of the table. I was beginning to gesture in an unsure, drunken manner when my right elbow slipped off the table edge sending my long, thin blonde hair falling over my left eye. I spent the next few minutes trying to continue with the scene as I kept shaking my head to get the hair out of my eyes. I could feel myself getting madder and madder and when the test was completed, I stormed off the set, my lips a thin line against the tears.

God, how I cried in my dressing-room.

"This goddamn shitty hair," I yelled at my image in the mirror, shaking my head back and forth violently in physical defiance of it.

I didn't even go to the screening room a few days later when the test was run. I couldn't face it.

But then came the phone call from Arthur Hornblow's secretary.

"Mr. Hornblow would like to see you, Miss Keane." Why? Why would he ever want to see me again?

I went of course.

"Constance," he said, after we'd exchanged the usual opening amenities, "I'm going to cast you as Sally Vaughn in I Wanted Wings."

I didn't cry. I laughed nervously, thanked him too many times and raced home to spread the good news.

I received professional acknowledgment of pleasure from my mother and that's when it set in hard. I could not come up with even the slightest and most remote reason why anyone would cast me after that terrible, botched-up screen test. And what about my hair? Surely that must have frightened even the most hardened Hollywood producer. The thought crossed my mind that maybe they were going to rewrite the part of Sally Vaughn into a low comedy role for an ugly starlet with unmanageable hair. But even that was all right, I decided, because who was I to question any reason for putting me into an important film with so many popular leading men of the day. I'd take the role under any circumstances and with any strings they would see fit to attach. Constance Keane was going to be a movie star, just as her mother wanted her to be.

I learned later from the film's assistant director that the screening room reaction to my screen test was less than unanimous in approval and enthusiasm. Everyone at that screening did feel, however, that I projected some sort of magnetism, the kind that stars emit on the screen. My hair had been a smash; it gave me something that would be remembered, imitated and talked about. It gave the studio's publicity people something to peg their stories on. And let's face it—all those things are great big plus factors for anyone looking for stardom in Hollywood.

You've got to have a gimmick, even in the nicest sense of the word. When you think about it, every big name from Hollywood has possessed something, even a little something besides his or her talent. Gable's ears, Widmark's wild and wicked laugh, Cagney's slipping pants that his elbows always managed to hitch up, Davis' swishy hand and hip roll, etc. Just watch any impressionist on television and you'll see capital being made of a mannerism or physical feature. The same with cartoons and caricatures of celebrities. Durante's marvelous nose gave artists something to work with. Hope's nose and its famed "swoop" configuration and Mitchum's bedroom eyes—and on and on with virtually everyone of star ranking.

And my gimmick, my featured feature was my hair, fine blonde hair hanging loose over one eye. Something I always considered a detriment to my appearance became my greatest asset. That's Hollywood, folks. And that's the nature of the film fan. Who am I to fight it?

You can't imagine the silly thoughts that go through your head when you realize you're about to appear in a major Hollywood feature film as a lead player, one that will play in theatres all over the world—and in Brooklyn, your home town.

It occurred to me one day that with my hair over one eye and the few years I'd gained since leaving Brooklyn, it would probably be impossible for anyone back home to know it was me, Connie Ockleman. After all, I was now called Constance Keane.

But what I didn't realize at the time was that even my Miami friends who knew Constance Keane were to be thrown a curve.

Arthur Hornblow, Jr., didn't like the name Constance Keane. The first time I was made aware of his feelings on the subject was in his office. He'd summoned me early that morning and I raced to his office assuming he had decided to change his mind. I'd had a long and bitter fight with my mother the night before and had cried a lot. I smeared my puffy eyelids with make-up and tried to look as cheerful as possible when I entered his office.

Mr. Hornblow looked as though he'd been up all night. He had.

"Connie," he began as I sat nervously on the couch, "it's pretty well agreed around here that we want a different name for you. *I Wanted Wings* is going to be one of the year's big ones, and it could launch you into a very large and important career. And the name you begin that career with is very crucial."

"Whatever you think, Mr. Hornblow."

"Now don't misunderstand me, Connie. Connie Keane is a fine name. It's fine as just a name and as a professional name."

I smiled.

"It always seemed all right to me, Mr. Hornblow."

He smiled.

"Of course it's all right. But you do realize how many factors are involved in the making of a star, don't you?"

"I guess I really don't."

"Well, you'll learn, Connie. But believe me, the right name, a name that the public can latch on to and remember can make all the difference. It isn't just a matter, though, of creating a name that can be remembered. If that were all it took, we'd just name you Maude Mudpie or Tilly Tits or something and they'd remember the name."

I nodded that I understood.

"No, Connie, picking a name involves coming up with something that associates in the fan's mind the person attached to that name. The name has to . . . well, it has to be the person, or at least what the fan thinks that person is. You know what I mean?"

"Yes." I didn't, but that was irrelevant.

"It has to do with images."

I nodded.

He sat back in his chair and rubbed his eyes.

"I've been up here all night, Connie, trying to come up with the right name for you. All night. And about five this morning I knew I had it."

I sat up straight and came to the edge of the couch. A new name was an exciting thing. It's not an exciting event when your name changes because you lose a father and your mother supplies a new one. But when it's created for you to project a desired image, it's damned exciting.

"Connie, here's how I came to choose your new name. I believe that when people look into those navy blue eyes of yours, they'll see a calm coolness—the calm coolness of a lake."

The first thing that crossed my mind was that I was going to be named Lake something or other. That doesn't sound very outlandish these days with Tab and Rock, but in those days names stuck closer to the norm.

Arthur Hornblow, Jr., continued.

"And your features, Connie, are classic features. And when I think of classic features, I think of Veronica."

Lake Veronica?

Oh!

Veronica Lake.

Of course.

And then it hit me. My mother was sometimes called Veronica. Of all the goddamn names in the world to choose. I could feel the tears welling up and the lump forming in my throat. I tried so hard to hold everything back but I didn't make it. I broke down and bawled like a baby into the couch cushions.

There had been no way for Arthur Hornblow to know about my mother. Nor could he have known we spent so many summers at Saranac Lake while my stepfather recovered from TB at nearby Saranac.

I never told him why I was crying. My feelings were deep but quickly soothed. I really didn't care about having my mother's name. It was just a shock for the moment.

I told my mother when I got home and I'm certain she considered it the rightful will of Hollywood's gods.

But there are bad gods, too.

6

WE BEGAN shooting *I Wanted Wings* on August 23, 1940. I wasn't particularly happy leaving Hollywood for the film's Texas locations. By this time, John Detlie had become a very large part of my life. I suppose you could say I'd fallen in love with him, if that's what a seventeen-year-old girl does.

I do know I had hot pants. And I wanted more than ever to get away from my mother. My stepfather seemed to be recovering although the recovery was a painfully slow one and didn't promise much for his future.

We left for San Antonio on August 15. John was working on the sets for a new film in Hollywood and saw no chance of breaking away even for a week-end to join me on location. I felt terribly lonely and out of my element in Texas, enough so to even wish at times that my mother could be with me. I tried to achieve some bit of rapport with the company of high pressure film people, but every attempt seemed to fall flat. They'd see right through my sham, and I soon decided to pull back, do my job as best I could, and not try to be one of the gang.

I was frightened to death of everything. The importance of the role was staggering to me. I was so nervous during the first few days' shooting that I knew I'd never be able to carry through with my role. No matter how hard I tried to avoid it, my legs would shake and my eyes would blink and my hands would tremble every time I was involved in a scene. Of course, my age had a lot to do with it. I was just a kid.

I found a solution to my problem. And while it did enable me to perform my role to the satisfaction of the director, it did nothing to endear me to the hearts of everyone working on the picture.

What I did was to develop a shell, a very cocky and snippy shell that seemed to work. I knew I had no professional business being there in that role. It was the Hollywood star machine that had ground me out like a product on an assembly line, and I knew my lack of confidence would ruin me. Thus, the shell. I'd be on time for each day's shooting, wait my turn for scenes, do the scenes as well as possible, and then withdraw until called upon.

But even with my detached attitudes, I got along reasonably well with the cast and crew. Well, with one notable exception—Constance Moore.

Miss Moore and I shared quarters in San Antonio. It was a set-up where we each had our own bedroom and a connecting bath and living-room. There was no problem with those arrangements except that Connie Moore was determined to go down in history as the last of the great Texas swingers. Every night Connie would throw a party for Texas friends. The champagne would flow until four or five in the morning and the laughter and loud talk would keep me awake all night. Now, I'm not a square at all. I love a good party and always have.

But here I was, seventeen, working in my first film and wanting desperately to do a good job. I wanted to look and feel bright on the set every day. And long, loud parties at night don't contribute to that end. I even went to the company doctor for sleeping pills but Connie Moore proved louder than any pill.

Losing my sleep was bad enough. But what really did me in was overhearing a conversation one morning on the set. Connie was telling a couple of grips about herself and her acting career.

". . . and I always have needed sleep. And I'm sure not getting any here. That damn Lake kid throws the wildest parties every night in the room and . . ."

I buttonholed the assistant director, a very nice guy who championed me on many occasions, and told him I wanted to move to another room.

He assured me he'd take care of it. The next day, I was moved to the sixth floor, five floors away from my Texas room-mate.

Connie Moore didn't know I'd moved. It was three days later that she found out from one of the wardrobe gals who knew why and when I changed rooms.

". . . that damn Lake kid," Connie told her. "She throws all-night parties. Like last night . . ."

"Veronica moved three days ago to the sixth floor," the wardrobe gal told her.

You'd think someone would swallow their tongue after being put down like that, but not Connie Moore.

I recall one day when she'd gotten on me for some trivial matter and pushed and pushed until I had to walk away to hide the tears. I made it to my room, picked up the phone and called Arthur Hornblow in Hollywood.

"I'm coming back, Mr. Hornblow. I don't want to be in pictures."

He told me to stop being such a baby and to begin acting like a star. Big help. But maybe he was right. I was subject to the emotions of my age, and if I was going to work in pictures, I might as well mature damn fast.

My age worked against me in those early days of my career. I was so in-between, so not this or not that—seventeen. I was too old to receive the understanding accorded the child stars when they fouled up or threw tantrums. And I was too young to function smoothly in the adult world of Hollywood. I couldn't accept so many eventualities and simple facts of movie-making life. Or life itself, for that matter. I was trying to act thirty and usually ended up acting fifteen.

Maybe Connie Moore was simply acting like a Texan. Her mother told me when we were introduced, "If this is your first trip to Texas, sweetie, you'd better watch out for those Texas crabs. They jump ten feet."

I reacted to her warning like any seventeen-year-old would. I assumed she was talking about land crabs. I never even heard of crabs that go with the sexual act. You can see how much I had to learn.

Crabs weren't the only thing I didn't know about sex. I didn't know anything. I did learn a few things by peeking through the windows of a whorehouse next door to us. We'd only been living in Beverly a few weeks when Helen and I decided the goings-on next door were very unusual. The shades were always drawn tightly and many men came and went at strange hours. One night, one of the girls working for the establishment got careless and left her shade open an inch or so. Helen and I spent an hour crouched in the darkness watching her go through her tricks for two different customers. It was an eye-opener, and it even looked like fun. She did look bored, we decided, but the men didn't and maybe she was just tired. At any rate, there are better ways to learn about sex than watching a pro earn her living. Then again, maybe it's the best way. Always learn from the very best, my mother would say. And this gal wasn't bad in retrospect.

I did eventually learn to cope with Connie Moore's Texas bitchiness and our director's tendency to grab your thigh or fanny every time you walked past him. At least I learned to put him off.

And filming *I Wanted Wings* was an exciting challenge to me. Especially the big café scene where we performed on a set with lots of extras, many of them kids I'd worked with before. Here I was, a new star with a pretentious name, sexy costumes cut down to here, careful make-up by the best and a lot at stake. I can remember their faces as clearly as if it were happening today. They sat there, faces set in a semi-sneer, eyes squinting against success or failure. They seemed to be saying, "Come on you cocky little punk from Brooklyn. We knew you when. Come on and show us what you can do. We dare you!"

I mentioned this to the assistant director. And he gave me the best advice I'd had to that point.

"Fuck 'em," he said with authority. I was shocked at the language but agreed with the thought.

What else?

Working in *I Wanted Wings* was more thrilling than most films might be for a newcomer. Not only was it a major motion picture, but it was being produced with the full co-operation of the United States Government. That added its own glamour and excitement. Naturally, the government wanted the film to be a huge success. It would be a vehicle to tell the world about the training of many gallant, young American men. You simply couldn't ask for more direct co-operation.

There was one day when officials at Randolph grounded over 700 airplanes because our director complained the noise of their engines ruined the sound track for that day.

They didn't skimp with supplying manpower, either. They assigned 1,050 cadets, 540 officers and instructors and 2,543 enlisted men to be at the director's disposal at any time.

I was terribly proud even to be involved.

7

THERE were bound to be mishaps during the filming of *I Wanted Wings*. It's tough enough making movies in studios where at least you have control of most of the essential ingredients and elements necessary to film making. In a studio, the director is sure of his light source, sound facilities and camera movement. His biggest potential unknown is his cast, and even it is more prone to behave itself in the confines of a Hollywood studio.

But being on location at two Texas military bases takes just about all the elements and ingredients out of your hands. And you still have the temperaments of the talents to worry about.

Both Ray Milland and Brian Donlevy were good pilots in their own right. Brian was an Annapolis graduate and one of the youngest World War One pilots. Ray had many hours at the controls of various aircraft. And Wayne Morris, who later died of a heart attack on board an aircraft carrier he was visiting, had been a red-hot Navy fighter pilot.

During many scenes, Ray and Brian would actually pilot their own aircraft. There would always be a military flight instructor assigned to keep tabs on their actions and to help them out whenever possible.

There was one scene in particular where Ray and Brian were to taxi a plane across the field. Our flight adviser, a Lieutenant Gray, would lie on a wing, the one hidden from the camera by the plane's fuselage, and hang on for his life as the plane was controlled by Ray or Brian. During this particular scene, things were going nicely until the throttle jammed on the aircraft. It began to gain speed, and as it went faster and faster, our Lieutenant Gray was flipped off the wing, his head just missing the plane's stabilizer. As it was, he did sustain minor head injuries. I think he was happy to receive orders to the Pacific where he only had to worry about flying his plane and killing the enemy.

If you remember the film, I die after causing my own plane, a B-17 Flying Fortress, to crash. I was a stowaway, and my tragic end was only fitting my wretched, nasty role. But stowing away on a B-17 could only happen in films. Security was very tight, and being caught peeking inside one of those monsters could get you in all sorts of trouble.

I began having trouble with our director. The trouble was primarily personal in nature, and I reacted strongly: "Either he goes or I go!"

Guts, huh? My first role and I'm telling them I'm walking out.

Not really guts. If I'd pulled it out of temperament, they'd have strung me up the nearest flag-pole and had all our cadet extras salute the hanging. But the studio wasn't particularly happy about his personal life, and they realized he was damaging the picture. Hollywood really doesn't care about anyone's private life until it begins to have an adverse effect on the dollar product of the studio. When that happens, you've had it.

So they shipped our director back home and called in Mitchell Leisen, a prodigious director who'd been Cecil B. De Mille's assistant at the age of twenty-one and who had such films as *The Volga Boatman*, *King of Kings* and another aviation picture, *Thirteen Hours by Air*, to his credit. Mitch was one hell of a fine director, but he'd been introduced to me by none other than my friend and yours, Constance Moore.

Connie was married at the time to Director Johnny Machio, who was a good friend of Mitch Leisen. They were on hand when Mitch stepped off the plane in Texas. You can imagine what they told him.

This naturally put Mitch on his guard with me. He was tough in every scene, but it was a professional toughness and that's always easy to accept. But sometimes I'd find myself getting weary of the early calls and late hours and demanding nature of the new director. And I'd yearn for John Detlie more than ever when depression set in.

We talked on the phone quite a bit during the Texas phase of *I Wanted Wings*. I'd hear his voice and I could feel everything inside me draining to a core down low, a sensuous low core of yearning for the man I loved. He told me he felt the same way and wanted to make me his for all time. By this time we were using coy nicknames.

"Will you marry me, Mousie?"

"Oh God, *yes*, Pops. Yes, yes, yes. I love you."

And we'd hang up and I'd spend the night and the entire next day tingling and feeling like some alley cat in heat. And I didn't have one solid piece of memory to help me imagine what it would be like to have John make love to me. He never had. And so many nights I wished over and over it had happened, even once, to remember.

Eventually we packed up our Texas gear and headed back to California. Before we left, though, one very significant thing happened to me.

Paramount had assigned a very active publicity unit to our Texas locations. There was always a photographer snapping stills for advance mailings plugging the film. And I was posed in my share of them.

One day, I was standing close to a B-17 as the photographer was doing coy set-ups with me. The pilot of the plane either didn't see us or held all motion-picture people in scorn. He started engines just as I was leaning over in one of those ridiculous poses that were such favorites with publicity photographers those days. My rear end was towards the plane, and I was peeking around to my right at the camera when the prop wash hit. It caught my dress and blew it up around my thighs. The photographer captured the moment, chuckled at what would probably be a funny but unusable photo, and went on to take others.

It ended up as the photograph the studio used in their advance mailing for *I Wanted Wings*. It was released to newspapers and magazines all over the nation. And it hit big. It ran in hundreds of papers, and people started writing in to the papers and Paramount asking for more information about Veronica Lake. Not a bad break, you'll admit.

I still hadn't achieved any great rapport with the other members of the cast and crew when we arrived back in Hollywood. I maintained my cocky shell in self-defense, and would do my scenes, sit quietly along the side or in my dressing-room when off, and come back when it was time. That kind of aloofness, no matter how I might have justified it, is never well received by the Hollywood pros. I suppose they wanted me to be a bubbling teenager off-camera with lots of "Gee whiz" and "Golly gee" talk. But if I'd gone that route, I'd never have lasted. I had to act tough and unapproachable to overcome my fears. I did, and it paid off.

But no one really liked me. We were sitting on the airplane back to Hollywood and I was thinking about how the first phase of shooting had gone. I was secretly pleased with my performance. I knew my faults, and they were legion. But I was fairly satisfied with the way I'd progressed in such a short time. But not enough to want to see the daily footage shot in Texas.

Just as I was beginning to feel this slight twinge of confidence, I heard one of the director's staff saying to an extra, "Lake's a cute kid, I suppose, but she ought to go back to the farm."

The comment shook me a little, but not as much as it might have a few weeks earlier. My self-inflicted shell of toughness was beginning to penetrate a little deeper. I found myself shrugging off the comment with a casual, "Oh, shit," under my breath. Besides, there was no farm in Brooklyn. Any fool would know that.

Our first California location was March Field near San Francisco. By this time I was right at home around the military. Or maybe I was just feeling more at home in general. John was there, and that made all the difference.

We didn't waste any time in carrying through on our marriage plans. It was the third night of filming at March Field. We made plans to elope to Santa Ana. I told John I'd meet him there at nine o'clock.

Filming that day seemed an eternity. It dragged along, one re-take after another, hurry up and wait while this light was adjusted and this camera angle was reconsidered. Didn't they know I was about to become Mrs. John Detlie? You bet they didn't. For some reason I found it impossible to confide in anyone about my plans. But that was part of my whole life pattern. Everything had to be hush-hush; there was no exception.

The company shot late that day and we didn't wrap until eight o'clock. That left one hour to cover the over 70 miles from Riverside, where March Field was located, to Santa Ana, where John was located. I rented a Tanner Livery car and told the driver to get me to Santa Ana as fast as he could. I was wearing a red Betty Grable dress from Paramount wardrobe and white moccasins to help ease a sprained ankle.

"Actresses are always rushing some place," the driver quipped as he raced along. "Where are you rushing to?"

"Just an emergency with an old friend," I answered.

John.

"We'll probably pick up a ticket goin' like this, Miss Lake."

"Don't worry about a thing. Just get there. I'll pay all the fines."

"OK."

John. I'll be there, John. Don't get impatient and run away. I'll be there.

"Can't we go any faster?"

"Ma'm, we go any faster and we'll both end up dead."

"Oh God, don't do that. I'd never forgive you."

The driver pondered that answer all the way to Santa Ana.

John was there waiting for me. I was timid about running up to him and throwing my arms around him with the driver watching. I think the driver sensed the situation because he hastily put the car in gear and drove off.

"It's a nice night to elope," John said quietly.

"Yes it is."

"Shall we?"

"Yes."

We spent our wedding night in a local hotel. It was probably the most beautiful moment I'd ever known. I possessed a childish pride at coming to this man I loved as a virgin. And I think he shared the pride with me, or at least respected the way I felt. I fell asleep fingering my wedding ring, a tiny panda with a diamond, especially designed by John. He knew I loved pandas.

We lay in bed together early the next morning, not saying anything but revelling in the moment. Finally, John turned to me and said, "You're on your way to becoming a star, aren't you?"

"I guess so, Pops. At least that's the way Arthur Hornblow feels. Does it bother you?"

"No. Not at all."

But I knew it did. I tried to make light of the whole thing and John played along with my flip comments about Brooklyn girl making good and the star-making machine.

But then he said, "I'm not even sure who I married. Constance Ockleman, Constance Keane or this Veronica Lake creature."

"You married me, you dope."

"Who are you?"

"Connie. Your Connie."

"Or Veronica. My Veronica."

"Or anything you want to call me."

"That's what I'd like to do. I'd like to call you something that no one else does. You'd be my special person then. Do you know what I mean, Connie . . . or Veronica?"

"Call me anything you'd like, John. I love you."

"I love you . . . let's see . . . I know . . . I'll call you Ronnie. I've been calling you that in my dreams and that's who you should be for me. Ronnie."

"I'm going to have to keep a list so I can remember who the hell I really am. Whatever happened to Mousie? I'm glad something happened to it. From now on, I'm your Ronnie."

And that's what John called me from that moment on.

Unfortunately, John had to leave four days later for Gallup, New Mexico, where the film he was working on started location shooting. I'd gone back to work at March Field the day after our marriage. And if I thought I missed John when I was in Texas, I was to prove myself wrong during that first separation as man and wife. We immediately rented a house near March Field and hired a maid and spent the few evenings we had together getting moved in and comfortable. And then John left for Gallup and I was left to complete *I Wanted Wings*.

With the March Field shooting completed, we moved down to Hollywood and the final phases of the film to be shot in the Paramount studios.

Mitch Leisen was still laboring under the guidelines established by Constance Moore and her husband about me. He was unmerciful in the studio. It seemed worse there in Hollywood because Mitch was working within the confines of familiarity. He was at home in the studio without thousands of cadets and officers watching his every move.

At any rate, he drove me and cursed me and belittled me until I came to the brink of breaking.

I went over the brink on a Wednesday. I was playing a difficult scene with Ray Milland in which we were dancing, and I flubbed a few takes. I could see Mitch starting to boil, but the harder I tried, the worse I became. Finally, he yelled, "CUT," and turned on me with all the ferociousness of an animal.

"You dumb little bitch . . ."

I broke all the way. Tears flowed. And Ray Milland put his arm around me.

"Hey shorty," he whispered in my ear. He'd been calling me that since my first day in Texas. "Never let them see you cry. They spot one chink in your armor and they'll never let up. Walk away—but *never cry!*"

I did what he suggested. I walked to my dressing-room. And then I walked out the door, drove out the studio gate and went home to another rented house, this one in Hollywood. Our maid was named Bridey, and she was home when I arrived.

"Bridey, I'm going to Gallup, New Mexico, to be with Mr. Detlie. You're the only one who knows where I'm going and don't tell a soul."

We had a Dodge coupé at the time, and after throwing on a full-length possum coat, I jumped in the car and drove off. I was still wearing my make-up and costume from the Milland scene, and I looked ghastly. At that time make-up for films was heavy, greasy and yellow. I looked like some yellow witch of the mountains as I pushed the car past the Los Angeles city limits and east to New Mexico. I never had much of a foul tongue up to that point (contrary to popular beliefs, there isn't a lot of swearing in Hollywood. I learned my four-letter vocabulary from the Merchant Marines and the legitimate stage), but I drew on my favorite and virtually only bad word as I drove along.

"Shit on you, Mitch Leisen. Shit on you," I muttered over and over as night drew its curtain of black over everything.

I drove all night and drove too fast. I was a nutty, upset, immature and married kid and I reacted like one. I kept my foot to the floor and laughed at the few near-misses I experienced. And then I began to feel exhilarated at the freedom of driving through the night towards my ultimate and permanent freedom, husband John. The cool-wet air rushed through the open windows and filled me with its freshness.

I pulled into Needles, California, at about seven the next morning. Thanksgiving Day. After many strange looks from the gas station attendant, I drove off on my next leg to rejoin John and to escape Mitch Leisen, Hollywood, the star-machine and especially Veronica Lake. There was a light, rolling fog over everything. It covered the gentle frost that had settled on the ground during the night. I was about thirty miles north of Flagstaff when I felt the car begin to go into a rear-end slide. I was powerless. I guess I did all the wrong things in turning the wheel away from the direction of the skid and jamming on the brakes, but I was reacting naturally. The slide was now into a spin on that narrow mountain road. I threw the gears into second, another improper and imprudent thing to do, and at that moment the Dodge went all the way around. It kept spinning towards the edge of the road and suddenly went over the ridge. It slid down the side of the mountain, jerking and bouncing and even tumbling. I hadn't done a thing right up to that moment but for some reason (maybe my nun-aunt and her faith) I switched off the ignition.

And kept falling. Nose first. Over and over—maybe five or six times. I was buffeted about inside the car, yelling and screaming until the car came to rest with my final, piercing scream.

Everything so quiet.

I was sprawled across the front seat, my head on the right side. I realized I'd also had the presence of mind to throw myself away from the steering column as the car started to nose over.

I took a few deep breaths and nothing seemed to hurt very much. And then my foot started to throb. It was my toes, and once the pain set in it was excruciating.

I think I laughed. I'd gone over a mountain and turned over so many times and all I seemed to suffer were broken toes. But then my knee started to hurt, and I could feel blood running down my left leg. But even that didn't frighten me. There was nothing major in my injuries. I was sure of that.

The fog was thick where the car had come to rest. I couldn't see a thing outside. I began to gently rock back and forth to see if I was on solid ground. The last thing I wanted was to squirm around in an attempt to get free and cause the car to roll further down that mountain. But it seemed secure.

I pushed against the door. It wouldn't budge. I pushed again with all the strength I could muster. The door held firm against my shoulder.

"You idiot," I mumbled as it dawned on me to roll down the window and climb out that way. I did, it rolled down easily, and I slipped my 95-pound frame out into the grey of the fog.

I checked the damage. My knee was cut, my toes were obviously broken and I was banged up pretty good around the face. I tore off half of my slip and tied it tightly around my bleeding knee. That completed, I set out to climb back up the mountain.

I got up to the roadside and waited by the side of the road. It was fifteen minutes before a car's headlights could be seen through the fog. I stood there and flapped my arms until the car spotted me and stopped.

Inside was a farmer, his wife and their small son. The boy was huddled up in the back seat against the morning's dampness.

"Howdy," the farmer drawled.

"Hi."

"What's the trouble?"

"I had an accident with my car. It's down there."

He thought about that for a moment. He took a long, careful look at me. So did his wife. I must have been a beautiful sight. My hair had been in a bun but now it hung down in strands over my face. My eyes were swollen. The heavy yellow make-up had run and streaked my face with yellow smears. The slip hung loosely from my knee. My shoes were down there with the car. And my possum coat added the final touch to the image I presented that morning to the farmer.

He whispered something to his wife and she whispered something to him. Finally, the farmer peered out his window again.

"'Reckon we'll take you into Flagstaff. Sure you ain't in some kind of other trouble?"

"Not that I know of," I answered. He should know about Mitch Leisen.

"Git in."

I climbed into the back seat just as the mother pulled her son to safety in the front with her. She wrapped a protective pair of muscular arms around him and never let go until they safely dumped me in Flagstaff at the Automobile Club. They let me clean up, had a local doctor look at my injuries, and arranged a ride to Gallup. My toes were broken, but fortunately my toes seem to be made up of almost all cartilage, which allowed the doctor to simply tape them together.

I arrived in Gallup in good spirits. John was very understanding and it was so good to be with him again. The shock of the accident didn't set in until just before dinner that night. I completely fell apart and had to be put to bed with sedatives.

It took Paramount three days to figure out where I'd gone. I'm sure Ray Milland or the studio never thought I'd walk that far.

Finally, the inevitable call from the studio came. It was from the front office, and they called me a spoiled little brat and an ungrateful bitch and other choice compliments.

"If you can't talk to me with a civil tongue, I won't talk at all." I answered and hung up.

Naturally, I went back. My first break in films and I walked out. Beautiful, huh? That just isn't done. I'd established myself in the hearts and minds of Paramount as a temperamental little brat with the arrogance of a nobody.

But I had a few things working in my favor. First, we'd shot so much of the film that replacing me would entail too much cost. Second, my candid photograph and its acceptance by the nation's press had established me as a star of great commercial potential. This Veronica Lake broad just might be a money-maker for the studio and they never turn their backs on money.

So I came back to work, finished the picture and waited. Filming had taken four months. I think John made me pregnant on the final day of shooting because my first child, Elaine, arrived nine months later.

Box office for *I Wanted Wings* proved excellent. I was billed seventh after the main titles, a proper place for a newcomer. But the star magic was working. Even a few critics were kind. The League of Decency gave the film a Class B rating, which meant it was objectionable in part. The part was Veronica Lake, who, the League said, wore suggestive costuming.

About that, Cecelia Ager, critic from New York's new daily tabloid, *PM* wrote: "Miss Lake is supposed to be a *femme fatale* and to that end it was arranged her truly splendid bosom be unconfined and draped ever so slightly in a manner to make the current crop of sweater girls prigs by comparison. Such to do has been made over doing justice to those attributes of Miss Lake that everything else about her has been thrown out of focus. The effect is too uncanny."

Another critic said I made Lana Turner look like a schoolgirl. But that's all *I* was, really.

Some critics thought I was a good actress.

Some didn't.

But everyone knew one thing.

Veronica Lake was a star. Paramount knew it. My mother knew it. And I knew it.

What more natural thing than to ask for a raise for my next picture? I asked for one thousand dollars a week. They offered three hundred. We settled for that.

Which is a hell of a lot better than seventy-five bucks a week, my salary for *I Wanted Wings*.

8

MY MOTHER was Constance Charlotta Trimble when she married my father. Like me, she was seventeen when she first entered into the holy state of matrimony. The wedding melded her Irish immigrant background with my father's German and Danish strains. He was Harry Ockleman, a seaman working on tankers for The Sun Oil Company.

My parents met in Brooklyn and conceived me in that same borough of New York. Naturally, I don't remember Brooklyn in my very early years. But I do remember attending kindergarten in Florida, my first recollections of Brooklyn at age six when we returned from Florida's warmth to Brooklyn's dirty, cold-wet snow. My very first snow. I didn't like it then and I don't like it now. I'm a warm weather girl, one who ventures north only when the lure is sufficiently enticing.

The first eight years of anyone's life are bound to be dull, unless you've been forced into Faginish activities or illicit, pre-puberty concubinage. I suffered nor enjoyed neither.

My first eight years were normal in every sense. I was a tom-boy. I remember that and so do some of the little boys in our neighborhood who, from time to time, felt the sting of a left hook from the toughest broad on the block. I could whip 'em all, much to the dismay of my victims and their collective egos. Besides, I always preferred the companionship of little boys to that of little girls. Girls would backbite and gossip and whine and cry but not boys. Boys would take a swing and you popped them back and that was that. Hands were shaken the next day and all was forgotten.

I suppose it would be advantageous now to launch into some heavy dialogue on how I had to fight my way up from poverty and misery into the glitter and fame of showbiz.

Sorry. That wasn't the case. We always had enough money, never an abundance but enough for comfortable middle-class living. Seamen made good money and still do. There were always plenty of toys, although toys never seemed to be a part of my growing up. It was a strange situation in our house. The toys would be purchased and brought home, but I wasn't allowed to play with them.

"Stop spending all your time playing with all those silly toys."

And more would be bought.

"You'll just go damaging the house with those toys. Put them away."

Another doll. Girl toys.

I wanted fire engines and boxing gloves.

I did enjoy a particular set of paper dolls with slots and things called "Baby Nancy." My friend Rosemary and I each went through six sets of "Baby Nancy." But it was the only doll I ever enjoyed. My mother naturally leaned towards female toys for me. She tried quite often to teach me little ladylike things but I was never very good at them. It was my job to wash out and mend my own socks. I used to take care of the mending by putting adhesive tape over the holes. Mother never appreciated that.

I actually gave away all my toys. It soon became a ludicrous situation because all the kids on the block waited anxiously for my dad to bring home toys and books and puzzles and games. They knew they'd have their payday from me soon after the loot arrived. And I seldom disappointed them.

No, my initial eight years of life can only be summed up in one word—normal, provided you ignore the toy situation. Our house on Lefferts Avenue in Brooklyn was ample and the neighborhood fair.

I made my acting debut at the age of eight. It was the lead in the school play, *Poor Little Rich Girl*. Prophetic in a way, but not indicative. Again, I cannot claim the role because someone discovered inner ability as a thespian. I was given the part because I had the longest, blondest corkscrew curls in the class. I sang two songs in the play and wore a white bunny coat. My stepfather came to see me perform, my real father never having had that pleasure. He died in a horrible ship explosion in dry dock in Philadelphia. The tragedy was compounded because he'd just received his Master's Papers and stood to make more money for his efforts.

It seems to me I spent a great deal of my childhood alone. Even my give-a-way program of toys didn't buy me any flock of lasting friends. Not that I minded. Being alone has always had its appeal for me, along with its inherent agonies. But I believe that if a vision came to me in the middle of the night and offered me an ultimate choice—people or solitude—I'd go with the solitude, resulting traumas be damned. Nothing really hurts you except people and old-age deterioration of the cells. And since people can't do anything to curb the cell thing, they really don't seem to serve much of a useful function at all. I like people. I really do. But they confuse me terribly—and disappoint me.

People are greedy. The more you do for them, the more they expect. It's just recently I find myself tightening up on what has always been an easy generosity. And that isn't like me at all.

I remember walking down a Brooklyn street one afternoon and coming upon a nice Italian kid on the block. She was just a wailing-wall of tears.

"What's the matter?" I asked her.

Nothing but tears.

"Come on. What's the matter?"

"I lost it."

"Lost what?"

"My veil . . . for communion."

"Oh."

"Momma will beat me. She will. I know it."

"Oh gee. Well maybe it won't happen. Maybe . . ." What else could I do? I went home, stole $1.35 from my mother's purse and gave it to the Italian kid. She bought a new veil, didn't get walloped by her mother and lived happily ever after. Me? I went home, got the beating of my life for taking the money (deservedly), and didn't live so happily ever after.

I stole one other time in my life. That incident came about because another girl in the neighborhood, who was quite a bit older than I, became very depressed over her junior prom in high school. Seems, folks, she didn't have a thing to wear to that prom.

I didn't steal any money for that gal to buy a dress. I just took my mother's brand-new dress, never worn, and her equally brand-new shoes that matched the dress and gave them to that sad girl. I hope she married the boy who took her to the prom. It's the only way to justify the beating I received when everything came out in the wash.

The beatings got through to me. I gave up my life of crime, got through grammar school and junior high and headed south with my mother and father, the new one. My step-dad's lung problems demanded a warmer climate and Florida seemed ideal. I learned to love it, its free and easy atmosphere, its warm sun and blue water and clement sand.

I attended two high schools. One was in Miami. The other was in Montreal while my stepfather was going through his TB cure at Saranac, near Lake Placid. I preferred Miami both for the climate in which it was located and because it was a public school. The school in Montreal was the Villa Maria convent school, a very Catholic institution with rock-solid religious views and no pity for those with even the slightest doubts.

We lived in at Villa Maria which insured against public contamination of the girls. And when you think about it, herein lies the crux of the world-wide success of Roman Catholicism. People don't rebel against something that is held to be absolute and does not even allow for probing into the opposing side. Catholics are not to attend services at other churches. What a revelation it might be for many of the fanatical faithful.

I did love dearly my Mother Superior. She was a warm and jolly woman taken to hearty gales of laughter at the misfortunes and *faux pas* of the students. So often, when I'd pull some stunt that enraged the other nuns, they'd send me to Mother Superior in desperation.

I'd walk into her austere quarters, look at her through the top of my head, always bow, and mumble some form of apology.

Her face would be set in firm resolution. And then the corners of her mouth would begin to crack and her eyes would take on a hint of sparkle and soon she'd put back her head and laugh with great gusto.

"Constance, Constance, Constance. What are we going to do with you? What a sense you have for finding trouble and entering into it."

Invariably she'd sigh and shake her head before telling me what she always told me at the end of these sessions.

"Do you know what, Constance? I look at you and watch you fumble through your growing up and I'm amazed at just how much you're like me when I was your age. Yes, I was pretty good at finding trouble, too. And do you know what else, Constance?"

"No, Mother Superior."

"Someday, Constance Keane, you'll be a nun. I just know it. And you'll be a good one, too. I'm sure of that."

I'd gulp a smile. And Mother Superior would lean forward, turn her laugh-lined face back into a proper and fitting frown and say with firmness, "But you must learn how to control that rebellious nature of yours. You must try to stay out of trouble in your life. Will you do that for me, Constance?"

"Yes, Mother Superior. I promise."

"You may go." And the frown would settle into a gentle smile as I'd back towards the door, head lowered, half-tripping over my feet in the presence of this woman whom I both loved and feared.

Stay out of trouble in your life? I couldn't then and still can't. It's the nature of the beast, I suppose. It's me. Except when I've tried to be someone else.

I used to try and affect a southern accent while at school in Montreal. I did it to amplify my role with the kids as a true southern belle, and don't you forget it, kids.

"Ah do declare ah believe ah bin told a lil' ol' fib or two," I'd say to them.

And three minutes later I'd slip into exaggerated Brooklyn speech. "That's smoiy apinion and it'll gittcha where ya wanna go."

I knew the other girls giggled behind my back but that never bothered me. I enjoyed being labelled the kook of the class and played the role to the hilt. Of course, I did the same thing when I was in Miami, only there I took on a charming French-Canadian accent. But I think I was normally well liked in both places, if only because I was the one who'd climb the wall for sandwiches after hours. And you could usually depend on finding a piece of cake in the veil bag we all carried in our sleeves. I suppose I was trying to prove something. And sensing Mother Superior's favorable attitude towards me gave me the guts to do many things outside the rule book.

Obviously, my exposure to Catholic teaching didn't make any first-rate Catholic out of me. In fact, it served to turn me away, completely away from the church and its teachings. And that's a shame.

There was an article written recently in which a poll was reported on various colleges and universities. In effect, each university was categorized in terms of the life-goals it would probably best provide a student attending that particular school. Girls, for example, who are in search of a husband, were advised to go to an engineering school where there is usually a preponderance of male students (how basic can you get?). And engineers make good husbands, the article claimed. Dull perhaps. But always there.

And the article also made the point that if you'd like your son or daughter to develop and maintain a firm religious sense, the last school he or she should attend is a church school, especially after the early grades.

But condemnations of the Catholic Church and its inability to serve the people of this age are best left to renegade priests, disillusioned laymen and church leaders themselves who every day seem to nail down religion's lid just a little tighter.

Suffice it to say I was a Catholic. I am no longer. And before we leave things mysterious, let me disclaim any particular disappointment in only the Catholic Church. It does not stand alone in its dogmatic refusal to bend.

I recently spoke with a former Catholic, now a member of his local Unitarian congregation. The Unitarian Church is, as far as I know, a self-professed pillar of non-dogma. Man at one with his universe, free-thought, freedom to believe and express those beliefs. It all sounds wonderful. But my friend, enjoying coffee after his first Unitarian service, was asked how he liked the sermon.

"Just fine," he replied. "But I really don't think I can accept what he said about. . . ."

Tight lips. Hard stares. Frantic appeals to reason by defenders of the non-dogma. Which all goes to prove that you have dogma at both ends of the scale. You can be as dogmatic in your liberalism as in your conservatism. There just doesn't seem to be any middle ground, at least not for me. I now confine my religion to televised discussions on the church's role in fighting dope addiction.

The decision to enroll me in Villa Maria was not one of long-standing need on my mother's part. I was supposed to attend public school right there in Saranac. We lived in a lonely little home with a small terrace and I had my own rock garden. My parents quickly became friendly with a few local priests, and there didn't seem to be a day went by when you didn't find one of them at our house having coffee with my mother and discussing the world and my stepfather's progress with his tuberculosis. My mother was always very proud of me when they were around and would encourage me to be friendly and demonstrative with our clergy friends.

I found it easy to like the priests and enjoyed being fussed over by them and, especially, by my mother. She wasn't given to that under normal circumstances.

There was one priest in particular who seemed to take an extraordinary liking to me, and he'd take apparent delight in walking with me and talking about growing up and the problems young girls face in what he felt was a rapidly deteriorating society. I'd listen, not really understanding the points he was making, and tell him funny stories about Brooklyn and my friends. The times with him were relaxed and enjoyable—good moments.

He arrived one afternoon and my mother called me in from the rock garden to be with him. We sat in the living-room and drank tea until Momma said she had to go downtown for something or other.

She left us alone. The priest was telling me jokes about ghosts and, supposedly to emphasize the point in one of them, asked me to come sit on his lap. I went.

I sat across his legs and he continued his story. But his voice had changed. It was hoarse now, and breathy.

Suddenly, he brought his hand around my waist and placed it on one of my breasts.

I gasped and sat up straight as his other hand slid under my heavy gray flannel skirt and pushed under the elastic of my panties.

I squirmed to get up. He pushed his mouth against my ear.

"You're such a pretty girl, Connie. I . . . I . . ."

The whole thing lasted no more than twenty seconds. I was up on my feet and running out of the room, out of the house to the familiar calm of my rock garden. I didn't dare go back inside.

My mother returned eventually and came to me in the garden.

"Did he leave?" she asked.

"Yes, Mommy."

"I hope you entertained him nicely, Connie."

"I did, Mommy."

"He's so nice. We're lucky to have such fine friends."

"He's very nice."

It was another priest who was responsible for my gaining admission to Villa Maria in Montreal. My mother began to feel I was falling victim to the pressures of modern life and asked this priest if he could do anything about getting me into Villa Maria. He did everything he could and eventually succeeded. My mother was very grateful to him. And she was relieved that I would now be under the moral wing of good church teaching.

I somehow find it difficult to even consider my brief time at Villa Maria as high school. You function day by day under the cloak of confinement and you're lucky to get out feeling only extreme fear of the after-life. It didn't seem like high school at all.

Miami was different. It still is. Miami offered me more of a typical high school life, with over-anxious boys and naughty girl-talk in the locker room after a rousing game of field hockey.

Miami High was a ball. The school was like a country club for juveniles, its classes slight but necessary interludes between beach romps, jai alai matches and football games. And always boys and girls racing somewhere in hopped-up cars. Miami High has changed since I attended. I understand it's taken on a much more pronounced academic atmosphere. Still, Miami's proverbial moon and glorious sand are the same. It's all so romantic.

But Miami and its romantic qualities didn't provide me my first crush on a boy. That happened in Saranac. He was the older brother, eighteen, of a close girl friend of mine. I guess I was fourteen.

The problem was he didn't know I existed. He'd race past us in his very own Chris-Craft and wave at his sister and I'd die a little. He was very handsome and had dark, wavy hair that blew around just so when he had the boat at full speed. Boy, I was nuts about him.

Unfortunately, the only time he ever gave me a second look was when my halter broke and fell off. He was bringing the boat in one afternoon while his sister and I were swimming off the pier. I gave him a big wave as he passed me in the water and the damned strap broke. The halter floated away and I squealed for help, careful to keep my breasts under the surface. It wasn't easy, and his face lighted up when they'd bob up and out of the water.

Like most men, my crush didn't try to help. He just looked. It was fortunate there were no other boats near him. He would have demolished them all. His sister swam out with a towel and, amidst much giggling, we came back to shore. My hero was waiting on the pier.

He laughed at me.

I turned my head and walked past.

He said hello every time he saw me after that. I'd mumble a greeting and walk right on by.

He called me for a date. I turned him down.

He'd become interested.

I never gave him a tumble.

I was becoming a woman.

The next crush I had was on the local high school football hero in Miami. He was a quarterback named Frankie Rentz. I'd seen him on the beach with his bulging biceps and cute, crooked smile. I was really nuts about him.

It wasn't mutual, of course. I never admitted that to myself. I've always been a dreamer of good dreams. Any bad dreams are turned away in mid-air. Only the happy endings were allowed into my head and I conjured up the happiest endings with Frankie Rentz. He'd carry me away to a little cottage and we always lived happily ever after. It didn't bother me then that every time Frankie was in my dreams, he was wearing his football uniform. And sometimes, when my dreams were especially prolific, we'd be surrounded with eleven little Rentz types, all in shoulder pads and diapers.

I was at an age where my sexual experience was mostly fantasy fed by juvenile fumblings in the back seat of a hot rod. I dated as much as most of the gals at school and went through the usual necking scenes. Nothing ever got out of hand, if you'll pardon the pun, but it was always Frankie in the car with me, not the fellow I was actually with at the time. Being inexperienced, I could never carry these flights of fantasy out of the back seat of a car. I could never carry them into the cottage and the bedroom. I guess I didn't know what to do with them once I got them there. But I just knew Frankie would bring me to the heights of which women could only dream. It got so bad I'd sit in class and contract my pelvic muscles and force a tingle or two. And Frankie Rentz, the real Frankie Rentz, wasn't even aware he was doing that to me.

My crush on Frankie lasted until I got a Christmas job at the Blue Cross Drug and Department Store on West Flagler Street in Miami. They gave me a job wrapping packages, a dull routine except for the little bell I had at my disposal. I could ring it—ding-ding—and a teen-age runner would appear to run errands for me. He would get me more wrapping paper or twine or Christmas stickers and the like. I was drunk with power.

I was doing fine in my job until Frankie came into the store one night just before Christmas. There he stood, so handsome and appealing as he browsed along the cosmetics counter. I had to make him notice me, but that meant leaving my wrapping post. He was below me, the wrapping desk perched on a small balcony above the main floor of the store. I had to force him to see me. Of course. The bell.

"Ding, ding, ding, ding, ding."

The runner came. "Hey, do me a favor. Watch the counter here for a minute. O.K.?"

"Sure."

I accomplished a very quick fluff on my hair, straightened my skirt and came down on the floor.

"Hi, Frankie."

He turned and smiled.

"Oh, hi, Connie. How's things?"

"Great. Great. I work here. You know that?"

"No kiddin'? I didn't know that. That's great." He turned back to the items on the counter.

"Yup. I work here. Christmas job, you know?"

"Yeah. That's great." He picked up a bottle of French perfume.

I thought quickly.

"Hey, Frankie, how about some help picking out what you need. I mean, I'd kinda know better what your mother would like. I mean, 'cause I'm a girl, too, and . . ."

"I already got my mother her gift. This is for my girl. I'm going steady. You know that?"

I shook my head sadly.

"Great chick. Hey, that'd be great, your helping me and all. I don't know a thing about this stuff."

I knew Frankie had a steady girl. But that never bothered me because in my dreams he'd always get mad at her and come running to me. But I knew it was over now. All over.

"Sure, Frankie. I'll help you pick out something."

I chose the most expensive perfume, said goodbye to him and returned to the wrapping desk.

I wrapped with a vengeance. I made extra fancy bows and double layers of paper and attached extra little silver bells on even the cheapest merchandise. Frankie was gone from the store but as hard as I tried not to, I kept looking back to that spot on the floor where we'd talked. Maybe he'd come back into the store. But I didn't believe that. Not for a minute.

I soon ran out of ribbon and rang the bell. No one showed up. I rang it again. Still no one. I was getting mad, mostly about Frankie Rentz, and leaned over the railing to yell for a runner. Just as I leaned, the guy below me behind the counter decided to switch on the ceiling fan. It went into motion and clopped me right across the bridge of the nose. It didn't cut my nose because it was just getting started, but it hurt a lot. I cried and got rid of Frankie Rentz for ever.

I think of Frankie Rentz every time I have a sinus attack. He's a successful dentist in Miami and I think his son was the star quarterback on Miami's team for 1967. I know it isn't very complimentary to Frankie to think of him only when I have a sinus headache or nose bleed. But my crushed passion for him deserves such a painful memory jog. I'm sorry, Frankie.

Who needed Frankie Rentz anyway? I was no wallflower in high school. I had a lot of dates, some with school BMOC's and some with fellows I just liked. And there was one I dated because I felt kind of sorry for him. He was so homely and fat. And he asked me to a school dance. I couldn't say "no."

This same boy also taught me how to drive. He'd pick me up every morning in his little Ford and drive me home after school, always taking time to let me practice my driving skills. He was a wonderful guy. Just unattractive.

I returned to Florida late in my Hollywood career to film *Slattery's Hurricane* with Richard Widmark. We were staying at a downtown hotel. I was browsing through magazines in the lobby after the first day's shooting when I heard a voice behind me say, "Connie?"

I turned and there stood this tall, well-built and very handsome man. I looked at him with a cocked eye and for a moment didn't place him. And then some features began to look familiar.

"Oh, no. Not Tom Moxley."

He grinned from ear to ear and we joked about high school and my driving lessons and the dance. We had lunch together and I must have said, "I can't believe it," at least twenty times, all to his genuine amusement. If only girls in high school could look into the future and see beyond the baby fat and acne. If only . . .

I also dated Gilbert Miller and Phil Fisher while attending Miami High. I just happen to remember their names. I assume they remember mine, at least the one I ended up with through Arthur Hornblow's imagination.

9

BEAUTY contests were born in Miami. Not that beauty pageants are new. Beauty has always been put on parade, publicly and privately. Most of the world appreciates a beautiful girl and, perhaps even more so, a contest of any sort.

But Miami seems to typify the beautiful girl in the bathing suit. I believe it was publicist Steve Hannagan who latched on to the bathing beauty gimmick to promote Miami into such a favored vacation land. He'd have every pretty girl in the area photographed at poolside or on the beach and ship the pictures off to every newspaper up north. And the photos had their effect, especially on the New York or Chicago businessman on the commuter train, puddles forming under his boots from melting snow, ears frost-bitten and eyes stinging from the cold wind. He'd sit there and feast his eyes on the warm girls in that warm, sunny climate and decide that's were he ought to be. Naturally, the pretty girls with their tanned navels play a big role in bringing about that motivation. But he knows it's unreal. His wife will be with him and looking will be all he'll get.

But there is that sun and sand, and enough folks up north reacted to bring Miami into the front of tourist destinations.

Beauty contests have played a very large part in my life. It wasn't by design that I entered the "Miss Miami" contest while in high school. It was because I was pledged to a sorority (I told you Miami High was different) and one of the pledge requirements was to enter that particular beauty contest. I did as I was told and found myself number 86 on the contestant roles. My emotions were mixed. I laughed at the whole idea for openers. But then my ego started to creep into the picture and I tried on several occasions to get out of the competition. But each time I tried, the members of the sorority became even more vehement about my obligation. Frankly, I wasn't that eager to lose in a competition of good looks. "Leave 'em laughing" was the way I felt about living my life and, at that time, I had a pretty good reputation with the Miami high school set as a pretty girl with a good figure. My chest was usually mentioned with solid approval and the boys seemed inclined to slot me into the acceptable girl category. Why have a bunch of leering men decide I wasn't so pretty? Why blow what I had?

Contest time came around and it had all become one large joke to me. Part of that was defensive; act like you don't care and losing becomes easier. In fact, I wanted so much to create the illusion that I didn't care that I decided to do something on stage that would elicit the desired comic reaction from my sorority friends.

I decided to ham it up.

The contest was like all beauty contests. There was Harry Richman as MC, bright lights, bad music and judges trying hard to look totally objective.

Eighty-five girls pranced before the audience and judges before Mr. Richman said with the same enthusiasm he'd mustered for all the others, "And now, ladies and gentlemen, contestant number eighty-six . . . The lovely Miss Constance Keane."

Christ, I almost died. I didn't think I'd be scared when it came my turn. I'd practiced at home, especially how I'd walk onto the stage and turn around. I practiced walking so my hips swung more loosely than usual. I stood in front of a mirror at home experimenting with ways to accentuate my breasts. I'd planned to inject a little bit of burlesque movement to delight my girl friends. One day I took off all my clothes and did bumps and grinds in front of the full-length mirror in my parents' bedroom. Somehow it all looked slightly grotesque and I quickly put my clothes back on.

All the practice, ridiculous as it might have been, did make me feel confident that I'd at least strut out on the stage without any fear.

And here I was backstage, my name announced for all to hear, and my damn knees were shaking and lips trembling and heart beating a frantic paradiddle. I forgot all about making fun of anything. Was Frankie Rentz out there waiting to see me trip over my own feet? I knew my mother was there and I cursed the inch-thick make-up she'd applied before I left the house that afternoon.

I knew I'd better get out there before somebody pushed me from the wings. I took a step, and then another, and suddenly realized I'd walked all the way to the center of the stage without falling on my face. My confidence began to pick up a little and I did my turns for the judge and kept a big smile plastered on my face. It was actually beginning to turn into a pleasurable experience. My dress, a long black satin one, fitted beautifully over my bathing suit. I forgot about my heavy make-up because I figured the bright lights would wash everything out anyway. I was catching on to the event and began remembering some of the things I'd decided to do once I was out on the stage. I put a little of the burlesque walk into my stride and made my rump really move.

The band struck a chord signifying it was time for the dress to come off and for the judges to have a look at me in my bathing suit. Part of their judging was to be based on how gracefully each girl could handle that transition. It's not easy to be graceful when you're taking off any item of clothing. But I had that all figured out.

My dress had a long, single zipper down the side. I simply grabbed the zipper, gave it a quick pull and the long black satin dress fell at my feet.

They were impressed. You can tell when an audience has reacted favorably, or at least with surprise. I did my walking and turning in the bathing suit, a white tufted one, and walked offstage to thunderous applause.

Once I got backstage again, the trembling set in. Had I gone too far? Had I disgraced anyone? Myself?

A couple of my sorority friends were back there waiting for me. They were giggling but said I looked great.

"I wouldn't be surprised if you placed as high as eighty-fourth," one laughed.

"Maybe even eightieth," the other girl threw in.

"Was I that bad?" I asked.

"Worse," they agreed. "But don't worry about it, Connie. The rest are terrible, too."

We proceeded to stand back there as the final few contestants did their turn on the stage. Girls in bathing suits were everywhere, most with anxious, grim faces as they awaited the first sorting out of contestants. That's the way it was to be handled. Keep narrowing down the field and keep bringing the remaining girls back until the three top winners were decided upon by the judging panel.

We passed the time analyzing the physical shapes of some of the other contestants within our view.

"That gal has a great figure," I said.

"With that big fat belly? She's a mess."

"And that one over there. The one with the little tits. Ugh! And that one with the fat can. She's got flat feet, too. What a lousy smile. I hate that stringy hair."

Lovely girls, huh? Not them. I mean us for talking that way. But it was a lot of fun. Like being back in the locker room.

The judges announced their preliminary choices. I was still in.

And it went on and on until late in the night.

Harry Richman never faltered in his enthusiasm for the task. One of the judges fell asleep a few times and another read a magazine. But it finally came to the end. Backstage was a terrible scene. Girls already out of the running were in various states of depression. Some were in hysterics. Some sat glumly staring at nothing. Mothers were consoling, or scolding, or crying with their daughters. Talk about the slave markets—flesh peddling. Those are better descriptions of beauty contests.

Finally, Richman strode to the microphone, flashed his smile and announced to the audience, "Ladies and gentlemen, the judges have reached their decision on who shall reign as our glamorous Miss Miami for the coming year."

"Remember," one of my sorority buddies whispered, "the sorority gets all of anything you win."

Drum roll.

Hush.

"Ladies and gentlemen, in third prize, the lovely Miss Constance Keane."

Afterwards, my mother came backstage and joined in my friends' enthusiasm for my placing third in such a large field.

"You did very well, Connie," my mother said rather flatly.

"Thank you, Mommy."

"Your make-up looked lovely. Just right."

We were interrupted by Harry Richman. He shook my hand and congratulated me on winning third place. My mother jumped right in.

"I'm Connie's mother, Mr. Richman. I certainly enjoy you when you perform."

"Thank you, Mrs. Keane. You know, this little gal of yours has an awful lot of class for such a little thing. Real showmanship the way she dropped that dress. It really caught our eye. You don't see showmanship in kids this age any more. You ought to try her in Hollywood. I think she'd make it."

My mother promised she'd do that. I giggled along with my friends who, behind their laughter, were truly impressed. Imagine me being told I'd make it in Hollywood by a big name entertainer. It was a thrill. I tried to hide it but I'm sure everyone knew how pleased I was to have such encouragement from Mr. Richman. And there was no doubt about my mother. A gleam came to her eyes and if it weren't so confusing back there, I'd swear she turned and looked westward with a long and promising sigh.

Entering the "Miss Florida" Contest wasn't as much an outside decision as "Miss Miami." For one thing, I was all in favor of becoming a contestant. I'd caught a mild case of winning fever and felt my chances in the next contest were quite good. But I wasn't without outside forces acting on me either. My mother was all for my entering. So were some of my friends.

This time I played it straight. No gimmicks, no dresses falling to the floor. Just me. And I won. First place this time. "Miss Florida."

I wasn't a winner for long, though. They found out I was under age for a contestant and took away my title. I didn't mind. Being disqualified after you've won something is a pretty good way to lose. All my losses should be that winning.

10

I WANTED Wings was a box-office success. I was in. Veronica Lake was a familiar name with millions of movie-goers. And Paramount started treating me like a valuable piece of jewelry.

We discussed what roles I might be considered for now that my appearance in a film would help insure its success. No decisions were made. But it was obvious that Paramount was not about to interfere with the formula. There'd be another siren role and that meant no gamble. I'd proven how good a siren I could be.

Beauty shops all over the country began advertising the Veronica Lake hair style. And *Life* came out with an article devoted to my hair and the sensation it had caused. They divulged such important information as the fact that my head had 150,000 hairs, each measuring about 0.0024 inches in cross-section.

Other pertinent facts were that my hair varied in length from 17 inches in front to 24 inches in back and fell about eight inches below my shoulders. They told their readers I had to get up earlier than most actresses because my hair had to be washed, set and dried each morning before appearing on camera. I washed it twice in Nulava shampoo, once in Maro oil and then, because Hollywood's water was so hard, I rinsed it in vinegar.

It was all true, although embellished some. And I am happy they pointed out the problems of having a head of hair like mine. It *did* constantly snag on buttons and in bracelets. I did snap a winding stem on my wrist watch trying to pull my hair loose. And it did get singed more than once while I was smoking.

I certainly would have preferred to have made my mark in Hollywood's shortest hair style. Everything would have been easier.

But it never would have given the Fuller Brush Company the chance to promote one of their lines.

One of the Fuller salesmen, a nice chap, came knocking on my door one day and asked if I'd like to buy a brush.

It so happens my favorite brush had just about had it. And Fuller carried a brush very much like my worn-out one.

So, I bought it. Great brush.

It wasn't long after that the company announced to the brush-buying world that Veronica Lake used a Fuller brush. Salesmen carried literature heralding that fact. I understand the brush sold quite well, a flattering finding, I suppose. At least it was a good brush.

The bandwagon was really rolling. The *Harvard Lampoon* voted me the worst actress of 1941. The studio had people thinking up names for me like Cyclops Cinderella and Lastex Lorelei. They described my hair as the Detour Coiffure and the Peeping Pompadour. And the comics had a field day.

> *Groucho Marx:* "I opened up my mop closet the other day and I thought Veronica Lake fell out."
>
> *Bob Hope:* "Veronica Lake wears her hair over one eye because it's a glass eye."
>
> *Tizzie Lish:* "Here's a recipe for Veronica Lake potato bread. Use one-eyed potatoes . . ."
>
> *Fred Allen:* "I was stopped by a cop the other night for driving with one headlight out. He looked at me and said, "Hey, whatta you tryin' to pull, a Veronica Lake?"

And the public caught on.

I was dancing at a party with John one night when a woman said to her husband. "Look at that dame. Who does she think she is? Veronica Lake?"

And a woman in a theatre mentioned to her escort upon seeing me, "That must be Veronica Lake, junior." No one realized how little I was.

By February 1941 I was getting itchy for another role. I was cautioned that impatience was an undesirable trait in Hollywood.

"The studio knows what it's doing," I was assured by a friend. "You're hot property right now, and they'll make sure the next role is right. They'll keep it rolling."

I accepted that but still felt my inner anxiety. That's symptomatic of actors and actresses, and, I suppose, anyone in creative jobs. You can't wait to finish what you're doing and then you begin worrying once you've spent a week of inactivity. It's simple insecurity, a plentiful commodity in Hollywood.

Fortunately, Preston Sturges was sharing my itch for activity. Preston was one of Hollywood's top directors, especially in the comedy field. He'd recently completed editing *The Lady Eve* and went to Paramount with an idea he'd been toying with for a long time. His concept was to build a film around the life of a motion-picture comedy director. This fictional director would be in the midst of preparing a film dealing with hard times and trouble. He decides to actually live the hard life to give him a feel for the film he's about to direct. He'll become a hobo and travel the rails in search of material. The name of this fictitious film to be directed by this fictitious director? *Oh Brother, Where Art Thou?*

There's a girl in the real film, a girl trying to break into the movies, who joins forces with the fictitious director and together they bum across the country. And, for some unexplainable, glorious and celestial reason, Preston Sturges suggested me for the part to Paramount's brass.

"NO!" That was the initial response. "She's a great siren but no comic. Sultry, yes. Funny, no."

"I think she could do it," Preston argued.

"She's not an actress," they retaliated. "She's a great-looking dame with a great chest and nutty hair. But she's no actress."

But Sturges persisted. God bless him. He kept hammering away at Paramount's literal view of me until they gave in. He sold them on taking a chance. Maybe I could act, and that would copper their bet with me even more.

"I want her for three reasons," Preston told them. "One, she's the hottest bet in Hollywood right now. Two, she photographs great. And three, I can do without temperament on this film. She'll do what I tell her and she'll do it fine."

Preston called me at home with the good news.

"I hate to fink out on you now, Preston, but are you sure I can do this?" I asked after a few preliminary shrieks of pleasure. What a time to have a momentary lapse of self-confidence.

"I haven't got a doubt in the world. And you shouldn't either."

I hung up the phone, did some silly dance steps around the living-room and plopped on the couch. How could I tell him I was pregnant?

11

"WHAT about this baby rumor, Ronni?" Paramount had picked up some of the gossip floating around town that Veronica Lake was expecting her first child.

"That's all it is. Honest. A rumor. You don't really think I'd go and get pregnant at this stage in my career? Come on. Give me credit for some brains."

The baby was due some time in the middle of August, according to my doctor. Shooting on the Sturges film, the title to be *Sullivan's Travels*, was to commence May 12, 1941, just three months before my baby was due.

"This is going to be a tough film, Ronni," Preston told me. "I'd never want to see a pregnant gal try to do it."

"Everything's going to be fine," I assured him. I was determined it would be.

Naturally, I was worrying about Preston, Paramount and me. I never stopped to think that my biggest problem would be my mother. It was just an oversight in the recent hectic activity. But the rumor reached her.

"For God's sake, Mommy. Calm down. I'm going to do *Sullivan's Travels* and no one will know the difference. Besides, if I want a baby and a home with John, that's my business. Not yours."

I could see my mother turning black with rage.

"It is a selfish, stupid thing to do," she yelled.

"Mommy, please stop shouting. Please."

"Can't you get anything through that head of yours? All the work and tears to bring you to this stage and you get pregnant. First you run off and marry him without even telling me. And now . . . now you go and . . ." I hung up on her. She called back.

The hassle on the phone went on in various stages throughout the afternoon. I'd just hung up on one of them when John came home from the studio. It was so marvelous to see him. Here was the logical person to set my mother straight. It was our home, our lives, our baby. I told him about the afternoon and my mother's reaction to the news. He didn't seem to want to hear about it. He was polite and listened to my story, but he shrugged it off and declined to call her back as I suggested.

He didn't have to. My mother called a few minutes later. I forced John to answer the phone. She ranted on and on about how horrible my pregnancy was for my career. John listened passively until she said, "Don't you realize what you've done?"

He laughed. "Of course I know what I've done. I was there." He laughed some more, obviously not in tune with my mother's mood. She wasn't looking for laughter.

"It's not funny, John," my mother said with great sorrow in her voice. "You've ruined her career. Did you stop and think of *that* when you were *there*?"

John winced. He seemed stunned at my mother's serious tone. He looked over for me to give some clue as to something further to say. I gave him a pleading look, a plea to yell at her, snap back and defend me, us, the baby soon to be with us. Defend anybody, for Christ's sake.

But all he did was smile and talk weakly into the phone.

"It's O.K., Mom. Honest. They don't know at the studio and I thought Ronni was all set. Maybe we can . . ."

Maybe we can *what*? I wanted to pick up the couch and throw it at him as he sat there uttering inane disclaimers and absurd attempts at finding a solution. I hated John at that moment. I wanted him to stand up to her and tell her to mind her own business. And the last thing I wanted was for him to apologize for making me pregnant. I searched his face for some sign of rebellion. There was none, only embarrassment and confusion. He looked over to me for something. Strength, I assume. I gave him tears.

"I didn't mean to do anything to Ronni's career, Mom. I mean, Ronni wanted to have a baby and we . . ."

I walked out of the house and didn't return until two days later. John offered apologies but for all the wrong things. We're all hurt by different things, each a conditioned soft core of our past experience. The fact that John, my husband, ended up by explaining away my pregnancy by blaming me was the greatest hurt I'd known. Maybe if he'd known my mother intimated to me years ago that I was a mistake, a mistake resulting in a very unwanted child, he'd have reacted differently to her. Maybe not. We never talked about it again. It simply took its place in the wall that would build between us.

12

SULLIVAN'S Travels was a joy to make. Preston Sturges displayed absolute genius, a fact recently applauded by many at the Preston Sturges film festival at Lincoln Center. There's no doubt he ranks with the great directors of Hollywood, and being given the no-name role of The Girl in the film was the best break I was ever to receive in my professional career. It enabled me to act in what I consider one of the best films of my career, and critics then and now concur completely with that feeling of mine. I felt very much at home with comedy and still do in summer stock.

Preston not only directed Sullivan's Travels, he also conceived the story and wrote the screen-play. It had that marvelous Keystone Comedy feel to it, many fast-cuts and kaleidoscopic sequences that worked due to a masterful editing job by Preston and Stuart Gillmore.

I was in my glory, pregnant or not. Here was a film in which I spent most of my time with my famous hair tucked under a cap, my famous bosom lost under a ragged man's coat. Baggy pants completed the costume for the film. All I had to do was act. I accepted the challenge and immersed myself in the role.

Preston quickly learned a few things about me. The most important thing was that I always gave a terribly stiff reading of lines that I'd learned long in advance of the day's shooting. I've always been quick to learn. It's easy for me to pick up patter of any kind.

The first few days' shooting found me going through a rigid and doltish acting job. It was terrible. I'd studied my lines over and over and knew them cold. And that was the problem.

Preston talked to me about it and allowed me to try a few days of looking at my lines just before shooting the scene. That kind of thing would be sacrilege for a stage actress—and an impossibility. But it works for me. I'd look at the script while the technicians were setting up and go out and do them. It worked much better.

"Don't ever walk on my set knowing anything about your lines or scenes," Preston told me after the first day under the new system. I didn't for the rest of the film and for most of the other films I worked in after *Sullivan's Travels*. The word got around I was better without advance preparation and most directors accepted that and worked with it.

Preston Sturges liked his heroes to be treated rough and slapstick. And he was a fast starter. The first day's shooting found my co-star, Joel McCrea, falling into a rain barrel, falling over a wagon tongue and crawling through a hen house. He also hid in the middle of a pig pen with 100 squealing pigs.

It was a wild movie to make. And it got wilder when Preston found out I was pregnant.

Keeping my pregnancy from Preston hung over my head like a cumbrous weight. I certainly didn't want to upset him and the fever with which he approached the film. And yet I was scared to death my condition would cause a problem later on and make completion of the film an impossibility. I knew I had to do something and do it quickly. But I couldn't get up the guts to simply tell him. So I told his wife, Louise.

It was in the first week of shooting. Louise Sturges, also pregnant, was sitting on the edge of the set watching the filming. Mary Martin was also there as a spectator. She'd just finished filming *Birth of the Blues*, was pregnant like the rest of us and jubilant that she could relax until November when her baby was due.

Preston spotted Mary and yelled, "This looks like Paramount's Stork Club." Everyone laughed. And I saw an opportunity to bring up my inclusion in the club. I leaned over to Louise Sturges and whispered, "Don't tell Preston, but I'm pregnant, too."

Louise turned to me and smiled. But her voice had no hint of the smile.

"I certainly will not tell him," she said flatly. "But I'll give you a two-minute running start to tell him yourself."

Sturges was hardly overjoyed. In fact, it took visible restraint to keep from boiling over at me. That evening, he consulted with my doctor and the studio executives. Once they assured him they were not overly displeased with this turn of events, Preston decided to go ahead with me in the role. I went through all the usual promises to myself and the gods that I would never again do this, or that, if only he would decide favorably. Naturally, I never kept those promises. No one does. When he told me I could stay in the role, my first reaction was to be thankful I'd told him about things so early in the game. I would have hated to think he kept me on because it was too late to come up with a replacement with so many completed scenes in the can.

The shooting schedule turned into a wild and woolly one. The whole success of the film depended on the pace Preston could maintain in the scenes. It had to move, and move fast. And his shooting schedule reflected the film's flow.

We did twelve different locations in sixteen location days, and that's damned fast when you consider the maddening set-up time in film making. The opening scene alone ranked as one of the fastest in feature film production. We did 390 feet in one continuous take. It included 95 separate speeches, 1,121 words and three actors—McCrea, Robert Warwick and Porter Hall. Hall had to give every speech in the film with a cigar in his mouth and went through 121 cigars during the shooting. Sturges himself appeared in the movie and even donated a set of his electric trains—he was a devoted hobbyist—to the special effects department for one scene.

Once a film is rolling smoothly, everything seems to work right. You pick up momentum and pieces fall into place and it's one hell of a feeling. I'll never forget filming the scene in which Joel and I are traveling in a car. We actually shot the scene between five and six in the morning, and did seven pages of dialogue without a hitch. No re-takes. An actor's dream. And a director's, too. Preston and I were getting along famously.

Besides enjoying the chance to work with Preston, I found the experience a fine education. He was sure, confident, and had the critical ability to express just what he expected from his talent in any given scene. Joel McCrea was marvelous in the role of the director turned hobo; his only apparent problem was how to get through all the dirty, messy scenes and still maintain his bum's outfit for the next day's shooting. That was solved by having two identical outfits. There was one period during which Joel had to play all his scenes soaking wet. The hot lights of the studio dried out his costume much too quickly to even allow one continuous action scene. But Hollywood is the great innovator. They soaked his clothing in oil which photographed as just plain wet but didn't evaporate under the lights. That's one of the kicks about film making. Nothing is what it really seems. Like the milk used in *Sullivan's Travels*. Again, the lights caused too much heat. And no one wanted to drink spoiled milk. So they substituted plain old whitewash. And cut away for a quick milk substitution when actual drinking had to take place.

There was also the scene in which Joel and I snoop around in garbage cans in an alley. We didn't go far. Paramount has a marvelous alley just behind its commissary. The half-completed power plant in the background was neatly covered up with a huge sign—"Erected by The Acme Construction Company."

Naturally, the studio publicity people were working overtime on ways to use me to publicize the film. But it wasn't easy. Sexy Veronica was dressed in loose-fitting, trashy clothing. Her famous hair was tucked up under a cap for most of the film. No cheesecake for them to work with.

But never count a studio publicity flack out. They simply turned around and made a big noise about how Paramount had hidden its greatest asset under baggy clothing. They praised me in releases for daring to prove I was an actress and not just a hairy sexpot. And they made it work.

My pregnancy never bothered me at all. But Jiggs did. Jiggs was a monkey working on a Dorothy Lamour film on the next sound stage. Poor Dorothy. She was always getting bitten and clawed by the animals.

I was sitting on our set one day dressed in my tramp outfit and minding my own business when I felt something grab my hand. I couldn't look. And then I felt teeth gently clasp on my fingers.

I couldn't move. I wanted to scream but didn't dare. Preston happened to look over and saw my plight.

"Don't pull your hand away," he said quietly.

I didn't move a muscle.

"Hey," Preston yelled to his assistant. "Get the trainer for that goddamned ape."

Jiggs just kept on holding my hand in his teeth. He never bit hard enough to break the skin; just hard enough to let me know he was there.

His trainer finally came running over from Dorothy's set.

"Jiggs," he snapped in what seemed a terribly human voice. But Jiggs understood his master. He let go and romped over to the trainer.

I sneaked a look at my hand and saw that aside from a regular row of white marks from his teeth, no damage had been done.

"You're lucky," his trainer told me. "He hates women."

"Great."

"But he must like you," the trainer went on. "When a monkey puts your hand in his mouth, he likes and trusts you."

"Well, the feeling's not mutual. Keep him the hell out of here."

The trainer was definitely hurt. He took Jiggs, trusting, lovable ape that he was, and led him back to familiar surroundings. Dorothy heard about it and howled.

"He missed my sarong," she told me. Judging from the gleam in that monkey's eye, I don't doubt it at all.

Although my pregnancy wasn't bothering me, I found a tendency on the part of the crew to treat me like some fragile piece of china. And the further along I became, the motherly protection became more intense. I loved them for it. That film seemed to have attracted the nicest people.

One of the final scenes we shot was photographed around a swimming-pool 100 by 40 feet. It was a private pool at a Hollywood mansion. The studio rented it from the owner for $500 a day, all proceeds going to charity. This was a common Hollywood practice with the wealthy.

The script called for me to push Joel McCrea into the pool with all his clothes on, and then stand at the pool's edge and tell him off.

I pushed. He went in the water. I did my lines and stepped back to allow my stunt girl to take my place. Joel was to grab her by the ankles and pull her in with him. He grabbed. She went in the water with him. The scene was wrapped.

I watched them frolicking around in that gorgeous water and decided, pregnant or not, I was joining them. I know that isn't a prudent bit of thinking for a woman in her eighth month. But I've never won any awards for prudent thinking anyway. So I jumped.

I went in the pool for fun. But Preston immediately had the cameraman start rolling again. My stunt girl was no longer in the water. Joel noticed the camera was in operation, and started going through the same water antics he'd performed with the stunt gal. He dunked me. I went under and came up. But I didn't come up the way the script called for No-Name Girl to surface. My petticoat had gotten twisted over my head and I couldn't shake it off. All Joel saw was a headless form bobbing on top of the water. He grabbed at the petticoat and finally managed to yank it off me as I sputtered for air.

They pulled me up onto the grass and waited for me to catch my breath. Preston was the first to speak.

"That was a pretty dumb stunt, Ronni."

"I know, Preston. But it looked so damned inviting and . . ."

"Well, I'm glad you enjoyed it. I caught all of it and it looked great. Go dry off, have lunch and we'll come back to the pool this afternoon. I've figured out a whole gang of water bits for you and Joel."

So we did water routines all afternoon. Most of them were used in the final film.

We completed shooting of *Sullivan's Travels* on the twenty-first of July. Elaine, my first child, was born on the twenty-first of August, just thirty days later. She was a bundle of health. The pool episode obviously had no greater effect than instilling in her an innate love of water. Could that be possible?

The reviews on the film were good. Interestingly enough, they've become even better lately as the film ages. It seems to be falling into that vague area of the film classic, and it pleases me greatly to see this particular motion picture reach some plateau of critical acceptance. It at least gives me a running chance to be remembered for my best work, the secret dream of any actress.

Preston Sturges and I remained the best of friends. He never directed me again, which was my loss. But he said many nice things about me, both to the studio people and to the general public. He told Sheilah Graham, "She's one of the little people. Like Mary Pickford, Douglas Fairbanks and Freddie Bartholomew when he started, who take hold of an audience immediately. She's nothing much in real life—a quiet, rather timid little thing. But the screen transforms her, electrifies her and brings her to life. I think she's the biggest bet in the business."

The problem with writing your autobiography is that you feel a reluctance to include puff like the above. But then you reconsider the whole situation and realize that it affords you a chance to counteract, in some small way, all the bad things people have said about you.

I can only thank Preston Sturges for taking a chance on me for *Sullivan's Travels* and for still liking me after it was over. Lest you feel I'm over-saccharine about remaining friends with someone, let me remind you that Hollywood friendships are notorious for their lack of longevity. A perfect example of that was Richard Maibaum, the writer and co-producer on *I Wanted Wings*. I'd heard he'd become quite ill and decided to visit him. His mother answered the door and led me to a small Spanish terrace in the back of the house. Dick sat there with his mother and we talked about *I Wanted Wings* and what I'd been doing lately. He brought up my elopement with John and I recalled with warmth how Dick had come to my dressing-room to offer his congratulations. He was so nice and comforting to a very young and scared girl in her first major role. A fine person.

"How's everybody?" I asked him at one point.

"I guess fine," he answered. "I haven't seen anyone in a long time." His mother raised her eyebrows to indicate dropping the conversation would be wise. I did.

I didn't stay much longer. Dick was in pain and grew quite weary. I got up to leave and went over to give him a kiss. He took my hand in his and said, "You know, Ronni, you're the only one who's come to see me. The only one." I left before the tears did more than just well up in my eyes.

I value friends. I don't have that many, but when I do latch onto one, I hold on as best I can.

13

ELAINE was beautiful. And, like most mothers, I took her beauty and waved it for all to see. John and I had, together, created a truly lovely little girl. And John, despite all his professed dislike for children, seemed to fall right into the role of father and ardent admirer. He did all the cootchy-cootchy-coo things and made all the funny faces to make the baby laugh. It seemed things were really shaping up for the Detlie family. My mother stopped ranting and raving about the child and its threat to her daughter's career. That, of course, let John off the hook. He wasn't forced to defend anything any longer, and this suited his nature and inclination.

The world might have been more receptive to the birth of such a lovely little girl. But war does not procreate the soft, frilly world of new-born babes. And Europe was at war. Its local tensions had inflated into a global tension. It did not bypass Hollywood. Our anxiety was climaxed, or released, depending on your psychological leanings, on December 7 when Pearl Harbor was attacked. By that time I'd begun filming *This Gun for Hire* with a new actor named Alan Ladd in the male lead.

Alan Ladd was a marvelous person in his simplicity. In so many ways we were kindred spirits. We both were professionally conceived through Hollywood's search for box-office and the *types* to insure that box-office. And we were both little people.

Alan wasn't as short as most people believe. It was true that in certain films in which his leading lady was on the tallish side, Alan would climb a small platform or the girl worked in a slit trench. We had no such problem working together.

Alan had played a small role in *Joan of Paris* as one of five fugitive British flyers, but *This Gun for Hire* brought him to the forefront of the movie-goer's imagination as to what a tough guy should be. Adan Ladd was a superb psychopathic killer. He could be cool, placid, all-observing and knowing or just plain nasty. He was all these things in his career and a nation reacted enthusiastically. There is no actor with whom I'm more closely connected than Alan Ladd. And yet we had less to do with each other than most other acting teams.

We'd arrive on the set early in the morning. Alan would nod and say, "Good morning, Ronni."

"Hi, Alan."

We'd go to make-up and wardrobe, play our scenes together, and go back to our dressing-rooms to take off the make-up and wardrobe.

"'night, Ronni."

"'night, Alan. See you tomorrow."

Both of us were very aloof people. We were a good match for each other. It enabled us to work together very easily and without any friction or temperament. Naturally, the public linked us romantically. But neither of us cared what the public conjured up about us. And we were just as indifferent to the studio's sly attempts to perpetuate the romantic rumors. It's all part of the game in enticing the public into the theatre, and the Ladd-Lake billing proved to be a powerful lure.

There were times when we came close to completely shedding our individual shells and joining forces in a closer and perhaps more normal relationship. Alan laughed easily and we'd occasionally sit and swap stories. I'll never forget his reaction to the War Manpower Commission's request about my hair. It seems too many female defense plant workers were wearing the Veronica Lake hair-do and getting it all fouled up in the machinery. The Commission, through the War Production Board, passed something or other which requested me to refrain from wearing my hair long for the duration of the war. It's all in the Congressional Record. Alan laughed for days over this unexpected request from our government. I must admit I was flattered to think I had become that crucial to our war effort. The last thing I wanted was to have caused a work force of one-eyed women fouling up the defense machinery.

At the time, *This Gun for Hire* didn't seem to be much of a film. Graham Greene had written the novel from which Al Maltz and W.R. Burnett scripted the screen play. For me, it marked two big milestones in my career. I received my first screen kiss, and I was making $350 a week. The money was no big deal when you consider the salaries stars were receiving. Let me be quick to say that I use the term *star* to denote someone with proven ability to draw people into movie theatres. It's not an expression of egotism as most people might consider it. I was a film star under the professional definition. And $350 a week was incredibly low pay for someone in that professional strata.

But everything being relative, I was thrilled over my salary increase. It meant more to me than receiving my first screen kiss from Robert Preston. No offense, Bob.

In the film, I played Elen Graham, a nightclub siren who also happened to be a singer, dancer and magician. I've been accused of late of being a magician at making a bottle of Scotch disappear. But I wasn't good at any sleight-of-hand then. I was all thumbs. Paramount brought in a professional magician, Jan Grippo, to teach me some basics. I didn't learn a thing. I just kept fumbling around while our director, Frank Tuttle, tried to shoot round the flubs.

To compound things, I had to dance and sing besides making eggs disappear. And my singing and dancing experience was as non-existent as my magic ability.

Filming dragged along at an agonizing pace, especially on those days when my act was in front of the camera.

We'd start late because I always had trouble with my false fingernails. I've always kept my nails short, but that wouldn't do for a nightclub siren doing tricks. They'd finally manage to get the claws attached and we'd go to work.

And everything would go wrong. We'd do a take and the dance director would say he wasn't satisfied. Another take would follow and the lighting director would inform Frank Tuttle there was a shadow someplace.

One day we did that horrible magic act of mine over and over and over until I thought I'd scream. If I didn't foul up, it was a crew member. And if we all came through on a take, it was Josephine.

Josephine, like Jiggs, was a monkey. And she was as much of a bitch as Jiggs was a bastard. She was a mean, snippy ape who possessed temperament like no actress on earth. And I was stuck with her as part of my magic act. She'd either whip me with her clipped tail as we did the scene or bite me. She bit me twice on the arm. And she also managed to bite a couple of extras appearing in the scene.

The day had started early and was running late. We were up to take number 51 on that same scene. We did it, the camera stopped rolling and I held my breath for the verdict.

"Print that," Frank Tuttle yelled wearily.

Everyone applauded. I kicked off my shoes and started walking towards my dressing-room when the sound man's voice stopped everything dead in its tracks.

"No take. She was out of sync."

"Out of sync?" I screamed at no one in particular.

"Sorry, hon," the sound man said with a maddening devil-may-care tone to his voice. He was enjoying his overtime pay.

I flipped. I cried and let loose a string of foul language that would have put even Broadway actors to shame. My last word faded and there was total silence. I looked around. Everyone stood there gaping at me. The extras actually looked hurt that I'd talk like that. And they made me feel hurt.

"Sorry, gang," I announced with as much cheer as could be mustered at the moment. But I kept swearing under my breath as I walked back to again go through my routine for the camera.

We did take 52. And 53. And up through 60 and finally, after take 64, we called it a day. It was ten o'clock at night, just in time for Los Angeles' first brown-out, a partial power failure. It seemed a fitting finale for the day.

I watched the developed footage the next day.

"All those early takes don't look so bad to me," I muttered to Frank Tuttle.

"I know," he agreed. "I'm using the fourth take."

"The fourth? After we did all the others?"

"Yeah. It looks great. Don't you agree?"

And that's film making, folks, the last sixty takes tossed in the scrap can.

But you get used to all the re-doing in picture making. You come to the point where you just sit back and wait until you're told to go through the motions again. Of course, if the scene is a particularly difficult one or disconcerting for you, it becomes more difficult to tolerate all those retakes. Like when I received my first screen kiss. It was such a big event that Harold Hefferman devoted his column to the moment. And I found the doing nerve-racking.

I was wearing a very tight black gown and a hat under which my hair was carefully pinned up. Bob Preston was to be the one to violate Veronica Lake's chaste lips. I was nervous. It seemed the word had spread that a great Hollywood happening was about to take place, and half the studio showed up to witness. Now I know why Doris Day will only work on a closed set.

I was experiencing real stage fright. I could sense everyone waiting and watching. What in hell was the big deal? I asked myself. And I'd answer myself by asking why I was so nervous if it was such a trivial thing.

It might not have been so bad if extras had been working the scene with us. But it was to be just the two of us. The previous scene had been at a carnival. Now, in close-up camera position, Bob and I were to kiss in front of the shooting gallery. Just us. All the extras, and there were well over 100 of them, became spectators.

The scene opened with me telling Bob I had to leave San Francisco. He was to allow an appropriate amount of time for the weight of the message to sink in. Then, in a grand gesture, he was to sweep me into his arms and kiss me hard and long.

It all went as planned. He grabbed. I grabbed, too, and hung on for all I was worth. My nose was pressed too firmly against his cheek and I couldn't breathe. I pulled back just a fraction to allow air to enter my nostrils and pushed back again. I suppose you could call it a continuous two-part kiss.

"Cut!"

A couple of wise guys applauded.

"Looked good," Tuttle said.

"Her eyes were closed," someone yelled to Tuttle.

"So what?" Tuttle yelled back. "Closed eyes are good kissing technique."

"She looked nervous. Closed eyes make you look nervous when you're kissing."

"Like hell. Print that take. I like closed eyes."

I sighed a sigh of relief. But I was premature.

"The take's no good." It was the sound man. "I picked up a pounding all through the kiss, Frank."

"A pounding?"

"Yeh, boom, boom, boom. Steady. All the way through."

"Must have been Ronni's heart," Preston quipped.

"Must have been," I agreed.

We did the kissing scene again. I shut my eyes, took a deeper breath this time before we started, and found I could make it all the way through without coming up for air.

"Cut! Good take. Print that."

"N.G." Again, the sound man. "I picked up a truck motor outside."

"Tell that truck to shut up," Tuttle ordered his assistant. The assistant told his assistant who ran very quickly to relay the message.

Bob Preston was all smiles. "Don't worry on my account," he told Tuttle. And he winked at me.

"Again," Tuttle said with resignation. He asked for quiet and everyone listened intently for any foreign noise to spoil another take. Silence.

The make-up gal re-applied my lipstick, gave Bob a towel to wipe his mouth, and we went at it again.

"Cut! O.K. with you, sound?"

"Nope. I think I'm getting a clunk from the ventilator."

"A clunk?"

"Yeah. Clunk clunk."

Preston was grinning broadly now. "Again, coach?"

"Again."

I was having trouble getting up a pucker now. Bob Preston believed in good old-fashioned kissing; hard and long. And he expected it in return.

"How's your heart?" he asked in a whisper.

"About as fouled up as that ventilator."

"They turned the ventilator off."

"I'll try it on my heart."

"Keep your eyes open."

"Frank likes 'em closed."

"Ready?"

"Ready."

It went beautifully. I assumed we were through with the scene. But Frank destroyed that illusion.

"Now let's catch the individual close-ups," he ordered.

"Do we have to, Frank?" I asked.

"I resent that," was Preston's response.

Tuttle turned to Preston. "You don't mind going on, do you, Bob?"

"Hell no. Why do you think I took this part? Now we do it for your close-ups, Ronni. Then we do it for mine. Luckiest day of my life."

I'm glad he was happy.

This Gun for Hire was released in May of 1942 and met with mixed reviews. Surprisingly, it too has fallen into today's mysterious realm of the minor film classic. Today's film buffs look for things in films that we didn't when I was making films. I'm naturally pleased that films such as this still give people pleasure.

The critics generally saw my role in *This Gun for Hire* as a wasted performance after *Sullivan's Travels*. Others were more in tune with today's critics, and felt it was a small personal triumph for me. The film became known as a sleeper in the trade, and was even compared with much of Hitchcock's success in the suspense medium. The chase scenes were exciting, much to the credit of cinematographer John Seitz.

As I look back on the film, I view it with mixed emotions. It certainly helped perpetuate Veronica Lake as Everyman's mistress which, in turn, assured me further work in subsequent films. My box-office was still climbing.

But I gave up something in return. I had obliterated any inroads I'd made as an actress in *Sullivan's Travels*. I was right back in the low-cut gowns and wearing the sexy hair. "Take the bitter with the sweet," is the way I suppose the mountain folk would sum it up. And they're usually right.

Alan Ladd died in *This Gun for Hire* with his head resting in my lap. *Variety* commented, "Better men have died with their heads in less pleasant places." I always meant to ask Alan about his feelings on the subject but never got around to it. He probably wouldn't have answered me.

The Lake-Ladd thing was moving in high gear now. And Paramount wasted no time in pairing us again, this time in a re-make of Dashiell Hammett's *The Glass Key*.

We did this film without incident except for my punching Brian Donlevy in the jaw and rendering him glassy-eyed. It happened while we were filming the opening scene of the film. The script called for me to punch him on the jaw. The idea was not without a certain appeal to me. I'd worked with Brian in *I Wanted Wings* and we'd never really become bosom buddies. I was certain he didn't like me and that made me nervous.

I threw the punch and connected with his chin. Now, Brian Donlevy is a very solid 200 pounds on a five-feet, eight-inch frame. He wasn't expecting much of a punch for two reasons: I was too little to punch very hard, he reasoned, and I certainly would know enough to pull a punch in a motion picture. He was wrong on both counts. I'd learned in my Brooklyn youth to lead with the hip when you throw a punch. Every pound I owned was behind it when it caught his jaw.

I saw his eyes go into a glassy haze the moment impact took place. He didn't move. He just stood there gazing straight ahead, his mouth hanging open.

I cried. I was terrified. And as he regained some of his lost senses, I could see right away he hadn't taken the matter lightly. His face seethed with a barely controlled rage.

"What the hell did you do that for?" he said through clenched teeth.

"I'm sorry, Brian. I don't know how to pull a punch."

"I'll give you until the next take to learn," he said with complete finality. I took his advice and pulled my punches from then on.

Hammett fans hated our version of their favorite author's classic. Others never liked the original version with George Raft and felt we'd accomplished an improvement on the story. Either way, it all came off for me as a humdrum affair sparked occasionally by the antics of William Bendix, one of my all-time favorite people. Alan and I attacked the project with all the enthusiasm of time clock employees, a pretty cocky approach for two people without acting credentials and only the instant star system to thank for our success.

I was happy just keeping busy. Unfortunately, things at home were rapidly developing into quiet chaos. There was no overt action of deed that could be sorted and destroyed. It simply was no longer a happy home. That happens despite what our divorce judges think. Why every divorce has to have some major crushing blow to render it eligible for legal severance is beyond me. You marry to be happy, and when the two people are no longer happy, the marriage is no longer worthwhile. I don't believe it a contradiction to further state that I hold marriage high in esteem. I believe there to be nothing more meaningful than a marriage in which each partner contributes to the other, both in happiness and in further development of the individual. I just think it should be easier to get out when it doesn't do this.

My age didn't help things. I wasn't able to read the signs, the hints, recognize and understand the causes and effects. I'd just get mad, or brood or sulk or anything else you might expect of a very young girl with a husband and child. And, we mustn't forget, I was a screen idol, a sex symbol, a cause for mass masturbation and heavy breathing in darkened theatres.

None of this pleased John. And I couldn't understand that. Not at all. I do today, and wince whenever I think of the unfortunate spot John had been placed in when he married Veronica Lake.

John never really expressed displeasure at my stardom. But it was there, deeply embedded in him and growing deeper as each day passed. As I said, I now look back through the magnification of age and understand. Had I understood when it was happening, our lives might have taken different courses from those they followed.

We walked into a restaurant one evening and John was greeted with, "Good evening, Mr. Lake." That's not easy for a man.

I'd receive letters from my fan clubs and many would ask questions about "Mister Lake." I was receiving over 1,000 pieces of mail a week and tried to answer one out of every five. I signed every one Mrs. John Detlie. But it soon got out of hand and my letter-answering chores were turned over to the studio. Every major studio had a letter-writing staff and usually one person, in most cases a female, who was expert at signature forging. She could sign anyone's name as well as they could, and I wonder how many millions of people all over the world have cherished photographs supposedly signed by their screen favorite. It's a good thing for society these signature experts used their skills for motion-picture studios. With slight leanings towards crime, they'd have made a fortune.

The invitations were for me, with my husband invited to attend with me. My face and figure were known all over the nation. Men wrote me letters, most simple puff but some lewd and shocking. And my earning power, although not realized as yet, was now far greater than John's.

My friends were no help either. I didn't have many, but I did start spending some time with other film people. And that meant movie talk—star talk. It all added up to a belly full for John, a belly full of talk and scenes and letters and people that chipped away at John's ego as husband and provider. There he was, college educated with honors and immensely talented, married to a runny-nosed tom-boy from Brooklyn who just barely finished high school and was a screen favorite just because Freddie Wilcox liked her chest or the way she walked or something called "having it."

Shit.

Everything happened against the backdrop of Hollywood's greatest and zaniest era. And there was a war that overshadowed everyone's life. But strangely enough, it was the war that intervened in our own private conflict and brought things back to an even keel for a period of time.

As an art director, John was potentially useful in camouflage design. Through a friend, he began designing camouflage schemes for military installations in our home at night. It was all very exciting. John was excellent in his designs, and threw himself into the work with an intense sense of mission. And so did I. I became fascinated with the work and spent many evenings helping him in any way I could. It pulled us together, a togetherness we hadn't felt for much too long a time. And it did wonderful things for John. He was contributing in a major way towards our efforts in the war. I could only function as his lackey in the work. It was his ability being utilized, not mine, and the stakes were far greater than providing a lap for Alan Ladd's last screen moments. I'd never seen John happier. Yes, there is a certain perversion in finding happiness in any war. But you grab happiness when it's around. I grabbed and held on tight. It was an opportunity to help our country in its war; two people not about to be drafted by Uncle Sam. It was happiness and pride and a lot of other things.

14

THINGS picked up for me, too. René Clair, a fine director, was casting for *I Married a Witch*. I was in love with the role of Jennifer, the fair witch, and told René I wanted to play the part.

"No!"

I went to Preston Sturges and asked him to talk to René.

"You know I can play comedy, Preston. Please do what you can do."

Sturges talked with René but René was completely against me for Tonnifor. He referred back to *This Gun for Hire* as an example of the kind of role I did best.

"What about *Sullivan's Travels*?" Preston asked him.

"One good role doesn't mean she's a good comedienne," was René's reply.

"And two good roles does indicate something," I pleaded with René. "I want that part."

Things remained unsettled for a few days. Finally, Preston called me at home with the good news. "I got René to give you the role, Ronni. He's still reluctant and you'll have to do a lot of proving with him, but you're in. And that's the big hurdle."

"Doesn't *Sullivan's Travels* prove anything to him?" I asked.

"It should, hon. But he hasn't seen it. Doesn't plan on it, either. As far as he's concerned, you're a siren starlet with box-office, but no actress. Prove it to him."

René was terribly nice to me despite his reluctance to use me in the film. And he was certainly a fine director. He had everything— timing, viewpoint, appreciation of the subtle things that made good comedy. And he had a hell of a heart as evidenced during the second week of shooting. He came to me after looking at rushes and said, "I'm here to apologize, Ronni. Preston was right. You are a hell of a good comedienne. I'm sorry."

I loved René for that.

And I hated Fredric March.

I don't believe there is an actor for whom I harbor such deep dislike as Fredric March. It's strictly personal. We all know and recognize what a fine and distinguished actor he is. But working with him gave me the feeling of being a captive in a Charles Addams tower.

He gave me a terrible time during *I Married a Witch*. I'm sure that despite what René thought, March considered me a brainless little blonde sexpot, void of any acting ability and not likely to acquire any. He treated me like dirt under his talented feet. Of all actors to end up under the covers with. That happened in one scene and Mr. March is lucky he didn't get my knee in his groin.

What he didn't realize was that this sexy, no-talent Brooklyn blonde has a vindictive streak in her. I set right out to give it back to Mr. March.

I got to do it twice, really. There were other very small moments when I felt I'd pushed back a little. But two incidents stand out in my mind as particularly effective examples of getting even with my co-star.

One scene had me in a rocking-chair. A picture falls off the wall and strikes me unconscious. I'm supposed to sit in the chair without movement while March desperately attempts to talk to me.

The shot was medium, showing only the two of us from waist-high. We were into the scene and he came close to me. He was standing directly in front of the chair.

I carefully brought my foot up between his legs. And I moved my foot up and down, each upward movement pushing it ever so slightly into his groin. Pro that he is, he never showed his predicament during the scene. But it wasn't easy for him, and I delighted simply in knowing what was going through his mind. Naturally, when the scene was over, he laced into me. I just smiled.

The second time I was able to give vent to my vengeance was during a scene in which March was supposed to carry me off into the distance. The cameraman rigged a forty-pound weight under my dress. We did the scene's opening business and then Fredric picked me up. Naturally, he expected no difficulty with tiny little me. But that forty pounds of extra dead weight made one hell of a difference. I could hear March grunt under his breath as he valiantly carried out the script's directions. We did the scene three more times and each one brought on a definite decline in his strength. He put me down for the final time and scowled at me.

"Big bones," I said and walked away. He heard about what had been done a few days later and the wall was built permanently, never again to come down. We've seen each other a few times since then and we never speak to each other. Oh, well.

Despite Fredric March, filming *I Married a Witch* was fun. With things at home eased and more stable. I was relaxed during the shooting. And I was doing comedy, something for which I was grateful and hopeful. Maybe with two good films under my belt, the studio would take me away from the siren roles.

I was also out of touch with my mother, a situation brought on during production of *The Glass Key*. William Bendix was in that film and I soon came to adore the guy. It was a platonic adoration for a marvelous human being. My mother, in a state of something or other, felt I was out to steal Bill from Tess, his wonderful wife. Tess and I had our problems over that before things were properly explained and settled. I never forgave my mother for that. I stopped speaking to her completely, a blissful state of affairs.

John was deeply involved in his camouflage work, I with my comedy role, and our home in the canyon was again full of warmth and happiness. We'd wake up to those big fat California mornings, smile, and go on our enjoyable ways. The evenings were serene. And Elaine was bringing up great joy as we watched her develop before our very eyes. There was a lot to be thankful for.

John never came to the set, and I was surprised to see him one late afternoon towards the end of our schedule on *I Married a Witch*.

"What are you doing here?" I asked.

"Nothing special, Ronni. Just thought you might like dinner out."

It sounded fine. We seldom went out for meals, preferring our home and my cooking. I've always loved to cook.

We went to some joint in Beverly Hills that tried very hard to emulate Don the Beachcomber but missed badly. John was pleasant but tense. He seemed to want to say something other than our general chit-chat but couldn't. Finally, after dinner and over coffee, John revealed his inner secret.

"I suppose there's no sense in prolonging this any longer, Ronni."

"Prolonging what, honey?"

"What I have to tell you. You know what I've done?"

"I suppose I could guess but that would take all night. Just tell me."

"All right. I've joined the army."

"You what?"

"The army. I've joined. And they've given me a commission. With the camouflage department, District Engineer's Office. I'll be leaving for Seattle very soon."

I could easily have slid under the table in shock. I'd had absolutely no indication, no clue to this turn of events. Things had been going so well with us at home. Why did he do this? What did it mean?

John tried to explain it over drinks at the bar. We had a concoction called Golden Cups, an exotic drink with the kick of a mule. After three, we called it a night and went home, each silent in thought. I got up the next morning with a balloon for a head. It was the first time I was ever late for shooting. I should have just called and said I was sick. It's funny, but I was never able to do that. A silly little hang-up I still have. I showed up late, blundered through the day and headed home for more talk with John.

The shock didn't wear off for at least a week. I was primarily mad at John. I was mad he'd done it, and even madder he did it with such secrecy. Like so many things, I'm now able to look back with a little more wisdom. His decision to join the army was a logical one for John. It brought him fully into a career in which he was a recognized expert. In Hollywood, and don't forget that we were both in the same business, I was the big deal—the star. As a Major in the Army's camouflage division, John entered a world about which I knew nothing. I probably would have done the same thing had the roles been reversed.

We kept the house in Beverly Hills. I stayed there with Elaine and Clara, her nurse, while John reported to Seattle. I promised to join him as soon as photography on *I Married a Witch* was completed. That took two months. We packed up and headed north. I was actually looking forward to being an army Major's wife. I still didn't understand but had gotten over the initial emotions. It would be a welcome change living in Seattle and I was confident our married life would be greatly improved. John would now be the important one, and I would be his wife and our child's mother.

But you never escape being a film star. You can escape if you really want to escape. But it has to be a total and energetic break with films. I not only wasn't capable of that clean a break, I really didn't want to sever my career for all time. There's some ego in the female animal, too.

We found a pretty house in Seattle. It was more expensive than the other officers could afford. And that started our first Seattle problem.

John was determined that we would live like an army family. We would live on his income, and never go beyond it in our style of living. I couldn't buy that. We fought about the house and its furnishings and my clothing and everything to do with money.

"Damn it, Ronni, why can't we live like an army family? I'm sick and tired of living over our heads."

The problem was John knew we weren't living over *our* heads. We were living over his head, and that was too bitter a pill for him to swallow. It destroyed everything that his new army career was to have achieved. He was to become the prominent member of our family. Spending the money I'd made plopped us right back in the old way of life. I should have played the game his way. I know that now. But I couldn't then. The money was there and I couldn't see any reason why we shouldn't enjoy the things it could buy.

"I just want a pretty home for us and a nice life," I argued with him.

"And I'd like to live like an army Major's family. Is that asking so much?"

"Yes, it is. What's wrong with spending some of the money I've made?"

"I just don't like it. That should be enough."

It was the same when I'd buy a hat or dress that looked expensive. We were in a worse rut than ever. And I had no outlet as I had in Hollywood. There was no studio to go to every morning. There was nothing but the army life. I was very dissatisfied. And John was miserable.

There was more than money, however, that chipped away at the Seattle phase of our marriage. Perhaps if Veronica Lake had been buried and put away for the duration, things might have had a chance. But there was no one to bury her. She was precious to the bosses at Paramount. And she was precious to me.

I wasn't in Seattle long when I was invited to be the guest of honor at a non-commissioned officer picnic and dance. I accepted. And John was furious.

The picnic was fun, the men terribly polite to this blonde film star who also was the wife of an officer. God, what pressure to be under. I endeared myself to them when two young officers arrived and tried to join in the picnic.

"Sorry, fellas, but you'll have to leave. This is for non-coms only." They muttered and left.

It was the same that evening at the dance. Many officers arrived, including one of the generals. He asked me to dance and I turned him down.

"Sorry, sir, but I'm an enlisted man's girl for the day. No officers allowed."

John feigned amusement at that story but it was purely a valiant effort. Veronica Lake had followed him to Seattle. There was no escaping her. I'm sure John loved me when I was just his wife. But Veronica Lake was an annoying image that would linger around him until the stake was driven into her heart.

Things just kept deteriorating. And one of the crushing blows came at my first War Bond Rally at Fort Lewis. I was asked to be the special guest on the reviewing stand the day of the rally. With me were all the brass from Fort Lewis. And John was *ordered* to be there with me.

It was a dreadful day. The troops marched by and we all looked on in admiration, although I kept stealing glances over at John. If only he didn't have to be there. He was humiliated, angry and hurt. And I was nervous. At one point during the troop review, a ranking officer leaned over to me and said, "You know what they're saying about you in Seattle, don't you, Miss Lake?"

"Mrs. Detlie," I corrected him.

"Yes. Well, they're saying that it's a cinch you aren't from Seattle. Not with your trim, thin legs. All the Seattle gals have thick legs from climbing all these hills." He laughed. I ignored him. What a bore some of these officers were. I began to feel light-headed. The reviewing stand, John's forced presence, the officers, the pomp and circumstance, the steady, drilling beat of the march music all were getting to me.

"It means a great deal to all the men to have you here, Veronica," the general whispered to me.

"John's a lucky man," I was told.

How I wanted to be off that damned reviewing stand and home with Elaine. And John.

There was a ceremony after the troop review and the general proudly introduced me.

". . . great motion-picture star, Veronica Lake."

I knew John wanted to be off that damned reviewing stand much more than anyone.

"And I'd like to introduce her husband. Major John Detlie."

Mild applause. How he hated to stand up. Why couldn't they have introduced him first, and then me as his wife? Because I was a star. And I was the big deal that day. And John was my husband, the star's husband.

When things really get bad and you feel there isn't anything to make them better, you sort of say, "the hell with it," and just go ahead with what you want to do. That's the way I felt in Seattle. I was what I was and that was that. I left on a national War Bond Tour in October 1942 that took me to New York. John greeted my departure with, I think, mixed emotions. He wasn't sorry to see Veronica Lake leave Fort Lewis. But he was mad to see his wife take off leaving her child and husband behind. He complained bitterly about my leaving. And we fought.

"Why is it so wrong for me to go on a bond tour, John? You left me in Hollywood to do something for your country and to satisfy your own needs. I'm just doing the same thing."

"You have a child and a husband. That should be enough," he answered accusingly.

"And I have my own life to lead. You knew that when you married me."

"I married a girl I loved. Not some sexed-up symbol named Veronica Lake."

The New York Trip was unpleasant. It was hard work, a constant schedule of shaking hands with people in factories and on the street, speaking at this rally and that, never with even an hour to yourself. I did get one night off and that proved the biggest disappointment. The night before, it had taken a full detail of police to get me through a crowd and into a 45th Street theatre. Now, alone in my hotel room, I didn't even know one person to phone. I wanted to get out and do something on my own. But it just didn't seem possible. I ended up ordering an extra large dish of strawberry ice cream from room service, ate it and went to bed by ten o'clock. The tour was climaxed by a huge rally at Madison Square Garden. I left New York tired, confused and afraid to return to Seattle and John.

It was a chilly reception in Seattle. This led me to become more fearful of what was to come and, like most people, I covered up my fear with aggressiveness. I presented a tough front to John, one in which I claimed to have every right in the world to pursue the career of my choice.

"You can go to hell, John," I yelled at him soon after returning. "I'm a movie actress and if another film comes along, I'll take it." It wasn't entirely fair of me. I knew I was being offered the role of Olivia D'Arcy, a powerful and challenging role in Mark Sandrich's new film, *So Proudly We Hail*. It was to be based on the lives of the nurses on Bataan and Corregidor.

When I broke the news, it resulted in a series of bitter arguments and even more bitter silences. We were both drained by the time I began commuting between Seattle and Hollywood to work on the film. I'd spend the week in Hollywood and return to Seattle on week-ends.

So Proudly We Hail promised to be a meaningful film. Mark Sandrich, who was known primarily as a producer and director of musical comedies, was very taken with the tales coming back from the war about the nurses who served so valiantly on Bataan and Corregidor. He told the people at Paramount, "We must make a picture of those nurses. I just hope some get out to tell us what happened."

Ten did escape, one of whom was Lieutenant Eunice Hatchitt. She'd been born in Prairie Lea, Texas, and had joined the Army Nurse Corps in Houston in 1936. She became technical adviser to Mark Sandrich on the film.

Mark flew to Washington with Allan Scott, a screenwriter, to speak with the returning nurses and to ask permission from the government to make the film. The nurses were to be there to receive citations for their service. The nurses told their stories to Mark and Allan and, from them, a fictional plot was developed. No fiction could truly capture what these girls went through. They were under fire constantly. They slept in jungle foxholes, survived on minimum rations and worked day and night with the wounded. They were evacuated from Bataan to Corregidor and, after that island came under heavy bombardment, taken to Australia.

Mark also signed on Colonel Thomas Doyle, a two-year veteran of the Philippines where he was in command of the 45th Infantry, Filipino Scouts, during the Bataan and Corregidor battles.

He was evacuated by submarine on May 3, just before Corregidor fell. Colonel Hoyle was to be responsible for all matters of Army etiquette during the filming.

My role in *So Proudly We Hail* was a small one compared to those of Claudette Colbert and Paulette Goddard. But it was a highly emotional one. My hair-do was to be hidden under a cap. I wore it parted in the middle and with a roll on the neck. Army regulations would never have allowed any nurse to wear that silly peek-a-boo style.

The first week of shooting went beautifully. It wasn't until the second week that the pains came. They came in the middle of the night, and by three in the morning they'd reached the severe stage. I was nauseous and my stomach felt in the grip of a huge vice.

They took me to the hospital where my doctor was waiting. He ran blood tests that indicated an unusually high white cell count.

"Ronni, I dislike asking you these things," he said, as he stood sternly at the foot of my bed. "But have you been sleeping around?"

I started to laugh, but it hurt more when I did.

"Hell, no. Why ask that?"

"Well, your white cell count indicated to me the good possibility of venereal disease. That usually brings about such a high count."

"V.D.? Me?"

"I just asked."

"Listen, I feel so rotten I'd tell you anything that would help. No, I haven't slept with anyone. Even John for a long time. It can't be V.D."

They decided later it was my appendix. They promptly went to work removing that useless little organ. I was up and around in a week and went back to filming *So Proudly We Hail*. I delighted in answering the question of what was wrong with me by saying, "V.D. Advanced case."

John and I quarreled every time I returned to Seattle. They were never loud quarrels. Neither of us was the loud type. But they were consistent and bitter, each filled with accusations and counter-accusations. I tried many times to appeal to John's obvious sense of duty to his country.

"*So Proudly We Hail* is more than just another Hollywood film, John. It's a salute to the military. I'm proud to be in the film."

But that point of view was too remote for him to consider and accept. Actually, we'd reached a point so many marriages reach; there was no solution possible, only the animal instinct to salvage what each of us could of individual pride. Individual needs transcended the mutual need of the marriage. The point of no return had long been passed.

The film took my mind off the bad marriage. It was an interesting film to make for many reasons. One had to do with the pre-production theories many people held about how Paulette, Claudette and I would function together. I think most people assumed I'd act like a little bitch on the set and fight the others all the way. I had acquired a reputation for saying what I thought. I hadn't played the Hollywood game very much and a certain resentment built about that. As I've explained, I'd adopted a cockiness to cover my obvious inadequacies. And I found that as my confidence increased, I saw little or no reason to change myself and my approach to functioning in Hollywood. I truly did not like the usual Hollywood life to which everyone seemed to gravitate. It left me cold. I don't believe I was ever difficult when situations were fair and logical. But when I felt something was wrong or when someone pushed me around, I pushed back. And that goes just so far in movie land.

At any rate, I got along famously with Paulette and Claudette. But they didn't get along with each other. I acted like a little angel on the set, always smiling when others were fighting about something or other. It wasn't always easy to maintain that front. There were times I wanted to lay somebody out. But I was determined to prove all those pre-production guessers wrong. I succeeded.

There was one incident about which I always laugh. It concerned an interview with Paulette Goddard. She was asked whom she liked best—Claudette or Veronica.

"Veronica, I think. After all, we are closer in age."

Claudette read the interview and flipped. She was at Paulette's eyes every minute, and Paulette fought back with equal vengence. I smiled.

And so it went. I had a dressing-room next to Bing Crosby and was serenaded every morning as Bing sang in his shower. It was also during this period that I began receiving nasty crank mail from west-coast Japanese sympathizers. And one of these folks, an actual living Japanese fellow, found his way into my dressing-room, took off all his clothes and fell asleep waiting for me overnight. I walked in the next morning and was greeted with his sleeping form as an eye-opener. He was cute lying there, all naked and curled up in the fetus position. I yelled for a guard and had him led out of there. He seemed very embarrassed.

The majority of the American movie public probably remembers me in *So Proudly We Hail* more than any other film. It also served to introduce a new male star to the American public—Bowen Charleton Tufts III.

Remember Sonny? Good old laughable, lovin' Sonny Tufts? He walked away with *So Proudly We Hail.* And he represented one of Hollywood's strangest personality stories. Some day, in the flood of biographies now so popular in American publishing, someone will do a Sonny Tufts biography. It's the incredible saga of riches to rags. Sonny was a lot of things, including a person seemingly infatuated with fire. Like one New Year's Eve at Jack Warner's house. We were all in the basement when we smelled smoke. We ran upstairs and there was Sonny, big grin on his boyish face, lighting all the drapes in Warner's living-room. There was also a rumor that Sonny piled all his motel furniture in the middle of his room and put a match to it. They say he placed a parrot in a cage in the middle of the upholstered kindling but you can't prove it by me. All I know is what I read about Sonny during the years before his death. It seemed there was a whole gang of perverted women claiming that Sonny had bitten them on their thighs. I just can't believe that ol' Kansas, his name in *So Proudly We Hail,* would do anything like that. Of course, someone like Sonny Tufts spawns rumors wherever he goes. Even in far-away places like London.

A Sonny Tufts biography is a must if Hollywood is ever to be understood.

We ground out *So Proudly We Hail* under Mark Sandrich and it proved to be a very big film. It opened at Radio City Music Hall to great acclaim, most of it directed at Sonny Tufts. But we all got good notices. To this day, people remember when I walk into the nest of Japs with the hand grenade in my bra. I recently had flowers delivered and the delivery man went into ecstasy reliving that scene for me. It was a fairly gripping scene. Mark Sandrich told me to play the scene like Mary, Queen of Scots, getting ready to go to her execution. He had a marvelous sense of imagery.

The appendectomy didn't slow me down at all. I felt wonderful until very near the end of the shooting schedule when I started to suffer from occasional nausea. I chalked it up to the operation. But as it became more persistent, I went to my doctor. This time he didn't suggest V.D. He knew exactly what my problem was. "You're pregnant, Ronni."

I went out and got drunk. I was thrilled at having another child. And I was petrified to face John with the news. Women should never feel that way. Why husbands who make love to their wives are upset when their wife becomes pregnant is beyond me. It's more easily explained today where contraceptive devices for women are more common than in the Forties. If a couple is depending on the wife to take care of things, a pregnancy would indicate she goofed, or decided to have another child. But with us, prevention was John's responsibility. Our sex activity was extremely limited, both because I was spending so much time in Hollywood and because when we were together, the atmosphere wasn't exactly conducive to love-making.

I then came around to believing that another child might cement our relationship. We all know how naive that kind of sophomoric thinking is, but it's an easy frame of mind to acquire when the pressure is on.

John's reaction was voidal, bland and non-committal. But John was a nice guy. He tried to feign enthusiasm and to fuss over me in my delicate condition. It was an empty effort on his part, but a A-for-effort sort of thing. He was a fine man, fine enough to try and place his wife above and beyond his true feelings. If our marriage was ever to be saved, this might have been the moment. This would have been the time for me to drop movie-making and devote myself to my family. With a second child on the way, I'd have every reason to declare myself retired. Had I done that, I believe I'd still be Mrs. John Detlie.

But I was totally committed to the career of Veronica Lake. My reasons for this are, I believe, understandable even to the most lay psychologist. The minute *So Proudly We Hail* was turned over to the editor, I accepted to a role in *The Hour Before Dawn*, a film version of W. Somerset Maugham's novel about pacifism and its ramifications. And, just as I recognized the pending birth of my second child as a crucial time in our marriage, I now recognize this film as the beginning of a great slide down for Veronica Lake. There I was at the peak of my popularity and with only a glowing future in store. Yet *The Hour Before Dawn* started me on a long series of bad films that never did a thing for my career. I never even knew I'd began the slide until it was too late to grab a rung and try to halt the fall.

You couldn't have told me then that things would not go well for me in the future. Personal problems aside, I was riding very high in my career. Two Marines in the South Pacific discovered a barren volcanic island and claimed it as Veronica Island. I never got to survey my new piece of real estate but I imagine it was lovely. *Life* voted me the top female box-office attraction. I won the Army Poll as the most popular female actress. You couldn't ride much higher at the time.

I wasn't loved by all. Louella Parsons made a habit of writing in her column that she didn't see what all the fuss about me was based upon. She said she didn't think I was very pretty.

I was sitting in The House of Westmore one day having a facial and hair set when Parsons walked into the salon. She sat down, looked over and didn't recognize me. "What a pretty girl," she told her attendant.

"Why don't you write that in your column?" I yelled at her.

Everything was roses. We completed the film schedule and enjoyed the good feeling that comes with the completion of any film. You're elated when shooting is wrapped up. It's like being freed from a cell and allowed into the fresh air again. Even when the filming is pleasant you discover yourself anxious for the routine to end.

I was scheduled for a rehearsal on the Groucho Marx radio show on the evening we finished shooting *The Hour Before Dawn*. The last scene in the can, I happily changed, rid myself of my make-up and gaily skipped across the set, now a frenzy of post-production break down. I never saw the light cable stretched across the sound stage. My foot caught in it and I went down with a sickening thud. It was an awful jolt. But after the initial pain, I got up with the help of some stagehands and continued out of the studio. I got as far as the exit door when the warm gush of liquid erupted from my crotch and splashed down my legs.

"Oh God, dear God," I moaned as I sank to the concrete floor.

An ambulance rushed me to the hospital where, after an extensive examination, my doctor expressed confidence that the baby wasn't injured in the fall. He did suggest I remain at the hospital for rest and observation, a suggestion I never argued with for a minute.

William Anthony Detlie arrived on July 8, 1943, two months earlier than nature intended. He was a beautiful little baby boy, perfectly formed and so sweet as he lay there in his hospital nursery crib. Naturally, he was little because of his early arrival. But so was I. And little people were "in" Preston Sturges had said. He told Sheilah Graham that I was one of the little people, and William Anthony Detlie would be one, too.

But my baby wasn't doing very well. Neither was I. The hemorrhaging had taken its toll with me and I was confined to bed for an indefinite period. The baby suffered from the placenta not functioning properly and was slowly dying of uremic poisoning. We fought our battles, mine looking better each day and his a daily matter of losing ground.

John was notified the moment I entered the hospital. He called me from Seattle.

"Can you be here tonight?" I asked.

"I can't, Ronni. I want to but I can't. You understand, don't you?"

"John, please. I need you here now. Please."

"I'll try, Ronni. As soon as things let up. O.K.?"

"It has to be O.K., doesn't it?" I hung up.

My doctor was furious at John. He knew how much I needed him at this moment. But I forbade him to call John. There was no more John. He died the moment I hung up that phone.

The baby died on July 15. John arrived that evening.

We attended the baby's funeral together. Neither of us spoke. I sat stunned in my wheelchair while John, in his major's uniform stood silently next to me. There was no need to attempt communication. The need to share was over. We each were faced with living with our own thoughts, our own individual emotions over this tragic event. The baby was lowered into the ground with all the finality of a closing curtain in a theatre. There would be no encores for him. It was over, and had never been.

John and I rode silently back to the house. The driver drove placidly in front, separated from us by a glass partition. We were almost home when John broke the silence.

"I'm sorry, Ronni."

I didn't want to cry. I bit my lip against it. "Why didn't you come, John? Why?"

He gazed straight ahead. I could detect a slight quivering in his lips, a silent cry that would never be heard.

"I had nothing to come for, Ronni. Nothing. I wanted to be with my wife, not Veronica Lake. I wanted to be with my baby. My baby, Ronni. My baby, not someone else's. It wasn't mine. It wasn't mine."

15

JOHN and I were divorced in December of that year. It was a peaceful divorce with little communication between us. I came to Seattle to straighten out affairs and returned to Hollywood. During the proceedings, John accused me of being an unfit mother, more concerned with her career than her daughter. He stated that my choice of friends was not fitting for a child's normal and healthy upbringing. And he mentioned repeatedly that I traveled too much to be an effective and loving mother and wife. I didn't argue. Maybe he was right. I'll never know. Perhaps if I'd been more of the storybook mother, my children would have had a better running shot at life. Again, I don't know. I just hope they never use me as a crutch for trouble they might run up against. Everybody has a crutch these days; a father who never took me fishing or a mother who played too much bridge or something or other. Or a psychiatrist to lean on—a paid listening buddy.

My divorce from John set me adrift on the Hollywood sea. It was a strange feeling being free of family commitments. I'm not forgetting Elaine. But you don't answer to your child when you're out all night and come in the next morning in a state of happy, drunk fatigue.

That didn't happen very often, but it did on a few occasions.

I was determined to leap into the role of the gay divorcee, footloose and fancy free, available and willing. It was hard. I'm not a swinger. And Hollywood was the land of the big swingers.

To better understand myself and the year I spent between John and my second marriage, it's necessary to take a good look at Hollywood itself, not geographic Hollywood but socially significant Hollywood.

One former female child star, revered by millions, described Hollywood recently as, "One big leech. Everybody was sucked dry."

I could never be that harsh on Hollywood. Yes, it was true that Hollywood consisted of too many people living off other people, people exploited and cheated and ruined. But Hollywood also was the stomping ground for a lot of very wonderful and honorable folk. There was solidarity in my Hollywood that was never allowed to escape through the image of glamour and dreams perpetuated by Hollywood and its show-business product.

I suppose it's easy for me now to defend and praise Hollywood. I was certainly never fond of the studios and their bosses when I was working under them. They were never especially fond of me, either. But I was a commodity called a star, a name, face and reputation that would lure paying patrons into movie theatres. And that's what it's all about.

Hollywood has and always will be profit motivated. So is every business. But while most businesses are quiet about their financial status, Hollywood fed an eager public with tales of incredible, almost distasteful wealth and living high. And it was O.K. with the public. It gave them a vicarious opportunity to live in the splendor of riches they'd never experience themselves. In effect, the very public private lives of Hollywood's community were as much an escape as the actual films. All of us were merchants of dreams, a product every bit as tangible as peanut butter and rivets.

The men who controlled Hollywood and its vast wealth deserved their positions. As hated as some of them may have been, no one could take away the guts, fortitude and foresight they displayed in building their empires. They came out of eastern ghettos, sweat-shop garment centers and mundane careers to bet their lives on a nation's need for escape. Those who succeeded reacted to their success as might be expected. They over-indulged in everything. They fed their natural egos, drives and insecurities with what their success could buy. And it bought a lot with the tax structure of the day.

It never bothered me that I wasn't adored by the studio brass. It was perhaps a little puzzling because of my short stature. Most of the biggest studio bosses were little men physically. I don't know why that is except that their incredible, almost superhuman drive might have stemmed, in part, from the proverbial little man complex.

Some of these little giants included Adolph Zukor who owned Paramount Pictures, Sam Katz, one of the truly big-time producers, Marcus Loew, owner of M.G.M. among other things and Carl Laemmle, founder of Universal Pictures. And, of course there was Harry Cohn, Darryl Zanuck, Sam Goldwyn and William Fox. These were the builders of the Hollywood empire, the men who truly created the motion-picture business of America. There were many others. But it was these founders and their individual outlooks that shaped Hollywood and its life. They were men possessed, loaded with idiosyncrasies that made wonderful gossip items and could make life miserable for those caught up in serving their whims. But no matter what hate fixations you could come up with about these men, you had to acknowledge their accomplishments and tip a small hat of thanks for creating an empire in which you yourself made more money than you could ever expect back in Brooklyn or Miami.

Hollywood was a unique pocket of fascism in democratic America. Democracy was late in penetrating the dictatorships of Hollywood. The studios were ruled by individual potentates. An example of this was at M.G.M. where, up until well after the end of World War II, studio policemen were ordered to salute any producer or member of management.

The studio bosses both created the aura of Hollywood glamour and lived by its rules. Studios had on staff such specialized people as vitaminologists to administer vitamin shots to management. Steam baths were as plentiful and plush as the lavish sets used for film making. The huge sums of money earned by successful films went to further splendificate the lives of management. Money was so plentiful it often seemed that much of it was spent in desperation moves to get rid of it.

A top producer would host a dinner-party and use individual $200 cigarette lighters engraved with the guest's name as place cards.

A film czar, bored with a dinner-party hosted for thirty people, would hire limousines and whisk everyone away to Mexico for a night of gambling.

Custom shirts at fifty dollars each were worn once and given away. Personal items—socks, shirts, ties and handkerchiefs—were monogramed with diamonds and other precious stones. Visitors to some offices were sprayed with perfume from a giant atomizer rigged in the waiting-room. Perfume reigned as a prize possession for the glamorous stars of the early days. Sam Kress, a druggist at the corner of Cahuenga Pass and Hollywood Boulevard, carried a quarter of a million dollars worth of imported perfume in his store to satisfy the perfume craze. Pola Negri reportedly bought one of each of the scents Kress carried and paid for it ail with a wad of bills. Wally Reid was constantly giving perfume to his friends and was limited in how much he could buy at one time from Kress. Some stars maintained a separate bedroom just to house their perfume collections.

Leather was another status craze for a while. Everyone tried to outdo the other in giving as gifts leather-bound editions of rare books.

In a word, the Hollywood of my time was madcap. It was flamboyance personified. It was the time of the expensive whore and elegant gambling. The very familiar faces of Hollywood could be seen at Billy Bennett's pleasure house or The Clover or Embassy Clubs up in the infamous section of hill country overlooking Sunset Strip. It was like a parade of famous wealthy faces in pursuit of pleasure, each trying to spend more and enjoy more than the others. And if you're about to roll the dice and your ten-year-old son comes up and tugs your coat, you turn around, hand him a thousand dollars and tell him to go play. I saw that happen one night at one of the plush gambling clubs.

The public eagerly fed the lavish tastes of the Hollywood community. It allowed the stars and studio bosses to live in total comfort, in Roman splendor in sections developed by the small Hollywood community in Los Angeles. It was interesting, I think, that while a nation drooled with envy for the Hollywood set, that same set was shunned and looked down upon by the natives of Los Angeles. It was so bad at one time that local merchants wouldn't honor a check from some of the top money-makers in Hollywood. They came around, of course, and there is a fairly stable relationship these days. But Hollywood in its growth years was scorned by Los Angelenos.

Hollywood reacted to this early snubbing by becoming almost communal in its living. It took vast areas of prime land and developed it with mansions and castles in which the affluent basked in luxury and the warm California sun. It was a money town and money did the talking.

The studios made the money. But ultimately the power was in the hands of the stars. A motion-picture star was the most important commodity any studio could claim. Each "major" scuffled to sign as many stars as possible. A studio's star stable meant everything. It's not that way today. Today's motion-picture star has found that under existing tax structures, he or she can do very much better acting as an independent performer hiring out to any studio with a specific property to be produced. My time in Hollywood was during the star system. As L. B. Mayer boasted, "We have more stars than heaven." He was probably right.

As a star in those days, you were expected to play the game a bit. The public wanted to read of your latest beau, your latest escapade in which you threw your mink into a pool of perfume, lost a million dollars on one throw of the dice and tickled your leading man's thigh under the table at The Brown Derby. Many stars did play this game. I'm sure some of them did it because they knew it was expected of them. But there were those who enjoyed the hell out of being able to act out their natural inclinations in a system of society where it would be condoned and even enjoyed. Every time a star would publicly deviate from the norm, the studios would mockingly shake their heads in shame and privately delight in another bit of appetite whetting for the public.

There were limits, of course, to which you could go in violating society's normal sense of right and wrong. Go too far and you suddenly found yourself without box-office lure. Come to that point and the studio washed its hands. You lost your value to them.

It was possible to party yourself to death in Hollywood. Anyone with any name at all was invited to six a night. Every studio had a crop of newcomers who were always available to be seen with an established name. The studios liked their stars to be seen in public. Gossip columnists thrived in chit-chat about who was where and why. And overriding everything was the implied promise of easy and frequent sex, not just the normal bedroom routine of husband and wife but exotic, frequent and varied sex. If some of the stars spent as much time in bed as the gossip columnists would have you believe, they would have ended up in a wheelchair at thirty, exhausted but with a happy grin on their faces. There were some who lived up to their reputations. The only one I really knew was Errol Flynn. Errol did try to get me into his infamous bed but he never succeeded.

It was the only party I ever attended at Errol's home. There was the usual evening swim with a few of the guests nude. Errol had stocked the house with an assortment of young and luscious starlets and they were available for any of his male guests who felt a sudden urge. It was all typical Errol Flynn; his clippings were not exaggerated.

I declined the swim and sat nursing a drink at the poolside, enjoying the occasional screech of feigned delight from one of the girls in the pool as a fellow grabbed and gave chase. Frankly, I was bored with it all and decided to go home.

Errol showed me to the door. He was handsome, that devil. He looked in my eyes and slipped his arm around my waist. His hand slipped down and clamped tightly on my rear end.

"I think we should go and make use of a special bedroom I have, Ronni," he said.

"I have a special bedroom I'm going to make use of, Errol," I replied. "It's my own and I'm going to sleep in it."

He took his hand away, kissed me on the cheek and smiled.

"As you wish, Miss Lake."

I left.

Errol and I would bump into each other from time to time and we were always friendly and warm to each other. Errol Flynn was a gentleman. I remember one informal cocktail party where some guy was trying to put the make on me. Errol jumped right in and protected me like a father. I suppose when you have as much success with the opposite sex as he did, one turn-down doesn't mean a thing. I always enjoyed his company.

Actually, I came in on the tail-end of Hollywood's glamour period. By the time I left, the glamour was being replaced by the grey suits and Harvard educations of more traditional business-men. Television had brought a competition to the entertainment world that demanded that Hollywood pull in its belt and approach its business with a harder head. They've done this and function that way today. My period began just as the film capitol was beginning its realization of the need to act more business-like.

There's no doubt I was a bit of a misfit in the Hollywood of the Forties. The race for glamour left me far behind. I didn't really want to keep up. I wanted my stardom without the usual trimmings. Because of this, I was branded a rebel at the very least. But I don't regret that for a minute. My appetite was my own and I simply wouldn't have it any other way. I conducted my marriage years going against the grain of Hollywood's pattern and approached my sudden single life without much change. "You can take the girl out of Brooklyn but you can't . . ."

16

I DIDN'T depend on the Hollywood fun machine for my kicks during the period following my notice of divorce from John. In California, you must wait one year until a divorce is final. I had no plans to remarry, although I wasn't committed to that course of action. If I was committed to anything, it was to find myself in a personal sense, and to lie back and enjoy things. During the previous year, I'd held one party. That was for a newspaper friend who was going into the Navy. I invited fifty of his friends, told them to bring their own booze, and broke up the party early. I certainly never had a reputation as the hostess with the mostess.

But I did become Hollywood queen of the kitchen party, my own brand of party, and I reigned in this capacity all during 1944, my footloose and fancy-free year.

Veronica Lake's kitchen parties were popular, so popular that movie folk began vying for invitations. I held them once a month, and on any given party day you might see Howard Hughes, John Garfield, Paulette Goddard, one or two U.S. Ambassadors, a couple of Supreme Court Judges and a sprinkling of newspapermen. All the women at these parties would be made to wear muslin aprons and help with the serving of food and drinks. They were marvelous affairs in their informality.

Howard Hughes became quite friendly with me during this period. He was a strange man which comes as no surprise to anyone. And he was a captivating person in his depth, so aloof and detached but with a trace of warmth for those fortunate enough to be touched by it.

Howard, for some reason, pretended he was deaf. I suppose he found it advantageous in business dealings, a technique to keep others off their guard while he took in everything they said. He was at one of my kitchen parties one day and sat stoically in the living-room, his attention never shifting to any of the groups engaged in heated discussions about one thing or another. People ignored him, both because they were slightly frightened of him and because many of them bought the story about his being deaf.

State Supreme Court Judge Blake and Ambassador Pawley were in the kitchen having a discussion of one of Judge Blake's recent cases. Howard evidently disagreed with something said because he yelled his opinion at them from the living-room. Everyone looked in surprise at the deaf man with such good hearing. It never phased Howard. He went right back to his act in the living-room.

I liked Howard Hughes. I liked his rebellion against everything that was expected of him. I respected him and was proud to be known as a favorite of his. He called me one morning at 5 a.m. on his direct line from the White House just to talk.

"What do you want to talk about, Howard?" I asked him in a sleepy slur.

"About anything you'd like to talk about, Ronni."

"I don't have anything to talk about, Howard. You called me."

"Well, think of something to talk about. That's why I called."

"I'll try." I think I sat there for a couple of minutes trying to come up with words. Howard didn't say anything. Finally, I heard him yawn.

"Well, goodbye, Ronni."

"Goodbye, Howard. Thanks for calling."

There was another 5 a.m. call from Howard Hughes a few months later. It was from his California home. "Do me a favor, will you, Ronni?"

"What favor could I possibly do for you at this hour, Howard?"

"I have to fly to Washington right away."

"O.K. Have a good trip."

"I have to get to my plane at Burbank."

"So call a cab." I couldn't stop yawning.

"No. No cab. Drive me to Burbank, will you?"

"Now?"

"I have to go right away. Drive me. O.K.?"

"O.K., Howard."

I fumbled around, eventually got dressed and drove to his home. I beeped the horn. Howard emerged from the house almost immediately. He was wearing a very expensive suit, white shirt and tie. And he wore sneakers with holes in the front through which his toes protruded. His luggage was a Corrugated Scott Tissue carton tied with heavy cord.

"Thanks, Ronni," he mumbled. It took me five minutes to stop laughing. We drove to Burbank Airport and there sat his TWA Constellation—his own personal one. He kissed me on the cheek, got in the plane and winged off for Washington.

A strange man, Howard Hughes.

There were no romantic implications between me and Howard Hughes. We just got along.

But I did become romantically involved during 1944 with a couple of interesting men. One was Bill Dozier, then an associate producer (*The Hour Before Dawn*), and more recently Batman's daddy.

Bill was one of many Hollywood people who tried in their individual ways to comfort me when I lost the baby. I remember waking up from the anesthesia and seeing a mink coat. I blinked a few times and brought things into focus. Inside the coat was Katharine Hepburn. I'd never met her before. She smiled at me.

"Don't worry, Veronica. You'll get over it. If there's anything I can do, please let me know."

She got up and walked to the door. "Remember, Veronica, the calla lilies *will* bloom again." Out she went. I found out later that her secretary was in the same hospital and Katharine just happened to be there visiting. It was nice of her to drop in on me.

Bill Dozier was also a visitor at the hospital. He preceded his visit with a gift—cherry pie and Grand Marnier, a whimsical favorite of mine. After the divorce papers had been filed, Bill started dating me. We went together for quite a while despite his secretary's warning that he was a player and that I shouldn't become involved.

I never heeded her warning. I liked Bill. And never had any traumatic experiences to cause me to break off our relationship.

We eventually stopped seeing each other simply because we decided to stop. I got a kick a short time later reading about Bill's courtship of Joan Fontaine. It seems he went to Canada where she was filming. Joan became ill and was hospitalized. She was interviewed by a movie-fan magazine and warmly told of how Bill had sent her cherry pie and Grand Marnier, a wonderfully sweet and thoughtful gift. They married. They're now divorced.

My personal female ego was at an all-time high during this period. I was pursued by some of the most eligible and not-so-eligible men in Hollywood. And they even came across the seas.

Aristotle Onassis constantly had ships coming into Los Angeles Harbor. The war rationing was on, of course, and Onassis kept me in perfume, steaks, good wine and nylons. It was like getting a weekly Greek Care Package, a complete reverse on Harry Truman's philosophy of mutual aid.

In the midst of all this male adoration and pursuit, I received a telegram early one Friday morning. I opened it and read:

> Will pay you 100-thousand dollars repeat 100-thou-
> sand dollars to marry me STOP Promise divorce within
> three repeat three days STOP Request immediate
> answer STOP Thank you.
>
> Tommy Manville

You know, I was tempted. I almost took him up on his offer. I was broke, the result of the low pay I'd received for my films and the astronomical medical bills from 1943. Had Elaine not been in the picture, I would have married Tommy Manville. It would have put me back on my feet financially and might even have been interesting. I've often wondered how things were with Tommy and his bevy of young wives. It might have been an education and a revelation.

After Bill Dozier (I wonder today if Bill would consider me for a role as The One-Eyed Monster in his Batman series), I began dating one of the Hakim Brothers, that powerful Egyptian film family of Hollywood. To this day, only the brother who actually shared my bed knows he's the one. I dated all the brothers, but only slept with one. It used to be like a scene from a high-style comedy to watch them together, each eyeing the other for some glint of a hint. To my knowledge, my Hakim lover has kept silent. And so will I. Of the brothers, I considered only one a true gentleman, a feeling born out by his discreet silence all these years. He was a marvelous lover and I totally enjoyed our moments together. I've always enjoyed sex. But I have always been a one-man woman. I don't mean you must be married to enjoy the thrill and satisfaction of sex. But I was always faithful to my husband and, for my own reasons, to whichever man I was seeing during any one time of my single life. I was faithful to Jean Negulesco, the director, during the time we dated. Jean was the one who told people at one of my kitchen parties that he was embarrassed whenever I looked at him.

"I always think my fly is open when Ronni looks at me," he told everyone. I don't think it really bothered him, though.

Some of my most pleasant memories of this period in my life came as the result of becoming acquainted with Lady Mendl, that fabulous Hollywood character who made a fine living convincing Hollywood personalities she was the last word in taste, both as a decorator and in general. Part of the secret of her success was to decorate homes cheaply and charge enormous prices, a practice that makes perfectly sound economic sense to any businessman.

I first met her under unusual circumstances. I was invited to tea with Lady Mendl at her home. I was escorted to her sitting-room by the maid. The maid opened the door and there was Lady Mendl— on her head.

"My dear Veronica Lake," she said upside down. I didn't know whether to lie down on the floor and twist my head as upside down as possible, or just to act normally. I decided on the latter course of action and said hello.

"How do you do, my dear?" she said. "Please have a seat. Tea will be served shortly."

I sat down where I thought her hand gestured.

We carried on a marvelous conversation for the next half-hour. Tea was served along with tiny cookies. Lady Mendl was in a charming hostess gown tied to her legs with a fine gold chain to keep it from flopping down over her head. I sipped my tea and tried not to look at her too intensely. It was disconcerting to be there, especially for the first time, and spend that time with an upside-down Lady Mendl.

She got off her head after a half-hour, gulped her tea and said, "I'm so pleased you could visit with me, Veronica. I do hope you'll come again."

"It was very enjoyable," I said and left.

Lady Mendl never stood on her head for me again. I visited often and we became good friends. Her husband, Sir Charles, was seldom there when I visited.

Once Lady Mendl greeted me at the door in a wheelchair. By this time we'd become much more informal. I didn't buy the "Lady" bit and she knew it. But she maintained it and I never overtly challenged. Except I began calling her by her first name.

"What the hell is wrong with you, Elsie?" I asked.

She sighed. "A nasty fall, Connie. And such unfortunate timing. You know I must go to New York, don't you?"

"No, I didn't know."

"Dreadful. But perhaps you'd be a dear and buy my train ticket for me. I simply can't get out of this chair and purchase it. Would you do that for me, dear?"

"Sure. Give me the money."

"The money. Oh, yes. I'm afraid Sir Charles and I have tied up every cent of cash we have in a business venture. You buy it and I'll reimburse you in a few days."

"Come on, Elsie. Get off it. Get out of that damned chair and buy your own ticket."

"That's terribly callous, Connie."

"That's me, Elsie. Callous Connie."

"Oh dear, please do this for me."

I did. I called Howard Hughes and he got me the ticket. Lady Mendl didn't pay me and I didn't pay him. And I kind of doubt whether he'll come after me now for it.

My financial situation was becoming progressively worse and I gave up my apartment and moved in with Mrs. Rita Beery, Wallace's ex-wife. I paid fifty dollars a month towards the rent and we shared all household expenses. Elaine was three years old and progressing nicely. There were times when it was obvious the lack of a father affected her. She was old enough to sense the void of John's absence although not acutely. I was spending a great deal of time with her due to an abundance of leisure time. I hadn't asked for the free time. In fact, as the months wore on, I became a little frightened at my inactivity. I did appear in *Star Spangled Rhythm*, a variety film in which many stars appeared as themselves for cameo performances. Each performer would do a song or be part of a skit, the end result a celluloid Ed Sullivan Show to boost morale during war time.

In *Star Spangled Rhythm* I did a skit with Paulette Goddard and Dorothy Lamour. We sang a song written for us called "Sweater, Sarong and Peek-a-Boo-Bang." It was dreadful, but fun. Later in the same film, Arthur Treacher, Walter Catlet and Sterling Hollo- way did a parody of the tune which was very funny.

Bob Hope and Bing Crosby watched us do the song and as I walked back to my dressing-room, Hope stopped me.

"Hey, Veronica, you saving your money?" he asked.

"Why, Bob?"

"With a voice like that, you'll need it." He was right. I never could sing.

Fredric March was also in *Star Spangled Rhythm*. It worked out nicely because I had a chance to confirm my dislike for him. I brought Elaine to the studio one day when Clara, her nurse, had to take care of some personal business of her own. Elaine stayed in the dressing-room and charmed everyone who came in to see her. Please accept me as an objective person and believe Elaine was an exceptionally beautiful child, a fact that later caused its own problem in my life. She was also a very agreeable child, quick and easy with a smile and warm to people. She held court in the dressing-room and delighted everyone. Well, everyone until Fredric March came in to see her. She took one look at him and got hysterical. She cried and screamed until he left the room. Kids know, don't you think?

Elaine never met Gary Cooper. She would have reacted favor- ably to him, just as her mother did. To me, Coop typified everything good and fine in a man. I never got to do a film with Coop. But I did get drunk with him.

Coop was unique in everything he did and stood for. I remem- ber living in the valley and seeing him out of our window on more than one Saturday morning. He'd be riding along on his horse, and the strange thing was he'd be slumped forward in his saddle. Every- one knows Gary Cooper always rode straight and tall. But not on Saturday mornings in the valley. The reason for this change in his riding posture was that he was fast asleep.

He'd get restless late at night and decide to go for a ride. He'd fall asleep in the saddle and the horse would know enough to walk along slowly and not wake his master. Talk about total relaxation.

We got drunk together in Chicago. It was on a War Bond Tour, one of many I made, and it was a dilly.

They kicked off the Chicago portion of the tour with a press conference at the Ambassador East Hotel, one of Chicago's most elegant hotels. I was introduced first.

I said a few inspiring words to the assembled newsmen and started to return to my seat when Cooper was introduced. I almost made it. I tripped over something or other and started down face first. I shoved my right hand out in front to break the fall and landed on my index finger. It was almost a perfect handstand.

"Aaaaaaaaaaaaah," I screamed in pain as the jammed knuckle started sending its dolorous message up my arm.

The room broke into laughter at my gymnastics, the loudest laughter coming from Coop at the podium. Sheepishly, I got up and regained my seat to thunderous applause. Coop went on with his speech as I sat there cradling my injured finger with my other hand and uttering fierce profanities under my breath.

As we were leaving, I heard an old pro reporter comment to a cub, "Whatta ya think of dainty little lady Veronica?"

"She's pretty clumsy for a little girl, isn't she?" the cub responded.

He should know how clumsy.

We went out on the town that night and enjoyed Chicago's legendary night life. There was Coop, myself, a few studio publicity types and Rita Hayworth. For some reason, we ended up in a strip joint on State Street. We were bombed by this time and in a giddy mood, the only mood to be in when you visit a strip joint. Up on stage was the club's stellar attraction, a flat-chested stripper wearing pasties, G-string and a boa feather to cover an old appendectomy scar. We proved to be an appreciative audience. We kept gulping the watered-down booze and yelled our appreciation at every bump and grind. Performers always work harder for an appreciative audience and the stripper in the spotlight wasn't any exception. The music got louder and we got drunker. And suddenly we were joined by a pasty-faced little girl wrapped in an oversized imitation fur coat.

"Hi," she said suddenly. "That's my sister up there." She pointed to the stripper to make sure we understood who she was talking about.

"I'll be damned," Coop said with great bravado. "Have a seat."

The girl sat down and accepted Coop's invitation, given very much tongue-in-cheek. And she immediately started telling us how badly she felt for her sister.

"Ain't that awful? My sister havin' to take off all her clothes like that for all them guys to play wi' themselves under the table and like that."

"Yeh, that's a terrible thing," Coop agreed. He had a concerned frown on his marvelous face.

"Awful," I added.

"Atrocious," one of the publicity fellows concurred.

"Sure is bad," the gal went on. "Guys all sit around lickin' their lips and all 'cause my sister let's 'em see her boobs and all like that."

"Rotten. No doubt about it."

She only stayed ten minutes, excused herself, thanked Coop for the drink and left the club. I'm sure she had no idea who we were.

We continued our pub-crawling, each successive move taking us into lower and lower dives, most replete with girl-on-stage-with-red-and-blue-lights-and-"Night Train"-with-loud-drummer. And B-girls enticing guys at the bar to buy water at two dollars a shot.

The final joint was no exception. The stripper of the moment was over the bar. We took a table just a few feet from the center of action and ordered a drink. It was Coop who spotted our pasty-faced little friend. She was sitting with a man at the bar and pleading with him to buy her a drink. He threw ten dollars on the bar and immediately ran one hand into the front of her blouse and the other up her dress. She giggled and performed a few phoney sighs of pleasure. And then she announced to him, "Honey pie, I gotta go dance now. Stay here and I'll give you a real good time when I git back." She blew in his ear, gave his bulging pants a squeeze, and left. Moments later she was announced as the sensational something or other and came on stage. It took her a minute to shed the cheap gown she was wearing and was soon down to G-string and pasties. She'd had no appendectomy and didn't bother with any boa feather.

"I'll be damned," was Coop's only comment as we paid the check and left. The dancer gave us an empty wave goodbye and snapped her G-string at Coop. He shrugged his shoulders and we all passed out into Chicago's night.

"I've had it with this bad whisky," Coop said as we stood on the sidewalk planning our next move. "Let's go back to the hotel and drink some good stuff."

We all agreed except one of the publicity men.

"I think I'll prowl a little," he informed us.

We made it back to the hotel and stayed up the rest of the night drinking and laughing at Coop's stories. He never told a dirty story, just cute and on the verge of being blue. An incredible story-teller and human being.

We were eating breakfast in the hotel dining-room when our prowling P.R. man came home. His eyes were black, his lips were cut and puffed and he displayed various other signs of a physical evening.

"Two guys mugged me, robbed me and dumped me in the gutter," he mumbled in answer to our questions. We were all appropriately sorrowful, but underneath it seemed a fitting climax to the evening.

17

I WAS enjoying the single life. At least I wasn't fighting it. But my financial position was getting me down and so was the thought of being out of work. I wasn't officially unemployed. The studio simply hadn't offered me a script in a long time. When they did, it was an inane musical called *Bring on the Girls*. I accepted the role for a couple of reasons. I wanted money, I was not that sure of myself and how the studio would react to any stubborn antics from me, and I had always wanted to do a color film. *Bring on the Girls* was to be a color motion picture, my first and last. Naturally, I had hoped for a good comedy role as the result of *Sullivan's Travels* and *I Married a Witch.* But for some reason, those films were never brought up or considered by management. To them, the formula dictated that I was to be cast in roles where low-cut gowns and loose hair would be featured.

Bring on the Girls proved nothing except how saccharine Hollywood musicals could be. Featured with me was my old friend Sonny Tufts. And there was Eddie Bracken and Marjorie Reynolds who made her screen name in *Holiday Inn.* And there was Spike Jones and his City Slickers and The Golden Gate Quartette and others of musical note. I didn't sing, which was the public's clear gain.

Bring on the Girls did have a lasting contribution to my life, however. It was during the filming that I met my next husband, Hungarian director André DeToth.

André was about to direct a film for another studio and asked someone there to check into the possibility of borrowing me from Paramount for the film. Paramount turned down the request but André and I did have dinner together to discuss the role. He was a charming guy, not unusual for a Hungarian, but overwhelming to me. I'd never been close to a Hungarian before. Had I, I would have known that along with their charm, they're also very childlike and, in many cases, sadistic.

André was called Bandi (pronounced Bundy) and was quite handsome and dashing. I fell immediately. And he knew it.

We married as soon as my divorce from John had become official. I became Mrs. DeToth on December 16, 1944, but only after a courtship that included such scenes as his belting me in the mouth and then offering me a carving knife with which I was to cut out his unworthy Hungarian heart. I didn't accept the invitation.

I made a lot of mistakes in my life.

Bandi was a moderately successful film director. Even the moderate successes of Hollywood made good money and he was no exception. My income had risen and, between us, things were fat. We bought a farm in Chattsworth and a ranch in Bishop. Bandi adopted Elaine and it looked like a bed of roses from that point on. I did another of those brief appearances in *Duffy's Tavern* in which I get my face pummeled by Howard da Sylva, and went right into the role of Sally Martin in *Hold that Blonde.* It was another in

Paramount's formula of the moment—put a comic and a popular sexy type together and folks will come see. All I really had to do was look good while Bracken romped through the silly story line of frantic chases and falls from window ledges and the like. But the money was good and I didn't raise any fuss. Inside, I was churning around with anxiety over the failure of Paramount to again give me a decent comic part to play. But Bandi tempered those feelings.

"You have a long career to go, Ronni. Be patient until I come up with the good films. I'm your ace in the hole and you shouldn't worry about a thing."

I believed him. I actually believed him.

In January of 1945, just one month after we married, I was invited to the White House for Franklin Roosevelt's annual birthday party. Many Hollywood personalities were invited and I was very proud to be included. Besides being a guest at the Birthday Ball, I was to appear in *Dear Ruth* which was to be performed especially for the President. The show was scheduled prior to the ball and the charter flight from Los Angeles to Washington was designed to arrive with time to spare. We were travelling on "Orchid Priority," top priority for any aircraft at the time.

But mother nature never heard of "Orchid Priority." The weather turned bad and we were forced to land at Kansas City. We finally arrived at 2 a.m., long after the ball and, naturally, the play. With no talent, the play was cancelled. The real sadness for most of us was that the President had to leave for the Yalta Conference at 1 a.m. and we missed him.

Mrs. Roosevelt held an informal luncheon the following day. I was thrilled to be seated at a small table with her and Harry Truman and his daughter Margaret. As usual, I talked too much.

Mrs. Roosevelt seemed terribly interested in Hollywood and my career to date. I went on at length about my new husband and Elaine and so many things. And I ended our conversation with, "You know what I'd love, Mrs. Roosevelt?"

"No. What is it?"

"A spoon. A spoon from the White House."

She laughed and discreetly handed me one right from the table. "I think I'd better spend some time with the rest of my guests," she said and went off to do just that. Mr. Truman and Margaret stayed with me and we had a very enjoyable chat about everything but politics. The Vice-President did confide that he felt the press were being unfair to him in the way they photographed him and quoted him out of context. I agreed, of course, but wanted to say that perhaps if Margaret and Bess dressed a little better, the press might be more kind. I've never seen any mother and daughter dressed in such bad taste. They were nice people, though, and I was pleased to see the press treat Mr. Truman a little better after he became President.

The White House photographer took a group picture later that afternoon and I treasured it for many years until a fire wiped out most pictures I'd kept of my career. In the picture, a space was left empty for the departed President. On one side was Mrs. Roosevelt. I stood on the other. Also in the photo were Myrna Loy, Gail Storm and Margaret O'Brien, at that point the darling of Hollywood and wherever else she happened to be. I think Mrs. Roosevelt wanted to adopt her.

But the most rewarding event during those hours at the White House came much later that afternoon. I found myself alone in one of the White House rooms with Mrs. Roosevelt. I don't know why we ended up that way but we did. And there were two things she told me which always seem to come to mind when I think about the Washington trip.

Mrs. Roosevelt said to me, "I want you to know, Miss Lake, that I was very happy to give you that spoon. I was happy because you asked me for it. Most people wouldn't bother asking. They would take them and walk out." I wish my mother could have heard that.

And then the nation's First Lady turned very solemn and gazed through the window onto the garden. I didn't dare interrupt her thoughts although I started to wonder if that wouldn't be what she was expecting me to do. She finally broke the silence by getting up and walking across the room. She stopped in front of a lovely cabinet and slowly perused the items behind the glass. Then she turned to me.

"The President is ill, you know." She said it so flatly, so without emotion or tone to draw emotion from me. I said nothing.

"The President has cancer of the prostate gland. He'll be operated on when he returns."

I sat there wishing desperately she hadn't told me that. It would have been bad enough if she'd been the wife of a dear friend. But she was talking about the President, a man as familiar to everyone as their closest friend.

"I don't know what to say," I said. "I'm sorry. I mean I . . ."

"And I don't know why I've told you this," Mrs. Roosevelt said with a smile. "I'm the one to be sorry. I suppose we all need to tell these things to someone. I chose you for no reason. No one knows of this except his physician and a few close advisers. Please respect my confidence."

"Yes, of course, Mrs. Roosevelt. Of course."

The President returned from Yalta and I waited day by day to read of him entering the hospital for the surgery. I suppose he wanted to but never got around to it in the press of his schedule. It all became meaningless on April 22 when he died of the cerebral hemorrhage in Warm Springs, Georgia. His death brought to me a strange and childish sense of importance. I never repeated what Mrs. Roosevelt told me. Never. I don't know why.

A few years ago, it would have been presumptuous for an actress or actor writing his or her autobiography to even get into a political discussion. Today it's expected and that's a shame.

We're paid to entertain, not run for office. Why in God's name certain show people think they should inject themselves into the nation's political stream is beyond me. I'm not at all opposed to anyone taking an active part in our nation and its future. And in many cases I'm certain many actors and actresses would be more capable than some of the professional politicians now in positions of power.

But Ronald Reagan? I never liked him as an actor and I think he makes a worse leader. And Shirley Temple attempting to hop on her own political *Good Ship Lollipop*. It's absolutely gross, in my mind.

You'd think that those theatrical people who do enter the political arena would at least benefit from years of good script writers. You'd think they might have learned the value of the understatement, the under-played scene, the subtle flow of words which are so much more believable than the grand statement of absolutes.

But no. They immediately play what they think is a necessary political game. They never admit indecision based on shaky knowledge of the facts. They're always completely for this and against that and never seem to realize that the people they're talking to aren't that way at all.

I've never been for or against Vietnam. I don't know enough to take a positive stand. And neither do most of the people who do jump up and down and march for peace or cry for escalation. I just know that war is hell, as they say, and it would be nice not to have any wars. But maybe we should be in Vietnam. Maybe if we're not there, we'll have a bigger war some day in our own country.

I've never been a political animal. I have taken an active part in campaigns when I was totally sold on the man for whom I worked. I'm not a political party person. I either like the man or I don't, and I don't bother voting if I feel it's just a matter of choosing the best of a bad lot. I felt that way when Wagner ran against whoever he ran against in New York. I'm afraid I feel that way too often. It's just that politicians all look alike.

I stumped Brooklyn for John Kennedy. I did the same in Dade County, Florida, for Adlai Stevenson. I'm interested in my country but have fallen into a lethargy of late due to a feeling that most politicians really aren't worth interest anyway.

18

THERE was no escaping Sonny Tufts and Paramount's formula films. We ended up together in a real tear-jerker called *Miss Suzy Slagles*, a story about medical students and their own set of particular hang-ups. I really wasn't interested because I was having some of my own with André.

It started at the earliest possible moment—our wedding night. We went for a wedding dinner at a favorite restaurant of André's in Hollywood. We entered and were greeted by his favorite waitress. She obviously became flustered at seeing us.

"Oh, good evening, Miss Lake . . . and Mr. Lake . . . I mean . . ."

When those kind of things happened with John, he'd simply fall silent and grind his teeth. But not André. He got mad, mad enough to walk out of the restaurant and leave me on our wedding night. Actually, it was better for Bandi to react so openly. Poor John never did, and allowed the thing to eat away at his spirit. André came home the next day as though nothing had happened. The problem was it did happen again and again with different variations, the sum and substance a constant red flag in front of his face. Again, I was the star, the name, and he was married to me. Damn, I sympathize with men in that position.

Another problem soon popped up its ugly head in our young marriage. I got pregnant.

Being pregnant itself wasn't a problem. It was Bandi's obsession with having a boy. We all know that prospective fathers dream of playing ball with a son. But with Bandi, it was a necessity, so much that I actually became afraid should the baby be a girl. I'm sure I would have had to pack up and walk.

Even my doctor became annoyed at Bandi's constant talk about what the baby must be.

"André, you're upsetting Ronni terribly with all this damned talk about a boy. Stop it, will you!"

But Bandi couldn't stop. He kept bringing up the issue until I blew my top one night near the end of my pregnancy.

"Shut up," I screamed at him. "Shut up with your damned talk about having to have a boy. I'm not some Arab bitch married to a king. We'll get what we get and you'll like it or get out."

Our argument went on for an hour before Bandi revealed what was really at the bottom of his obsession. I was really pushing him when he broke.

"I am sick and tired of hearing about that beautiful Elaine, that beautiful Elaine, that beautiful Elaine. So your first husband gave you a beautiful girl. Well your second one is going to give you a beautiful boy."

I couldn't believe it. It had become some sort of competition with Bandi. With a boy, there would be no comparison between the children. With a girl, his might not be as pretty as John's. Absurd, of course. But sad. I understood now and did everything possible to straighten out the situation. I couldn't do anything to insure a boy but would have if it was possible. The fact that it turned out to be a male baby was pure chance.

André beamed at the news. And he proudly announced our son's name.

"André Anthony Michael DeToth III."

"No," I insisted.

Bandi was insistent. "That is the name I want and that is what his name shall be."

"Can we call him Mike?" I asked impishly.

Bandi gave that a lot of thought and decided some giving in was indicated, especially where I was involved in some way in the birth.

"All right," he agreed reluctantly. "You can call him Mike." The name rolled off his tongue with disdain.

Little Mike was a problem from the first day. He loved to cry and never hesitated. He was a handsome baby, but there was a look in his eyes that was frightening to me at times. I could never put my finger on what I felt, what I saw in those pale blue eyes. It was something at odds with itself, a tension threatening to ulcerate and upset the balance of things. I expressed my feelings on a few occasions to Bandi and he dismissed them as foolish female neurosis. And I was sure he was right.

Living on the farm at Chattsworth was wonderful. We surrounded ourselves with animals—15 Doberman pinschers, a camel, chickens, rabbits, ducks and horses.

It was a perfect setting for children to grow and develop, 24 acres of rolling farm land and a spacious and comfortable home in which to live. Things were fat again, the mornings glorious gangs of splendor, the evenings cool and peaceful. Everything was right. Except the living-room wall.

"There's something wrong with this room, Ronni," Bandi protested to me soon after we'd moved into the house.

"What's wrong? I love it," I argued. I'd decorated the room in my favorite Chinese red and white. It was a huge room.

"It's too small," Bandi declared.

"Too small? Come on. It's like a barn."

But Bandi had decided. He walked to the far end and tilted his head back and forth as he looked at the wall.

"It has to go," he said.

"Go where?"

"Out. Maybe two feet."

I was getting annoyed now. The last thing I thought we should be worrying about was pushing our living-room wall out two feet.

"But . . ."

"I want it out."

He called in the contractors and they knocked out the wall, all 18 inches of it. It cost a fortune and the room didn't look one inch bigger. But Bandi was pleased.

Mike was almost four months old when Bandi and I accepted Howard Hughes' invitation to join him on TWA's inauguration of coast-to-coast, over-the-weather service. We left early on the morning of February 15, 1946, with a plane full of celebrities and Howard himself at the controls. On the flight with us were Cary Grant, Virginia Mayo, Walter Pidgeon, Mr. and Mrs. William Powell, Jack Carson, Jack Warner, Linda Darnell, Edward G. Robinson, Tyrone and Annabella Power, Harry Cohn, Janet Blair, Paulette Goddard, Myrna Loy, Johnny Maschio, Frank Morgan, David Selznick, Randolph Scott and his wife and Gene Tierney. Constance Moore hadn't been invited but climbed on board and came anyway.

It was like all press flights, wild and woolly and with everyone oiled by good booze. We landed at New York's LaGuardia Airport at 1:08 p.m., one hour and seven minutes ahead of the scheduled flight time of nine hours and forty-five minutes. New York was quite a change from Los Angeles' 71 degrees. It was 30 degrees and windy when we arrived, but Howard's free-flowing whisky provided warmth for just about everyone. One newspaperman on the flight tried to walk off at LaGuardia with a full bottle that was left over. Howard grabbed him by the arm and took the bottle away from him. The newspaper guy bitched and moaned to no avail. I immediately thought of Mrs. Roosevelt and her philosophy towards people who just grab instead of asking. I'm certain Howard would have given him a case if he'd only asked.

We had fun in New York until our last night in town. Bandi and I topped off an evening of nightclubbing with a drink at the famed Stork Club.

We didn't stay long. After chatting briefly with Walter Winchell at a nearby table, we said goodnight to the Stork's owner, Sherman Billingsley, and started to leave. We were almost out when a young man reached up to touch my hair. He was about twenty years old, perfectly sober and perfectly harmless. He never even reached my hair before Bandi wheeled around and started hitting him. He must have punched him four or five times before an army major got to Bandi and pulled him off.

The young man seemed badly hurt. He'd slumped from his chair and leaned against the table leg in a limp daze.

"You son-of-a-bitch," the army major snarled at Bandi. "I'm going to take you outside and kick your teeth in."

"Get your hands off me," Bandi snapped back. But he wasn't about to take on the major, a solid guy who obviously wasn't afraid of anyone.

The major started to push Bandi outside when Billingsley came over, calmed the major and escorted us outside.

"What a despicable trick," Sherman told Bandi once we were on the sidewalk.

"I don't want anybody touching her," Bandi answered.

Billingsley's last words were "Stay out of here, DeToth. Forever." The incident made the papers but it didn't seem to bother Bandi. He just shrugged it off.

We returned to Hollywood and I began shooting on *Out of this World*, another musical with Eddie Bracken. Bing Crosby's sons were also in the film. It was no different from any of the other Paramount pap I'd appeared in. The only saving grace was the money. I was getting more per picture than ever before and had to deliver less to earn it. Not a bad deal on the surface unless you happen to want to work harder and deliver more for that same money. But there was no talking to Paramount about that. These formula films were all doing quite nicely at the box-office and a change was definitely not in the wind.

Maybe if the money wasn't such a necessity I could have held out, made demands, threatened to stop working unless they came up with better parts for me. But again in my life, money was getting tight despite our combined incomes.

To begin with, Bandi wasn't making very much any more. He became temperamental and started turning down film after film. Too often, even when he accepted a film, he'd become enraged at something on the set and storm off in a childish display of temper. They'd pull in another director and we'd slip a little further in debt.

Bandi's theory of economic survival would make many an economist turn in his fiscal grave. With him, the less you had, the more you should spend. And that's how we got our first airplane.

Actually, I gave him the plane, a Navion, for Valentine's Day, 1947. A tie would have been a more reasonable gift on our dwindling budget but André served notice he was going to buy an airplane. He picked it out and justified it with Valentine's Day.

"You'll be buying me something for Valentine's Day, Ronni. Right? So instead of choosing something I really can't use, make the plane my gift."

Maybe a simple, stripped-down Navion would have made more sense. But Bandi loaded it with 10-thousand dollars-worth of extras. It had everything any TWA Constellation had and maybe more.

Plane in hand, we both took lessons. Our instructor was Stan Reaver, pilot with Hollywood's famed Paul Mantz. Stan was a hell of a pilot and instructor, a very conservative teacher despite all the daredevil flying he did in films as a Mantz stunt flyer. But as conservative as he was, he was always getting annoyed with me for being over cautious. I was ground shy. I loved being up in the air but dreaded coming down and having to touch earth with the two tiny wheels hanging below. Despite that small phobia, I received my license. So did Bandi, although Stan told both of us that Bandi had all the makings of a bad pilot. He was very quick in everything he did and could never bother taking the time to think things through. Dead pilots are made of this.

Our airplane was purchased with the money we made from the first motion picture Bandi and I did together. No one remembers it, which is just as well. It was my first picture as Veronica Lake outside

Paramount's jurisdiction and was a western with Joel McCrea, Preston Foster, Charles Ruggles, Lloyd Bridges, Don DeFore and Donald Crisp called *Ramrod*. I'm certain Bandi stayed with the film all the way only because I was involved. The crew hated him and was quick to let him know about their feelings. I don't know how many times I had to smooth his ruffled feathers, usually with him turning on me whenever I'd even hint at taking someone else's side in whatever dispute happened to arise that particular day.

Bandi wasn't my only problem during the making of *Ramrod*. My stepfather died on September 10, 1946, and I felt his death deeply. I loved him very much. I must admit his death also brought out a practical emotion in me. With him gone, I wondered what the event would cause in terms of my mother. Things had settled into a very comfortable arrangement since my mother and I stopped having any contact. I didn't want it to change in any way. Now that she was alone, she might make attempts at re-establishing contact with me. That was the last thing I wanted.

My stepdad's death saddened me. But there was life to be thankful for very shortly after his death. So often, a child is born to temper death's tragedy. In this case, it was a life saved that brought joy to me.

John Farrow, *Sorority House*'s director and my teenage Catholic hero, returned from military duty in the South Pacific. He came to visit me on *Ramrod*'s lot.

"What do I call you?" he asked after giving me a huge hug. "Connie, Ronni or Veronica?"

"The choice is yours." I beamed at seeing him again.

"You've come a long way. I'm pleased for you."

"It's so wonderful to see you back, John. So good."

"I wouldn't be here if it weren't for you, Connie. That's a fact."

I had no idea what he meant. It seemed like a bit of hack dialogue from an old movie. I think I even laughed a little in my confusion. "Why do you say that?"

"Remember that medal you gave me during *Sorority House*? The one you said your aunt sent you?"

"Of course I remember it."

He turned very serious.

"It saved my life."

I didn't know what to say. You know how those situations are. Usually, you begin with a nervous laugh and hope it isn't offensive. Then you stutter for a moment and finally come back with, "I don't understand."

"It saved my life. That's all, Connie. It stopped a bullet."

I felt as awkward as when I gave him the medal. And it dawned on me that to take the story too lightly would be an attack on John's deeply-rooted religious convictions.

"I don't know what to say, John."

"I'll just say thanks and we'll leave it at that."

"All right."

"Thanks, Connie."

"O.K."

It was enough to shake me back into some semblance of my former devotion. It lasted a few days with me. It's the most I've reverted since.

Bandi kept spending everything we had. He found it increasingly difficult to get rid of the money at home so he started taking long and frequent trips abroad, reportedly in search of properties and future film stars. I accepted it as necessary and stayed home to continue my acting career. Also to make money to support the farm, ranch, airplane and Bandi's travels.

Paramount put me back with Alan Ladd in *The Blue Dahlia*, an interesting whodunnit that also featured Bill Bendix.

There was hardly time to remove my make-up before Paramount had me working on *Saigon*, again with Alan.

It wasn't a bad film and featured such excellent actors as Morris Carnovsky and Luther Adler. By this time, working with Alan was like carrying on a conversation with an old friend. There were no surprises between us and no friction. We continued our aloof but friendly relationship and it was smooth sailing all the way.

The lights hadn't even cooled on *Saigon*'s set when I began working on *The Sainted Sisters* with Joan Caulfield and Barry Fitzgerald. It was a silly comedy about two confidence dames who, while fleeing to Canada, end up in Barry's house in a small Maine border town. Barry uses us for the good of his town and reforms us in the process.

I was tipped off early in the filming that some devious Paramount brass were waiting for Caulfield and Lake to come to blows. One of them was quoted as saying, "Let's put Lake in with Caulfield. Caulfield will fix her ass."

I played it so cool. And professionally bitchy. Everyone would come down to see the rushes and walk away shaking their heads at the scenes in which Joan and I appeared together. Every time Joan gave lines, I'd just stand there and stare at her. I was good at that, so good that people in the business began talking about my ability to steal scenes without doing anything. And no one appreciated it more than Joan Caulfield. There were times she'd leave the screening room in a rage.

"She can't do that to me," she'd complain to Bill Russell, our director.

"What did she do?" Bill would ask.

"Stand there like that," Caulfield would sputter.

"You want her to do something?" Bill would ask.

"NO! I want her out of my scenes."

"I can't do that," would be Bill's response. "I can't do that."

He didn't and we finished filming with very few words between the two female stars of *The Sainted Sisters*. Actually, Barry Fitzgerald stole the film and deserved that honor. Without him and the role he created, the film would have been far worse than it actually ended up being.

It was a good year for me financially. I made enough to run the farm and ranch, keep the plane in fuel and pay off airline bills. But just barely.

19

"YOU'RE pregnant again."

That was my doctor in February 1948. Bandi was pleased. It was another way to spend. Besides, my conceiving in some way justified Bandi's performance in bed. He was European in so many ways, especially with women and money. But he was no European lover. Bandi believed in man being a functional animal, and woman was a depository for man's function. Whoever made up that joke with the punch line. "Wham, bam, thank you, ma'm," must have had Bandi in mind.

Bandi went to Australia in May of 1948 on some strange and unexplainable mission. I was in my fifth month and depressed. Bills flooded the desk, I wasn't feeling very well and Bandi's more frequent trips away from home began to irk me.

"Let's go to New York, Marge," I told my secretary one day as we sat around the farm.

"For what?"

"Just for the going."

Marge shrugged her shoulders and said, "Sure. I'll get the tickets. When do we leave?"

"We don't need tickets," I told her. "I'll fly us there."

Marge went pale.

"Don't worry, Marge. I have 75 hours now of solo and we'll do fine. Of course, if you don't want to go, I'll just go it alone."

Marge displayed loyalty above and beyond any that should be expected.

"O.K. I'm with you, Ronni."

I didn't bother filing a flight plan. I took sectional maps the day before and carefully plotted our course to New York. We'd only fly in good weather and during daylight hours so I could fly contact using ground reference points as navigational aid.

We took off on a gorgeous day in Los Angeles. Lifting the little Navion off always gave me a sensation of freedom, freedom of earth's tenacious hold on you. You push forward on the throttle and there begins a battle against what nature intended. The wheels fight to free themselves of the runway's hold, their ally the wings and the engine striving together to force enough air under the wings for lift, buoyancy, clear flight into air's vast void. You win the battle and freedom is yours. Everything falls below, toy-like, and the clouds beckon you like marshmallow puffs in a fairy tale. I've screamed with delight on take-off, cursed the inherent limitations of its duration and fallen sullen when the tingling stopped and the thrill dissipated.

With Marge in the next seat, I collared my emotions and tried to look professional. The take-off was perfect, and we banked east for the first leg of our journey.

"How do you like it, Marge?" I asked.

"Fine. Fine."

"Beats flying the commercial planes, huh?"

"I wouldn't know. I've never flown before."

That's a brave girl, I thought, as I settled down to the business of staying on course, maintaining air speed and level flight and keeping an eye on instruments in case anything should malfunction.

Our first stop was Phoenix. We could have gone further but I didn't want to stretch my fuel at any time. Phoenix had good facilities and seemed a good spot for our first stop. I was in the pattern when Marge indicated her first apprehension.

"Have you gotten any better on landings, Ronni?"

"What do you mean, better?"

"I remember Stan saying you were bad on landings."

I laughed. "Don't worry about a thing. I just don't like hitting the ground. I like to just touch it."

"Oh." She gave me a forced smile, behind which there lurked the face of fear.

It was a perfect landing at Phoenix, much to Marge's relief. Mine too, I guess. A bad one might have sent her scurrying across to the nearest commercial plane.

"Will they all be like that?" she asked.

"Of course. Can't miss."

We made another good landing in New Mexico and headed on to Dallas. It dawned on me as we bore east that Marge had done a fine job in keeping the press from knowing of our plans. I expressed my pleasure to her. Marge always responded to compliments and this was no exception. She smiled, gave me a little salute and settled back in total relaxation for the first time. We fell silent and just watched the ground slip by below us.

It was the happiest I'd been in a long time. I even forgot about my pregnancy until Marge reminded me.

"How are you feeling?"

"Great. Just fine." It was true. I'd been having an unusual amount of nausea during this pregnancy and I had been concerned at how flying would further upset me. Obviously, it was the thing I needed. Maybe all pregnant women should take flying lessons when they're with child. We could start a club.

We touched down at Dallas with the smoothness Marge had come to expect of my flying skills. More fuel was poured into the Navion and we climbed back into the plane. It was Marge who first spotted the cars arriving in front of the terminal.

"Ronni. Look."

I looked. They were press people. You come to sense press people from other people. There was no doubt about this crew.

"Come on," I said hurriedly, urging Marge into position. "Let's get out of here."

I started the engine, waved the attendant into a faster job of clearing the chocks under the wheels, and quickly gave the plane some power. I held the left brake hard and the plane spun around to its left. Brake released, it started moving straight ahead. The prop wash caught the press people, maybe four or five of them, head on. One was a photographer with a Speed Graphic. I'm certain all he got on his negative was a lot of dust. "Just in time, huh, Marge?"

"I don't know how they knew," she muttered. "Probably some local creep looking for a three-dollar pay-off for a news tip."

"Probably."

We landed again at a small airfield not far from Dallas and spent the night there in a crummy motel. The next morning was a beauty, and we resumed our trip, now heading north with Springfield, Missouri, as one of the scheduled refueling stops.

Marge and I became engrossed in a long and heated conversation about Hollywood and some of the people with whom I was involved. The conversation ended when I realized we might be lost.

Marge looked down and spotted a set of railroad tracks.

"Aren't those the ones you said we'd be following pretty much?"

I looked. I wasn't sure.

"That river. Over there; Is that in the right place?"

It struck me funny. "It better be or some people are going to be very upset."

"We're lost, aren't we?" Marge asked with a quiver in her voice.

"Maybe not." I pulled back on the throttle and started a long winding descent. Soon, I was at no more than 1,000 feet and heading over a small town which stood alone in the middle of farm land.

"Can you read it?" I asked Marge.

"Read what?"

"The water tower. Over there." I pointed to a rusty tower that stood with uncertainty over the small town. We squinted against the day's brightness to read the letters on the side of the tower, partially obscured by many years of rust smears.

"No," Marge answer glumly. We passed the tower and came back for a second look. This time we were able to make out enough of the town's name to locate it on our map.

"Pretty fancy navigating," I said proudly as we climbed back up to altitude.

"I'm impressed, Ronni. I'll make a note to send the mayor of that town a letter when we get back."

"Tell him we'll pay to have his damned water tower painted."

"That's the least we can do." I'm sure Marge was relieved enough to actually make the offer.

We arrived over Springfield that afternoon.

"I don't see any airport," Marge said.

"I don't either."

We scanned the ground below and saw nothing that even resembled an air strip. After circling for ten minutes or more, I spotted a long, clear area with a building standing to one side of the clearing.

"Maybe that's it, Marge."

"It doesn't look like an airport to me."

It really didn't to me, either, but I didn't see anything else that made any sense. We had to land. Fuel was running low.

"That must be it," I said with great confidence. "I'm just not used to looking for turf runways."

"What's a turf runway, Ronni?"

"Same as a regular runway. Only it's grass instead of concrete."

"Is that harder to land on?"

"No, of course not."

"Have you ever landed on one?"

"Well, no. But it can't be any different. Relax, O.K.?"

Marge agreed to relax, which is like agreeing to stop hurting. I spiraled down to landing pattern altitude and began my left-hand approach. And then it happened. All that grass started to meld into one great big green mess. There was no runway. It was just a big green cow pasture with no definition, no landing strip—green nothing.

"How are you doing?" Marge asked.

"Great. No problem." I was starting into a mild panic but didn't show it. I just kept making my left-hand turns as though I knew where the runway was. I came into the last leg and lowered flaps. The Navion settled earthward at just the proper rate. I still didn't know whether a runway was under me. I sat and waited, cut power when the wheels were almost on the turf, and felt the small plane make contact. It was no concrete. The bumps and small ruts made sure I knew it wasn't. I brought the plane to a stop and swung around in the direction of the operations building. Marge and I went inside while they fueled the plane. One of the airport workers came over, pen in hand.

"How about your autograph, Miss Lake?" I signed his piece of paper, careful to add Mrs. André DeToth under the Veronica Lake signature.

"Thanks, Miss Lake. Thanks a lot. By the way, beautiful landing. I watched you all the way in."

"It was?"

"Right down the middle. Real smooth. Well, thanks again."

I couldn't believe it. My face must have indicated my surprise at the compliment because Marge picked it up right away.

"Just an old pro on turf," she said with a wink.

Pittsburgh was next on the schedule and I thought of Stan Reaver, my instructor, who just that year had won a cross-country race in a P-51 but had gotten lost over Pittsburgh. How would anyone get lost over Pittsburgh, I wondered?

I soon found out. Pittsburgh was covered with a low overcast, the result of industrial haze and low clouds. I gave some consideration to by-passing the city and going on to another airport.

"I'm all for that," Marge said when I told her of the idea.

"I am too, Marge, but I've gotta go." My bladder was as cramped as any pregnant gal and reacted accordingly.

It would have to be Pittsburgh, haze or no haze.

The landing was fine. I came in with full flaps and fluttered down very gently because of the increased lift the flaps created. But I couldn't get them up. I pumped that damned handle and the flaps just stayed where they were on landing.

Fortunately, there was a Navion service facility at Pittsburgh and they promised me an hour service. Marge and I ate after first making the necessary stop in the ladies room.

We were sitting talking about the bad luck of having the flaps go on us when it hit—the tornado. No one expected it in the area and it tore through the airport like a mad monster on the loose. There's no doubt we would have been up in the air just minutes when it hit if we'd stayed for only normal servicing and refueling. The faulty flaps turned out to be a blessing.

Marge still regained her composure. After such a trouble-free beginning to the flight, things seemed to be developing into a series of problems. But we were almost to New York and there was no reason to expect any further ordeal. Except for Salisbury, New Jersey, and who would think that pleasant little town would cause trouble.

I had friends in Salisbury and wanted to stop off and see them before reaching New York. I knew the airport was tiny but adequate for the Navion.

I brought on my own problems by flying past dusk. Night seemed to suddenly shroud everything and all visual contact with the ground was a thing of the past. We weren't far from Salisbury when darkness came, and I was certain it lay only minutes ahead of us and our path of flight.

The sight of red lights a few minutes later made me feel very good. Undoubtedly, they marked the end of the runway at Salisbury. I quickly went into my pattern and found myself floating down on the final leg. I was low, too low for a night-time landing, but I wanted to be sure and touch down at the very beginning of the strip. It wasn't until I was almost down that I realized the lights weren't runway lights at all. They were automobile tail-lights. And they didn't mark the end of the runway. They marked the airport boundaries. I reacted out of pure fear and pulled back on everything. The plane stalled and plopped down onto the strip. It took a big bounce, threatened to skid once or twice, but held steady and reacted positively to my braking. The red tail-lights rushed at us; they couldn't have been more than four hundred feet away when I landed.

We stopped five feet from the lights. Marge broke out in a nervous giggle and I swore at myself and the airplane and the world in general.

We had a pleasant time in New York. When it was time to go back to California, Marge came to me with a terribly honest expression on her face.

"Ronni, I know this will make you mad but I have to do it. I'm not going back with you."

My first reaction was that I was losing this great gal to some newly-acquired New York paramour. She quickly put things in understandable order.

"You're a fine pilot and all, Ronni . . . Honest . . . It's just that . . . Well, I thought maybe I'd take the train."

"Why do that?" I asked. "I've already decided to drive. You're welcome to ride right seat for me again."

A rush of appreciation filled Marge's face. "Maybe we can stop in that town and read the tower again."

"Could be. I drive worse than I fly."

Driving back went without hitch, although it seemed to me that Marge was more tense in the car than she'd been in the Navion. I suppose that's because there wasn't a damn thing she could do in the plane. All she could do was accept what I did as correct. She drove the whole trip back to Hollywood with her right foot working that imaginary brake on the right side. I hired a pilot to fly the Navion back and all was well. Of course André went into a Hungarian rage when he got back and heard of our trip.

"That was my baby you risked," he yelled.

"What baby, Bandi? The Navion?" We started talking again the following week.

20

BANDI sold the Navion when they yanked his license at Burbank Airport for reckless and irresponsible piloting. He turned to even more extensive travel to compensate for his loss and I went back to trying to make enough money to keep things going.

I couldn't begin another featured role because my pregnancy was showing. I did manage to get in a celebrity bit part in *Variety Girl* and signed contracts to do *Isn't it Romantic* before my doctor decided I'd better spend my last few weeks of pregnancy in Good Samaritan Hospital. I hadn't been feeling at all well and welcomed the rest.

The total inactivity did me a world of good. I passed the first week reading and chatting with friends and catching up on correspondence. I felt strong again, and waited with happy expectation for the arrival of my third child.

The serenity and calm of the second week was shattered when my lawyer arrived.

"This is too ludicrous to even bring up at a time like this, Ronni, but I'm compelled by law. Your mother is suing you."

It was too ridiculous to be a joke. "Suing me for *what*?"

"For a lack of filial love and responsibility."

I knew filial had something to do with parents and children. But I had no real understanding of what my lawyer was talking about. He explained.

"Your mother claims you promised back in 1943 to pay her $200 a week for life. She says you stopped paying her anything last May and owe her the money. She wants $17,416 in back pay and $500 a month for life."

André turned his temper on the lawyer. "You go back and tell her she's crazy."

"I'd like to, André, but she's filing the suit and there's very little we can do about it unless you want to settle with her out of court."

Bandi really blew. "Settle? She can't win a suit like this, can she?"

"I feel confident we can beat it. But that's one thing you learn early in the legal game. Never second-guess a court of law. They hand down some strange decisions sometimes."

André was beside himself. It was good because I was incapable of expressing any emotions. I felt all the strength of the last week drain away from me and I lay there in the hospital bed without saying a word. It was all too incredible, the notion, the timing, the meaning of it.

"Please leave me alone," I asked Bandi and our lawyer. Bandi was sweet and he tried to soothe me.

"Don't worry about a thing, Ronni. This is just some stupid crank thing she's doing. Just forget about it."

It was a long time after they closed the door to my room that I broke down. Once I did, there was no stopping. A nurse came in, summoned Bandi, and together they tried to help me stop. But it was useless. I just cried until it stopped by itself and sleep came.

My mother was serious in the suit. The following day she issued a statement in which she said, "My daughter has tossed me off like an old shoe. I'm destitute, indigent and dependent upon the charity of others. I spent my life savings of $10,000 to send Veronica to drama school. Now she earns $4,500 a week and hasn't sent me a thing since last May."

The press were all over the hospital. André kept them away and spoke for me. He was also forced to speak for himself because my mother named him as a co-defendant in the suit for "aiding Miss Lake in evading her responsibility."

"I don't even know the woman," André told the reporters. "We've been married since 1944 and I've never met Mrs. Keane."

"Veronica's having labor pains in there," Bandi told them, "and she's crying and sobbing all on account of this terrible thing."

Labor hadn't begun as yet but it was nice of Bandi to think of the line. I snapped out of my crying late the following afternoon and had a long talk with our lawyer.

"Did you ever agree to pay her a certain sum of money every week?" he asked me.

I had to admit I did. I never signed anything but had pledged support to her. And I made the payments faithfully until recently when our expenses made it impossible.

"She ought to be lucky she got what she did," I protested. "This business of spending her life savings on drama school for me is a lot of crap. And everybody knows that."

"Be that as it may, Ronni, there obviously was a contractual obligation to her. A verbal one. And your regular checks to her in the past bear that out, or will in a court of law. We may have a problem here."

"What the Christ does she expect. I'm supporting my grandmother, my mother-in-law, two children, a nurse, servants, Bandi's expensive whims, two goddamn homes and now another child. What the hell am I supposed to do?"

"I'd suggest we settle with her. Why drag everyone through a court when we can avoid it?"

I could feel the tears well up again. I strained against them but it was a losing battle.

"I'm sick and tired of living my life under threats," I sobbed. "Sick of it. Give her whatever money she wants. I'm just sick of it all."

We settled. It was settlement for legal purposes only. Everyone came to my moral and emotional aid, including Hedda Hopper who blasted the whole idea of the suit in one of her columns. Hedda and I never got along but I always think kindly of her for taking my side in the mess.

Diana was born on October 16. Like Elaine, she was a beauty. Bandi beamed with pleasure at the winner we'd created. "This should make you forget your mother," he told me.

I looked down at our child of two days and said a silent prayer to someone that this small creature could indeed make me forget. And as I looked, I slowly realized there was a hint of my mother in her face, just a slight hint, but enough to make me remember.

"She's beautiful, Bandi. Thank you."

21

"You're drinking too much, Ronni."

I can remember Bandi standing there, his finger pointed at me, his face a mixture of concern and disgust.

"What the hell do you mean I'm drinking too much?"

His finger again. "You're drinking more than you ever have. That's what I mean. And I think you should stop."

I lit a cigarette. There was a tiny tremble in my hand. Very tiny.

"Don't be silly, Bandi."

"You're in for trouble, Ronni. You start that kind of thing and you're in trouble."

It was getting to me, his accusing tone, his calm statement of the fact. I wanted him to stop but I couldn't think of how to bring it about.

"Why are you drinking so much, Ronni?"

"Jesus Christ, Bandi. Shut up, will you?"

I got up to go to the kitchen. Damn it, don't let him notice I'm unsteady. I'm really not. Just tired. And tense.

"Do you mind if I relax, Bandi? Do you mind? Do you mind if I relax while we go bankrupt?"

Bandi smiled one of his you-silly-girl smiles.

"Bankruptcy? That's absurd. I didn't want to tell you something but maybe I'd better. You and I are going to do another picture together. What do you think of that?"

"What picture?"

"A Herman Wouk story about Navy pilots and hurricanes and narcotics. It's called *Slattery's Hurricane*."

I poured myself a drink.

"And I'm a nightclub singer. Right?"

"Wrong. You're a secretary."

"And a dope addict."

"And a dope addict. Maybe we should make you an alcoholic."

"Up yours, Bandi."

"You're drunk and you're foul tongued, Ronni."

"And you're Hungarian."

Bandi stormed from the house to ponder my dislike for his nationality. I've met many Hungarians since Bandi and find all of them are charming. Really, the Hungarian thing has become a running joke between me and my good friend and editorial adviser, Sam Post. Sam is of Hungarian background and I love to tease him. It was mostly teasing with Bandi, too, but it proved to be a monumental sore point with him and, as we all know, everyone loves to pick at a weak spot in anyone's armor.

Bandi stayed away all night and returned in time for breakfast. I was hung over and he was tired. It made for stimulating breakfast conversation.

"Why do you hate Hungarians so?" he asked me between bites of toast.

It broke me up. "I *love* Hungarians, Bandi."

"Oh."

"Where did you go last night?" I asked.

"You would never believe it."

"Maybe I would. Tell me."

"I drove all night long. And I picked up a hitchhiker."

"A hitch-hiker? What kind of a hitch-hiker?"

"A girl. A young girl."

"That's convenient."

"It was terrible. Terrible."

"Really?"

"Yes. I picked her up and started to drive her to where she said she was going. We were passing through the Hollywood Hills when she asked me to stop the car. I stopped—what could I do?—and she got out of the car. And then . . . Well, then she took off her clothes and started to dance around."

"And then, Bandi?"

He shrugged. "And then I told her to put her clothes back on."

"And she did. Right?"

"Believe me, Ronni, she did. I drove her to her address and let her off. That was the end of it."

"You rotten . . . rotten . . . rotten Hungarian bastard."

"Ronnie, please. That was the way it was. Did I have to tell you anything? Believe me. That was all."

I yelled some more just because I felt I should yell. But I believed Bandi. I always believed him and in him where other women were concerned. Maybe I'm queen of the naïve broads but I do believe all of my three husbands were faithful to me. And I know I was faithful to them.

Bandi and I had many laughs over his dancing-girl story. It was good because laughs were few and far between. As he promised, we did make *Slattery's Hurricane* with Richard Widmark, Linda Darnell, Gary Merrill and John Russell. It was an interesting film if you liked flying and hurricanes. The story concerned the Navy's nine-plane Patrol Squadron 23 which handles most of the hurricane reconnaissance from the Naval Air Station in Miami. These Naval aviators pulled some pretty hazardous duty in tracking hurricanes in advance of their striking and hopefully saving life and property on the mainland. It was a special effects man's dream, and the effects were excellent. The script did create the infernal triangle between Richard, Linda and me. But the soap opera portion was just that. The film's appeal was in its excellent depiction of these pilots and the violent weather they braved.

I enjoyed seeing Florida again. And there was Tom Moxley, homely boy turned handsome man. And other old friends from high school and the neighborhood if you can call Miami a neighborhood.

The film did quite well and helped bail us out of the worst of our debt. It made no lasting impression on film buffs but did herald one of the most controversial innovations known to modern man—in-flight entertainment on commercial airliners.

The Navy, proud of *Slattery's Hurricane* and the salute it gave to Navy pilots, previewed the film in its 90-ton giant aircraft, the *Constitution*. The plane was one of those with rocket take-off assists and was the largest air transport plane in service anywhere in the world.

Eighty-six people made that flight and circled around Manhattan for three hours, ate lunch and watched *Slattery's Hurricane*. A temporary projection system had been installed as well as a silver screen in the front of the plane. The date of the flight was August 11, 1948, and some writers covering the flight speculated on what use in-flight films might have in commercial aviation. If they only knew. I think out of nostalgia and a sense of history, some airline ought to re-run *Slattery's Hurricane* for its passengers.

The completion of *Slattery's Hurricane* marked the beginning of a period of greatest professional frustration. Being offered bad scripts was bad enough. But now I wasn't offered any scripts. None. It was depressing, to say the least. And Bandi's traveling, now in high gear on the money from *Slattery's Hurricane*, became impossible to tolerate. I tried to reason with him from a dollars and cents point of view but money meant nothing to him. After I came to realize that fact, I decided I might as well join him.

"I'm going with you on this trip, Bandi."

He'd shake his head and refuse. "I'm going on business and it is not a wife's place to come on business." Off he'd go, leaving me in California with the children, animals, thoughts of a career obviously down the drain and, more and more, a bottle.

Our creditors were becoming impatient. I soon found myself spending half of each day pleading, or threatening or combining tactics. It was a degrading experience, especially because it was unnecessary.

It lasted for two years. I did nothing. I didn't try to do anything. No pushing back. No asking why I was no longer in favor with Hollywood. Just a long spiral down into a bottomless well, the only buoy a bottle—of Scotch. I was no alcoholic. But how those two years sent me scurrying for an easy answer; Bandi offered no answer.

I flew to New York and did Sid Caesar's *Show of Shows* in November 1950. But doing the show was only part of the reason for the trip. It was, in effect, a free ticket to New York to raise money to beef up our disastrous finances. I sold some jewelery at Cartiers, hocked a few other things around town and came back with enough cash to keep us out of jail. But it was only a temporary dam against the flood of debt.

Bandi was in London when I was offered a role in a Mexican movie called *Stronghold*. It was a dog but the pay was decent and I accepted. Zachary Scott and Arturo de Cordova were in it with me. And our director was Steve Sekely, a Hungarian director. With an accent, yet.

I laughed through the whole filming of *Stronghold*. Every time the director would give me directions, I'd hear that accent and break into laughter. It didn't endear me to him in the least.

The laughter lasted until Bandi arrived unexpectedly from London. He was furious I'd accepted the role. He went through all sorts of dialogue about how he was saving me for great things and I had cheapened myself by entering into such a grade-B production. He yelled and screamed and, in general, motivated everyone to raising a knife, blunt, against his throat.

It wasn't all professional dissatisfaction with Bandi, however. He was jealous, convinced I was playing around in Mexico. I denied it at first, but when the accusations got out of hand, I just yelled back.

"That's right, Bandi. I take on seventeen Mexicans a night and a double shift on Sunday."

He'd beat his fists against his head and go very dramatic. I'd laugh at him and that would really send him into a furor.

We got out of Mexico with a bad picture and a gulf between Bandi and myself that would never be bridged. The only thing that kept us together after that was the need to pool resources and imagination against the world to which we owed money.

We declared bankruptcy early in 1951 after the income tax people seized our home in April to satisfy over 60-thousand dollars in unpaid taxes. If that sounds like a lot of back taxes, keep in mind that we owed as much as 123-thousand dollars shortly before that. I made another trip east to hock what was left and Bandi and I called it quits. We officially separated in June 1951.

But my marriage wasn't the only thing I was to break away from. I decided it was time to make Hollywood a thing of the past. At this point, cynics will say that quite the reverse was true; Hollywood decided it was time to make Veronica Lake a thing of the past. I might have accepted that latter reading of the situation except for what happened right after Bandi and I separated.

It wasn't two weeks before scripts began coming to me. They weren't good scripts, mostly second-rate ones that would prove acceptable box-office with a name actor or actress. I received three in one week. I couldn't understand it after the drought of the past two years.

I decided to call one of the producers who submitted two of the scripts. He solved the question of the past two years very easily.

"I figured now that André wasn't around, we might have a crack at you again. Everything I gave him to try on you he rejected. He kept saying they weren't good enough for you."

I was stunned, not only at Bandi's gall but at his logic. There we were in the midst of financial disaster and he was turning down lucrative work for me. Perhaps his motives were honorable. Perhaps he truly wanted me in good properties and not the mediocre ones the studios submitted. I just wish he'd taken me into his confidence before telling the producers to go away.

I was furious at Bandi. But my fury was tempered by my own turn of logic. There I was with films to make for the first time in two years. And I realized I really didn't want to go back through the grind of playing sexy sirens in grade-B thrillers all for the silk purses of the studio management. I wasn't positive I felt this way. It was just another chapter in Veronica Lake's confusion. I needed time, quiet time, to think things out.

I packed up a few things, rented a cabin on St. George Mountain in the Sierras, hired a mule in a small town near the cabin and went into a three-month hibernation, my only link with the world a once-a-week trip into town with the mule for supplies. It was a marvelous three months, so free of pressures and conflict and Hollywood's peculiar slant on living. I could feel confidence and strength seeping back into me as I spent each day strolling the mountain and basking in the peace of its isolation. I did miss the children, although I was surprised at how little I missed them. There's a shame to be felt in my lack of concern for them. I've felt that shame and still do, the intensity of it varying with the successes or failures of Elaine, Mike and Diana.

I came down off the mountain, packed up what was left and flew to New York with the children. As corny and overly dramatic as it may sound, I actually did utter an official farewell to Hollywood as I stood ready to board the plane.

"The hell with you, Hollywood," I said to myself. "And fuck you too."

I set foot in Hollywood again in June 1952, to obtain my final divorce from André. I've never been back since.

22

I ARRIVED in New York as a celebrity. I felt good. Television, the newly-arrived enemy of Hollywood, welcomed me with open arms. This electronic marvel had driven a stake into filmdom's theretofore confident heart. Berle, showbiz wrestlers and neighborhood prize fighters reigned supreme in a growing number of homes. My acceptance by TV did marvelous things for my ego. My months on St. George Mountain had been a physical tonic. Drinking was once again an occasional thing of social enjoyment, its previous over-indulgence a temporary tranquilizer against the stormy years of my second marriage. The kids and I settled into a comfortable brownstone in The Village and I went about setting up and fulfilling the many television commitments offered me.

I found TV a challenge, and a lucrative one. You did your bit and walked away. The money was good, especially when you considered it against the grueling process of making a feature motion picture, with the months of work and early hours and endless re-takes.

TV had its frightening aspects, too, however. *Live!* Either do it good or flop. No chance to give a scene another try. No editor to snip out the flubs, take the best of many takes and blend them into an acceptable scene. One shot for all to see. But exciting, as the stage is exciting. These days, with video tape, performers are sure. But the performer live before his jury brings a vitality to the audience experience.

I worked the Berle show once. I was substituted at the last minute after the scheduled actress begged off for one reason or another.

Berle was unique. A lovable jackass, brass, confident, maddening. The scene I was to do involved a wealthy woman coming in for her welfare check. They dressed me up to the hilt with a full mink and lots of stage jewelry. We rehearsed one day and things went moderately well. Berle didn't laugh at other people and you were never quite sure just what he was thinking of your performance. He appeared to accept me with disdain. He didn't complain; he didn't have time.

We were into the live show and I made my entrance into the welfare office. I was half way across the set when, for no conscious reason, I grabbed my mink and pulled it up over my head like an Italian street woman's *babushka*. That simple bit of business caused me to adopt what I suppose was a terribly pitiful expression. It struck Berle so completely that he went into convulsions of laughter and held the show up for at least a minute.

After the show, he told me, "Veronica, that damned bit of putting the mink up over your head was great. Just great."

"Thanks, Milton. And thanks for the twenty-five hundred. I'm available any time." It was the easiest money I'd ever made.

Berle followed through on his compliment. The next day, I opened my door to be greeted by a florist's delivery boy. He had the biggest basket of flowers I'd ever seen. I knew immediately it was from Berle. No one else would ever choose anything so garish. Every conceivable kind of flower was in that huge white basket, the effect the gaudiest bit of nature ever devised. And one of the most thoughtful.

I did at least nine TV shows during my first three months in New York.

TV was fun. I even enjoyed the panel shows. But I soon had run the field of available television opportunities and turned to the stage for the first time in my life. It scared me to death. And I soon found out I had good reason to approach stage work with fear in my heart.

To begin with, the legitimate stage is undoubtedly the most demanding situation any performer can tackle. Like TV, it's live. But even in television's life orientation, the camera can be swung away from an embarrassing situation. Not so on a stage. You're there for all to see, judge—accept or reject. No wonder legitimate actors term television and movies bastard mediums. If you can make it on the stage, you can make it anywhere.

My entry into stage work was complicated by the children. How would I travel and still see about their welfare? It was solved in a variety of ways, none ideal, but all necessary under the circumstances. I took them with me on some tours. Other times, they went back to California to be with André. And there were friends or paid helpers in New York to look after them. Unfortunately, that's a damned unsettled way for any child to grow up. But I felt more guilt about it then than I do now. I had to make a living and my living was acting. Actors travel. Children had been brought up under worse circumstances and survived to go on in the world as responsible, stable adults. Maybe some of my children's problems in life would have been avoided had their mother been with them more. Then again, it might have made them worse. I sometimes find myself going through that whole, "What if . . . ?" routine. You could go to the grave wondering. I don't intend to. I have made bad and numerous mistakes in bringing up my children and I accept that blame and suffer appropriate remorse for the mistakes. But I ask my children to throw away my faults as a crutch. I tried, failed when I failed and succeeded when possible. Perhaps *they* should ask themselves, "What if . . . ?"

My first stage job was in Atlanta, Georgia. The play was *Voice of the Turtle*, and not only did they bill it as Veronica Lake's first stage appearance, they announced to the city that it would mark the first time running water was to be used in theatre-in-the-round. These two monumental firsts of American theatre, their order debatable, brought in a full house and plenty of critics.

The running water didn't run. I found that out when I started through a scene in which I was to wash dishes. All eyes were on that sink and I died a little upon turning the faucet handle. Not a drop. I turned it back and forth, praying that the promised water would spew forth and splash all over me. Back and forth I turned it and the giggles started from the audience. I was getting nervous and confused about what to do. I suppose some seasoning on a stage would have helped me accept the problem and ignore it, but at that time, it posed a monumental crisis. I reacted by doing what came naturally.

I faced the audience formally and announced, "It doesn't work. Tomorrow night will be the first time in stage history that running water will be used."

I turned back to the sink and pantomimed the washing of the dishes. The audience applauded.

Actually, the running water episode was the minor problem during my first stage appearance. It was the simple fact of doing theatre-in-the-round that caused me my greatest concern and agony. For those of you who aren't familiar with theatre-in-the-round, it means simply that the stage is in the middle of the room and the audience sits on all four sides. And they sit very close, close enough to rest their feet on the set or reach out and touch an actor. You're surrounded, with no place to hide. It's tough.

I'd received a marvelous ovation when I made my first entrance in Atlanta. It wasn't until I'd settled into things that I noticed just how close the audience was to me. I first knew it when I heard a fat man in the fourth row whisper to his buddy, "Hey, those bubs are for real."

I heard a woman from an unknown section tell her companion in a very loud whisper, "Her hair is real blonde."

One man, seated directly behind a desk on the stage, reached in and flicked out his cigarette in the ash-tray.

And one bore in the first row picked up a glass from the set into which whisky (actually colored water) had been poured and announced to everyone around him, "It's fake booze."

I soon got over the audience's proximity and things were going along nicely until my leading man, a young actor named Cary Betz, didn't show up for one of his cues. Cary was a very good actor, a handsome fellow and totally egocentric.

I was in the middle of a long speech during which Cary was to make an entrance. I gave the whole speech and waited. He didn't show. I fumbled around and did some stage business. Still no Cary Betz. Finally, in sheer desperation, I told the others on the stage, "Make yourselves drinks. I've got to go tell the janitor something."

I walked off the stage and up the aisle to the dressing-room. I threw open the door and there was Cary, self-professed matinée idol, combing each hair into place as he admired his image in the mirror.

"You conceited baboon," I yelled at him. "Get your pretty ass out there on that stage."

Cary was terribly annoyed I'd spoken to him in those terms and actually complained to the director after the performance.

"I won't put up with that has-been actress" (the word rolled off his tongue with scorn) "yelling at me like that. I will not have it."

The director, with a week to go with the show, soothed Cary. He asked me to show patience during the play's run for the good of the show, promising to keep Cary Betz in line. I agreed. Whatever else I might be, I am a pro. I fully understand management and its problems, especially in the shaky and fickle world of summer-stock theatre. I know the financial problems that beset stock companies and theatre operators, and have always tried to bend their way. It's paid off in large and steady demand for me as a summer-stock attraction, and the points I may lose by bending, to say nothing of the money, are made up for in increased work.

I put up with Cary for the rest of the show. Actually, I kind of enjoyed him and respected his budding talent. He did show up on cue every night after that one time, his hair precisely positioned earlier in the evening.

I kept busy with stage work and grew more confident with each show. Financially, I was relatively secure and stable. There was no excess of funds but enough to live comfortably. Elaine and Diana seemed to be progressing nicely and normally for their ages. It was Michael who worried me with his inner turmoil and apparent frustration that drove him from one troublesome situation to another. Nothing major, nothing to cause enough alarm to do something about it. So much happens as a child grows up that you chalk up to his age and temperament. Nothing serious. Just a rambunctious boy feeling his growing pains and missing California's wide open running spaces.

We took *Voice of the Turtle* to Birmingham, Alabama, and then back to Atlanta for a return engagement. And then on to an eastern tour with the show and another play, *The Curtain Rises*. The tour opened in Barnesville, Pennsylvania, and closed in Olney, Maryland. In between, we visited such spots as Fayetteville, New York, where I finished painting the walls of the set one hour before curtain time. And there was Matunuck-by-the-Sea in Rhode Island where the curtain collapsed during my performance. And Watkins

Glen, New York, where the resident staff walked off leaving me to answer phones all day and sell tickets right up until show time. I loved every minute of it. Gone was the plush façade of Hollywood. Replacing it was honesty, raw and meaningful vitality that shone bright in the murky memories of California and its film factory.

I came off the tour and rested for a month or so. It was a good time to be with the kids and we spent a lot of time together during the break. It was nice relaxing together, but the fidgets set in during the beginning of the second month and I found myself looking hard for another show. I found one.

"Peter Pan?" Elaine said with great disbelief.

"Sure. Don't you think your mother will make a wonderful Peter Pan?" I couldn't help giggling with her. Michael giggled too because his sister did. It certainly wasn't an encouraging beginning for me going into *Peter Pan*. Peter Lawrence had signed me for the lead role in the show and I didn't have any reservations about my playing it until the kids reacted with such incredulousness. It was the national company of the show and would open in Baltimore.

The first thing that concerned me was the need to whip myself into good physical shape. After all, Peter Pan is the spirit of eternal youth. Despite his pixie face, he's all boy and a leader. I wanted *my* Peter Pan to be able to jump higher and run faster and to be best at everything.

Before I set about the task of toning up seldom-used muscles, I went straight to the hairdresser and had my hair clipped into a pixie cut. I'd worn it in an unbraided pigtail in *Voice of the Turtle*. I walked out of the shop with short, straight hair brushed straight back. No one knew me, not even my friends in the Village. I walked around the streets and ran up a few and soon found myself feeling more and more like a boy. It was a little frightening.

I didn't fool around getting in shape for the role. The month of inactivity had led me back to harder drinking than usual. The first thing I did was cut out the booze completely. I'd get up every morning, eat a half-pound of grapes and start doing calisthenics. I did them all and for long periods of time each day. I also took fencing lessons. Soon, the benefits began to become apparent.

I felt tight and energetic. I could never go that route as a steady diet, but for the short duration I enjoyed feeling healthy. And with conditioning came confidence that I would be a hell of a Peter Pan.

We opened in Baltimore to an enthusiastic crowd. As usual with the show, the audience was a broad range of ages, a perpetual tribute to James Barrie's writing. I felt no obvious stage fright, an unusual state of affairs for me and one considered misleading by pros. Stage fright is good when it's controllable. Become blasé and you lose your edge, like when you eat a big meal before a show and turn in a sluggish performance.

Even the rigging didn't faze me. If I thought this was a children's book, I wouldn't even get into the rigging apparatus used in *Peter Pan*. It would be like pricking the Santa Claus bubble. But that's no problem here.

People fly in *Peter Pan* because of a London firm named Joseph Kirby Ltd.

The Kirby firm has been supplying flying equipment for Peter Pans ever since the very early 1900's. For our show, they supplied a wonderful gentleman named Peter Foy who, with three associates, operated a specially patented rig of wires, pulleys, drums, ropes and custom-made harnesses. All of us wore a harness under our costume and, when it was take-off time, they'd hook a wire onto the harness. Then Foy would tug on hemp ropes attached to steel aircraft cables thirty-five feet long. There's a whole intricate mess of counterweights and pulleys and the cables wind around four drums way up above the stage. It's all very complicated and, until I became Peter Pan, Joseph Kirby Ltd. boasted of never having a single mishap. To them, making us fly on stage was nothing. They specialized in aerial ballet in London where a whole chorus kicks and does somersaults in mid-air. It was all very comforting.

Besides, they told me, the apparatus would support one ton. I weighed ninety-eight pounds, which isn't much to lift, even for Peter Foy. He weighed 140 pounds and claimed he lost a pound at each performance. I believe it.

Anyway, there we were in Baltimore and the audience was warm and receptive and I felt as confident as I'd ever felt. Things were going beautifully until we came to the scene where three others and myself were to be airborne simultaneously. It would have worked except Mr. Foy attached the wrong cable to my harness. We all went up and I knew immediately something was wrong. I was sailing in the wrong direction, certain to cross wires with another of my flying friends. I looked backstage in horror and saw Mr. Foy dangling four feet in the air as he tried to counterbalance the weight on the stage. But this was usual; he always used his own body against the pull from the other end of the cables.

The actor coming at me didn't sense a thing. He just sailed right by dumb and happy, a contented grin on his face. He didn't know a thing until my cable made contact with his. He looked back and saw me swing around his cable in a large, flowing circle and start to head back towards him.

"God," I heard him say.

I didn't have time to say anything. I reached out on the way back and grabbed a hold of the ship's mast. It damn near tore my arm out of the socket but I held fast and found comfort in hanging on, my legs wrapped around the pole.

I really don't think the audience realized what was happening. I suppose many of them just assumed it was part of the show. But a few responded with laughter and that started everyone else off.

Mr. Foy was hanging on for dear life backstage. I frantically looked around for some sign of help. There was none. Stage hands stood with mouths open. Other cast members just looked bewildered. And then it dawned on me how ridiculous I must have looked hanging on to that silly pole with a theatre full of people looking on.

"For Christ sake," I yelled in a husky stage whisper to the nearest off-stage person. "Get me off here."

My simple plea broke the inertia backstage. They closed the curtain and brought out a ladder for me. I could hear the muffled laughter of the audience through the drawn curtain and I cursed them as I untangled myself and climbed down to the waiting arms of a crew member.

I walked right over to the stage manager and shook my fist at him. "I don't mind getting twisted up on that perch but why didn't anybody move to help me?"

He looked at me and shrugged his shoulders. "You're Peter Pan. You can do anything." He shrugged again and walked away.

We finished the performance and the audience forgave Mr. Foy and his wires. It never happened again and I suppose never will. But that's a bit of the story of my life. I seem to attract "firsts."

We finished touring with *Peter Pan* and I felt like a million bucks. The children, always a worry when I was away, had gone back to California to be with André. As much as I wanted them with me, I knew California was better for them. Only André wasn't over-joyed. He soon shipped them back to New York, an occurrence to be repeated too many times for their good.

I came back to New York feeling good. But there was something wrong, one of these somethings you can never pinpoint, never explain, but there nonetheless. Probably, and it was veiled at the time by the natural ego of the moment, the depression creeping up on me was natural and to be expected. It's amazing and under-standable how a public soon forgets the names it was familiar with. The time since my last film was slipping by and there must be a simple formula that spells out lost drawing-power in rela-tion to time. I didn't feel any different. But, obviously, producers did. Veronica Lake was becoming yesterday. And today was here. I found work. I'll always be able to do that. I did *The Gramercy Ghost* at Matunuck but had to drop out when a severe virus laid me low. I worked in *I Am a Camera* during its summer run on the New England Coast and *The Curtain Rises* for a summer. I remem-ber the latter because the zipper on my dress broke after taking a prat-fall. It was during a chase scene and the guy running after me kept trying to zipper me up as we went. It happened in Maryland, I think. And there was *Cat on a Hot Tin Roof* where I encountered another temperamental male co-star.

Our performance of that Tennessee Williams play simply wasn't destined to go right. To begin with, I fell off the stage in rehearsal and landed in the orchestra pit. Result—a badly sprained ankle with torn ligaments and tendons and everything else dear to the heart of the local osteopath. He fixed me up with a cast, the walking variety, and gave me permission to perform the show each night. It hurt a great deal and he took care of that by injecting three shots of novocaine in the ankle before each performance.

"You take these injections better than most men I know," he'd mutter every night as I bit my tongue.

The male lead in *Cat on a Hot Tin Roof* also wears a cast, a phoney that splits up the back and can be easily taken on and off by the actor. It was a stirring sight to see both of us limping all over the stage, my cast concealed under long negligées and smeared with leg makeup.

It was the third night of the run when my co-star, a local actor, decided his cast didn't feel quite right. He fiddled and fussed with it as curtain time became a thing of the past. The director told him to hurry up but this thespian simply wouldn't appear unless his cast was properly in place and comfortable. Time went by and soon the audience started clapping hands and stomping feet and chanting, "We want a show. We want a show."

I knew right away that the audience was thinking it was that temperamental movie star, Veronica Lake, who was holding things up. I expressed this to the director. He understood perfectly. He went out in front of the curtain and announced to the audience, "Ladies and gentlemen, our star, Miss Like, hurt her ankle during rehearsal and performs each evening in great pain. However, our problem tonight isn't Miss Lake's ankle. It's our other *star*." He said that last word with all the sarcasm he could muster.

I received a standing ovation when I made my entrance. They booed my co-star. At the show's end, my applause was deafening during the curtain call. His curtain call was met with thick silence. It did my heart good. I was especially pleased because I fouled up quite badly during the show. I completely forgot my lines at one point.

"This damned bayou country makes me thirsty," I told the others on stage. I quickly ran off and searched for a script. They went through some aimless chit-chat on stage until I had a chance to review my lines. I went back, told them the drink of water tasted good, and we went on with the play.

Obviously, I think of legitimate stage work with more fondness than motion-picture work. There's good reason for that and I think most performers will agree. The stage is so of the moment, so new each evening that the human factor comes much more into play. In films, everything is so clinical, so much the technician's art that mistakes aren't funny because they're so quickly erased, edited, snipped into a hasty past. On stage, the performer and his person mean something, for better or for worse, and the most memorable stories always seem to come from stage experiences. Watch the shows like Merv Griffin or Johnny Carson and you always notice the funniest people have worked a great deal in front of live audiences. Of course, burlesque was the greatest of all stage work but that was simply because it flourished in an era when things were always funny. Everyone is so much more serious these days.

And maybe that's what I loved about Joe McCarthy. Joe's father was quite a famous song writer. Everyone remembers and hums "I'm Always Chasing Rainbows," "Alice Blue Gown," "You Made Me Love You," or "Rio Rita." Joe, my Joe, was a song writer, too, having sold his first song before he even graduated from Juillard. He was a marvelously talented young man and we seemed to talk so easily together. It was never evident to me at the outset just how difficult it was for Joe to find any identity under his father's shadow. He seldom discussed it and was generally free and easy in everything he did and said. But underneath boiled hostility that increased in pressure without benefit of a safety valve. We were two of a kind, two people looking for an identity and that's why we seemed to understand each other. I could talk for hours to Joe and I always felt his apperception and compassion for what I was thinking and feeling. I fell in love with Joe McCarthy. I married him on August 28, 1955, in Traverse City, Michigan, where I was appearing in *Affairs of State*. We were married on the day of my final performance and I staggered to the show that evening full of love for Joe, warm canapés and too much champagne.

Meeting Joe and falling in love with him was a stimulating experience as compared to my previous love-leading-to-altar affairs. And I'm certain it had to do with New York and the different backdrop it provided for falling in love. Despite what the tourists from Kankakee say, New York possesses a warmth unknown in most every other place I've been. There's no doubt in my mind that Los Angeles will never gain that kind of Manhattan warmth.

I was introduced to Joe by another song writer, Austin "Ginger" Johnson, who collaborated with Joe on what I feel was one of the most beautiful things ever written—"Over the Weekend." Joe and I lived the madcap, Manhattan pub-crawling life in the early months of our marriage. The children had been on the coast with André when Joe and I began our courtship, but soon they were back with us in New York. We had a brownstone on Ninth Street in The Village, a dwelling undistinguished but for Mike's aversion to its front entrance-way. Mike refused to enter through the door. He used to shinny up a skinny tree in front, make his way along a branch and jump through the living-room window. It was one of the little things that drove Joe nuts. And me too, on occasion. Especially when strangers started doing the same thing.

I was entertaining some important theatre people one evening and we'd just gotten around to some serious discussion on Broadway possibilities for me when it happened. *Shazam! Holy Mother of Batman!* This strange gook leaps through the window and lands at our feet.

We all let out our own little expression of shock as this uninvited guest scrambled to his feet, brushed off the lint on his suit and gave us all a big smile.

"Who the hell are you?" I asked. It seemed appropriate.

"Oh, hi Miss Lake. I live upstairs. Forgot my key. I've seen Mike do this a million times and thought I'd try it. Didn't think you'd mind."

"You bet your ass I mind. Get the hell out of here."

He really looked hurt. But he shook a couple of hands, bowed to me and left. The silly thing was I became upset at the wrong thing. I apologized to everyone for the interruption until one of my guests asked how long the man had lived upstairs.

"Upstairs?" I reacted. "He doesn't live upstairs."

I never saw him again. For all I know he was an I.R.S. official on a spying mission.

It didn't take Joe and me long to begin not getting along. In fact, it was almost immediate. What had been a warm and relaxed friendship soon became a tense and rocky marriage—two new room-mates not destined to share the same space under a common roof. The kids drove Joe to distraction. He's a sensitive guy, soaked with talent and the emotional hang-ups that accompany that kind of talent. The classic, vicious knotty nuptial circle. Joe would get bugged and I'd get bugged. Instead of stopping whatever we were doing to upset the other, the reactions to the wrongdoing would spur us on to even greater heights of bitchiness. It was awful. The only time there was any peace was when we would make a tour of the joints and drink ourselves into a happy but temporary truce. This alcoholic appeasement was fine until the resulting hang-overs made things even worse.

God, how we fought. The children, as so often is the case, were both contributors to the battle and victims of its rage.

Of course, nothing is all bad. Joe and I did share certain moments of relative peace and even flashes of happiness. Perhaps the most memorable and happy times came when we'd visit an old friend of mine, Henry Gardner, up on his estate in Mill Stone Point, Connecticut. These were summer visits, warm days on the beach of Niantic Bay, a former quarry filled with sea water from the hurricane of 1938. I was always a good swimmer and loved leisurely dips in the bay's water and long sunning sessions on the rough sand. There would always be other house guests at Henry's house, never too many, but enough to bring the feeling of pleasurable companionship to the beach during our visits. It's shameful, I know, to admit much coddling and affection for the children of others while your own kids aren't included.

I never brought the kids to Henry's. But I lavished love on the other children who enjoyed those days on the bay. I guess I was a sort of aging, frustrated camp director. I enjoyed arranging the days for the children, scheduling treasure hunts or organized games. And I needed some scheduling myself. It was my job to collect the seaweed at the end of each day to put in the lobster pits. I loved that job and the smell of the seaweed. And then the lobster would cook in the pits and we'd drink and wait for it to be done and sit closely and maybe sing or just think. And so much talk of nothing and everything.

There were times I just stayed on the beach all night, heady with a belly full of lobster and gin, the night's coolness a blanket of tranquillity. I'd just sleep right there and smile at the thought of the water sneaking in and carrying me away to a place where peace was always present and never interrupted by life. You could see life. I'd sit in a big leather harness on the end of a long rope. The rope came from the sky and the end was never in sight. But I'd sit there and look down at life and all the people bumping into each other and the big buildings spitting out everyone at five to go home to smaller buildings. And fights. I was never smug up there on the end of my rope. I was filled with compassion for life below, but content I was a watcher.

Those kind of thoughts all sound very suicidal but I've never been a suicidal person. It just seems such a tragedy you can't have a place in life's stream to pull off and rest awhile. Sort of a living highway rest area where the juices get charged and they fill you up with high-test for the next hundred miles. And change your oil and check your pressure.

Generally, I didn't sleep on the beach. I slept in Henry Gardner's house with Joe. And I reigned queen on Sunday mornings when everyone would get up and go to church. I would always decline their invitation to join them, and as soon as they were gone I'd head for the kitchen. I always included blueberry picking as part of the children's daily activity because I'm queer for blueberries. Any berries. But mostly blue ones. I'd get out the pancake batter, eggs, berries and milk, pour myself a stiff eye-opener of gin in a water tumbler, and go to work. Everyone would return, their souls filled with something, and they'd dig in to fill up the other empty space. I loved those mornings. I had them fooled for a long time into thinking my trusty water glass was filled with water. They didn't believe me when I told them it was gin. One taste convinced them.

Henry Gardner was a nut. I say that assuming you will accept that description in the complimentary way it's meant. And I don't know why I refer to him in the past tense. I suppose it's because I haven't seen Henry in quite a while. I will again, soon, I'm sure. Henry is truly one of the world's great people. And he loved a joke and anything madcap that he could enjoy without getting too deeply involved.

Joe and I were walking along one day on Fifth Avenue. Right there, in front of Bergdorf Goodman, it came. A goose. A real live goose from Central Park. She was lost. And frightened to death of the cars and people. It was a Sunday morning and traffic, mechanical and human, was at a minimum for the city. That was good for the goose if not for her pining gander back in the park.

Anyway, Joe and I chased the goose up the street and finally cornered her. Once we had her, it became apparent that we now had to do something with our catch.

"Let's talk about it over lunch," Joe suggested.

"O.K. But what do we do with the goose while we're having lunch, Joe?"

"We'll put her in a box."

"O.K., Joe. But where do we get a box?"

"Over there." Joe had spotted a doorman. He went to him and convinced him to go back into his apartment house and find us a box. He did. We put the goose in in the box.

"What do we do with the box, Joe?"

"We'll give it to him."

"The doorman?"

"Yes."

"O.K., Joe."

Joe went back to the doorman.

"Would you watch our goose?" he asked.

I think the doorman thought he was on *Candid Camera*, if that was around then. Maybe *Candid Microphone*, the forerunner of the TV show. He laughed nervously, looked around cautiously, accepted Joe's offer of five bucks, and took on the awesome responsibility of entertaining the goose until we'd eaten brunch at Reuben's.

Joe and I had a serious discussion at Reuben's. It was agreed that the last thing we needed at our apartment was the goose. But somewhere during the conversation, I remembered that Henry Gardner had geese on the estate. And, if my memory was serving me correctly, he had always wanted to mate a particular favorite male goose of his.

"Let's call Henry."

Joe was agreeable to calling Henry, but he asked why. "Maybe he doesn't want a city goose," he suggested.

"Screw him, Joe. He'll have to be happy with what he gets. Pretty geese like this one just don't happen by every day. Not on Fifth Avenue, at least."

We called Henry. Henry was not as pleased and enthusiastic as I might have hoped. But after some gentle arm twisting, I managed to extract a commitment from him.

"What'd he say?" Joe asked when I came back to our table.

"Great. He'll take the goose."

Joe seemed genuinely pleased. But then thought lines crossed his face.

"How is he going to get the goose, Connie?"

"He's flying down."

"When?"

"Now. Come on. We have to meet him at LaGuardia."

"With the goose, I suppose."

"Of course. Hurry up. Henry said he was leaving right away."

Our cab pulled up to LaGuardia's Marine Terminal just as Henry's sleek little plane with Henry at the controls taxied up to a parking area. Our cab driver, his nose screwed up against the goose's natural scent which was heightened by too long in the box, graciously accepted Joe's tip and drove off with all windows wide open.

Henry was pleased to see us, feigned enthusiasm at our catch and asked us to fly back with him. We agreed and happily piled into the plane, the goose in her box behind the two rear seats.

Henry had received his taxi clearance when I asked him to wait a minute.

"What's the matter?" he asked.

"The goose."

"I know," Henry said quickly. "She smells like hell. Maybe she's got a problem."

"Not that, Henry. When a goose has to go, it has to go. I'm worried about the direction she's facing."

"What the hell for?" Joe snarled, now beginning to weary of the goose adventure.

Joe's attitude annoyed me. It didn't seem he fully understood the ramifications of this situation. I don't now but I did then.

"I think we should make sure she's facing front all the time, Henry," I said with great seriousness. "It would be awful if she knew where we're taking her and tried to make it back. You'd lose your goose, Henry."

At this point, Henry would have agreed to anything. He, too, was losing interest.

"So turn her around," Joe sighed. He was in one of the back seats.

"You turn her around," I suggested. After much quibbling, Joe agreed. We took off, flew low and landed at the strip near Henry's home. By the time we arrived, the smell in the cabin was overwhelming. Henry was gagging and Joe had taken on that uncertain look of sickness.

I don't know whether it was all worth it. I never did learn if the city goose mated successfully with the country gander to create a superior race of geese. Henry complained right up until the last time I saw him about the smell still permeating the airplane's cabin.

Joe McCarthy and I were married about three and a half years. We spent a year and a half of that time separated. It never never worked and probably wasn't supposed to work. I was me and Joe was himself and we never meshed. Chalk it up to the solar system and a lot of other things.

Compounding things was Mike and his headlong dash to trouble. It was getting to me, despite my ready acceptance of blame for Mike's confusion. But sometimes it was a bit much. Like when I came home one afternoon to find the apartment in total shambles. Mike and a few friends had taken kitchen carving knives and carved murals in the mahogany-panelled living-room walls. That cost me $1,000 for repairs and was one of the factors leading to my eviction. Joe was living elsewhere at the time, which was probably just as well. He and Mike never got along. In fact, our final separation came when Mike, all fourteen years of him, took a kitchen knife and tried to kill Joe, his stepfather.

Joe and I had been arguing. It was early evening and Mike stayed in the kitchen while we fought. Unfortunately, the verbal hassling got out of hand.

It had all started when I tried to make a telephone call from the phone in the living-room. It wouldn't work so I knocked on the bedroom door. Joe didn't answer; I walked in. He was sitting on the bed writing something, and as I reached for the phone he leaped up like a madman and started screaming at me.

"Jesus Christ, Joe, I only want to make a phone call."

His answer was to kick me in the back. It knocked me down and I thought my back was broken. I got up and went out into the living-room. Joe followed, his eyes ablaze and a stream of filth coming from his mouth. He picked up the dead phone in the living-room and that's when Mike appeared from the kitchen with the knife.

Joe's face went into shock. He tore from the apartment and ran down the stairs. But he'd forgotten about Mike's tree-climbing on Ninth Street. Mike went out of the window, down the tree and was waiting at the front door when Joe emerged. Joe ran up the street and Mike gave chase for a few hundred feet.

In the meantime, I called the police and had them issue a warrant against Joe for simple assault. It all ended up in court and the judge ordered Joe to stay away from me and the apartment.

"But it's my home, your honor," Joe offered in court.

"You make it very difficult for me," Judge Gladwin said as he handed down a bail of $500. He'd offered to just let Joe go if he promised to stay away from me.

I dropped the assault charges a few days later and Joe and I filed actions for separation. Joe had hurt my back and I crept around for a few weeks. Mike seemed pleased with the way things worked out but it had to leave its mark on him. And I think you can withstand just so many such marks in a young life.

I never asked for any alimony from Joe. I never believed in alimony for various reasons. Joe had money from his father but little himself. He wasn't a writer of commercial tunes and his income never rose very high. But to this day some of Joe's tunes come back at the strangest times to haunt me. He wrote some of the things Mabel Mercer did so well, and there is one song in particular, "Why Try To Change Me Now," that always seems to sum up our marriage. We both would have benefited from some change but you reach a point in life where change just isn't to be expected.

I was evicted from the apartment on Ninth Street. The landlord had had enough with carved living-room walls and people coming through the window and all. I got the word from a city Marshal one day. He knocked on my door one morning and handed me the eviction notice.

"Gee, I'm sorry, Miss Lake. I mean, you've given me so much pleasure so many times. I feel sorry for this, I really do."

I smiled through my tears and thanked him for being so kind.

"Well, you just take your time, Miss Lake, and don't be upset. You've got until the end of the day to get out, you know."

He actually came back a few hours later with two assistants and they helped me pack. He really felt worse than I about the eviction.

That night Mike and I moved in with an old friend named Charles. We stayed with him four days. And then a stroke of luck came my way. I was signed for summer stock at $1,000 a week.

With the girls in California with their father, I decided to take Mike on the tour with me. We opened in Chicago and held the majority of rehearsals in that city. I found it a strain to learn several parts and keep an eye on Mike at the same time. It all caught up with me and I landed in bed with a vicious virus. Some friends in Chicago offered to take Mike until I got over my bug. Mike loved the idea of staying with my friends and I was all for some rest. Unfortunately, the virus just got worse and I was sent back to New York to see my own doctor. Mike stayed in Chicago and I was put to bed in New York for a week.

I was just getting back on my feet at the end of the week when I received a call from the Chicago police.

"We have your son in custody, Miss Lake."

Mike hadn't done anything wrong. The police found him wandering around downtown Chicago at two in the morning and picked him up for his own safety. Thank God they picked him up. Who knows what trouble he might have found.

"We called the boy's father in Los Angeles," the policeman continued, "and he suggested we fly him back to you in New York. Mr. DeToth has wired us the money for his air fare to New York."

I was so frightened. And confused. Maybe I was just feeling the fright and confusion Mike must have been experiencing at the moment. I hung up the phone and just sat there shaking for an hour. Finally, I pulled myself together and went to the airport to meet Mike. I made a decision on the way. I couldn't cope with him, at least not for a while. I was weak from my virus, mentally discouraged and defeated, and afraid of Mike and life and even myself. I wanted Mike to have some discipline, the kind only a man can provide. I wanted him back with his father, André.

Mike got off the plane with a big grin. He said he was sorry for being picked up by the police but that he hadn't done anything wrong.

"I know, honey, I know."

I explained to him why I wanted him to go back with his father for a while. He seemed to understand but I could see a fatigue set in his eyes, that kind of fatigue that you only see in older people, weary of coping with a hard life.

Mike smiled and said he understood. I put him on the first plane to Los Angeles and went home to the solitude of myself and a bottle of booze. And I sent André a telegram.

Cannot handle Mike. Please help. Will arrive at 12 noon.

André was at Los Angeles Airport to meet his son. He greeted him, booked him on the next plane back to New York and said goodbye. Mike never even left the airport. In 48 hours Mike had crossed the country two and a half times. The feeling of rejection must have been brutal.

André never told me he was sending Mike back. The first I heard was when Mike phoned me from Idlewild. "Ma?"

"Michael?"

"Yeah. I'm back."

"Where?"

"In New York. I'm at the airport. Dad sent me back."

I went to Idlewild, found Mike after a long search, and we both sat down on a public bench and cried our eyes out.

I was staying with a friend at the time and I took Mike back with me. The fatigue was deep for both of us, now, mine a natural result of my life, Mike's also a natural result of *my* life.

"God forgive me," I said before falling asleep on the living-room couch.

I asked Mike how he slept as we ate breakfast the next morning.

"O.K., Ma. O.K. I dreamed a lot though."

"What did you dream about?"

"About nothin', I guess. Nothin'."

He dreamed so much after that.

23

I BROKE my leg the day after Mike's travel ordeal. Why not?

All of Mike's travel had taken place on Labor Day, 1959. Charles, our friend, persuaded me to come to the tennis matches at Forest Hills with him.

"You need a little diversion, Connie," he argued.

I agreed. The gal in whose apartment we were staying planned a day with Mike, and I went off to the matches. I enjoyed them, and afterwards Charles and I were invited for drinks and dinner at a friend's house in Forest Hills.

It was a nice party, and right after dinner someone put records on and everyone started dancing. Charles, all 210 pounds of him, had been a college athlete. But that didn't help him as a dancer. He clumsily tried to spin me around and we both fell to the floor, all of his weight landing flush on my foot and ankle. The ankle cracked like a piece of dry kindling. The pain was excruciating. I screamed and cried and they called my doctor but he was away.

"I want to go to a hospital," I sobbed to Charles.

An ambulance was called and they took me to Queens Memorial. A nurse greeted us.

"Where does it hurt, honey?"

The question struck me so funny I completely forgot about the pain and laughed. And then it hurt again and I got mad.

"Where the hell do you think it hurts? Where would a broken ankle hurt?"

She turned stone-faced and the doctors finally came. They set two bones and put me in a bed. I probably would have been content except that the doctors seemed so concerned and said a lot of dismal things about me and the ankle.

"That's a bad break, Miss Lake," one told me. "A very bad break."
He was right in so many ways.

The next morning I arranged to be transferred from Queens
Memorial to a hospital in Manhattan. They transferred me at nine
and my doctor had a bone man come in and see me late in the afternoon. He agreed with the gravity of my situation.

"It will be a long time before you'll be walking on that leg again,"
he told me. "You'll probably limp for the rest of your life."

I spent the next eight months in fourteen casts of varying size
and description. The first three months were spent in a traction
cast up to my hip. It weighed twenty-five pounds, which was about
one-quarter of my weight. I knew when I left the hospital that I'd
have to get a place of our own in which to live. I arranged to rent
another small apartment in the Village and paid a year's rent in
advance out of some summer-stock savings. I also scraped up
enough money to enroll Michael in the Grove School in Connecticut. That left me nothing with which to pay the soaring medical
bills. The final cost of my fling on the dance floor was in excess of
four thousand dollars.

Days on end crawled by me as I spent them dragging myself
from the tiny bedroom to the tiny living-room at a snail's pace. I
had no way of knowing whether my ankle was healing properly. But
my biggest concern was over the financial plight I once again found
myself facing. There wasn't a cent, the generosity of a few friends
buying the groceries and paying the light bill.

It was during this period that I met Nat Perlow. Here is one
of the sweethearts of the western world. To this day, Nat and I
remain the closest of friends. Nat is the editor of New York's *Police
Gazette* and probably sits on more interesting tales of New York,
past and present, than any other guy in the city.

Nat was truly my shining knight during that year. He always
seemed to show up at the right time, usually with a bag of groceries or some cash to pay a few bills. Every time I'd slip down to my
lowest point, I'd hear a knock on the door and there would be Nat,
stoop-shouldered, big cigar in his mouth and some goodies in a bag.

Like one day early in 1961, a year and a half after my accident.
Nat had been away on business for an extended period and things

weren't going very well for me. I was out of the casts but could barely limp around with the aid of a cane. Naturally, I hadn't worked at all during this period and the bills were piling up higher and higher. I'd let the rent slip for three months and that was my landlord's cue for action. He banged on my door, and when I answered, he snarled that I had 24 hours to get up the back rent or get out on the street.

I got so mad, mostly at myself, that I slammed the door in his face. And the ceiling fell down. A great big hunk of plaster shook loose above me and came down on my head. It hurt. I cried and stamped my good foot and cursed the world. I just wanted to slip through the floor boards to some never-never land and give it all up.

And then there was another knock on the door and there was Nat, large grin, pleasant greeting and brown bag full of food.

The orthopedic doctor who worked on my ankle calls it to this day his Michelangelo. I have no limp, no impairment whatsoever, and only the slightest twinge of occasional arthritic pain. He was a good doctor. The best.

I got through 1961 in one way or another. Nat continued to offer his generosity and, at times, I accepted. But I also tried to find work. I'd been away from acting for so long that it was difficult to renew interest in summer-stock producers.

I did find work for a time in a factory on South Broadway where I pasted felt flowers on lingerie hangers. That was a laugh a minute. When I wasn't pasting flowers, I was pub-crawling around New York with this friend or that friend.

It was during this period that I did something to heap tons of new-found notoriety on me. And I will go to my grave wondering at people and the things that pique their interest.

It seems everyone remembers when Veronica Lake was discovered working as a cocktail waitress in the Martha Washington Hotel in New York. It made headlines all over the world. It was major subway and bar chit-chat for days. Letters poured in to me from hundreds of people and from as far away as Japan, Australia and Sweden.

The Martha Washington Hotel is located on East 29th Street and is a cheaper woman's residence hotel for women than the Barbizon. That's why I decided to move into the Martha Washington after I felt I'd outlived my stay with friends. I took a room and applied for a job as barmaid to pay the rent. They hired me and I went to work.

When the *New York Post* broke the story, people felt very sorry for me. But you know, I really enjoyed that job. Sure, I needed the money. But I liked the people there, the merchant marine seamen, the occasional hookers, the broken-heart guys and the problem drinkers. All of them.

The regulars were confused about what to call me. Some used Connie, some Ronni and some used the formal Veronica.

There was a TV over the bar and sometimes a movie of mine would light up the screen. You could hear a pin drop. Everyone watched so attentively, much to the dismay of the bartender; no one drank when my movies played. I remember one week-end when *Star Spangled Rhythm* played on Friday, *Blue Dahlia* on Saturday and *Sullivan's Travels* on Sunday. It was a great week-end for me and a lousy one for the till.

I only missed work one night and that was the fault of the management. They were tough at the Martha Washington about paying your rent. Miss it for more than an hour and they locked you out using a special half-key that prevented you from using your key to open the door.

I was a day late with the rent that afternoon. I'd slept until two, got up, showered and made ready for my shift at the bar. I went to open the door. It wouldn't budge. They'd locked me in. It was so damned silly I went back to bed and went to sleep. The bartender checked my room, found what had happened and arranged with management to let me out and go to work.

I paid the rent on the spot.

That four-month job at the Martha Washington resulted in many things. I received checks and cash from people all over the world after they read the story in their local paper. I sent every cent back, not because I didn't need it but because I simply couldn't keep it. I'm not claiming high moralistic or ethical values. There was a hell of a lot of pride involved, as you can imagine.

I left my job proficient in the art of tending and mixing drinks. To this day I consider myself an expert at the art.

And I met Andy while tending bar. He's dead now. And I loved him very much.

24

ANDY came into the bar with two friends. I knew immediately they were seamen, my ability to recognize salt honed by a lifeline of father, grandfather and uncle making their living by the sea. They were wearing suits which didn't throw me off in the least. Suits on merchant seamen never fit right; they always look the way suits look on Anthony Quinn.

Merchant seamen look a certain way. Spencer Tracy? All the senior airline pilots in the world? All people cursed with premature wrinkling? Leathery skin? Romance through squinting eyes? I don't know. But Andy was undoubtedly a seaman and so were his two friends. It wasn't even debatable.

They were drunk when they arrived and proceeded to advance the state. I served them four or five rounds and soon they'd gone over the edge of drunken glow to extroverted loudness, boisterous, rowdy and wonderful. But the bar's manager wasn't at all pleased.

"Toss them out, Connie."

"Why? They're just having fun."

"Just get them out. They're too drunk and they'll just be trouble."

I think my boss was afraid of them. But I wasn't. Great big boys having fun. Pushovers. But I didn't want to tell them they had to leave. Why should I have to tell them their fun was over? They'd probably just returned from a long haul during which they fought weather and loneliness, all their problems magnified by their kithless boredom. What a wonderful thing to go to a bar and get gooned.

I ignored them as long as possible. But the boss called me over and threatened me with, "Get them out of here, Lake, or I'll do it and you can go with them."

I reluctantly went to the table. Andy never looked up. The other two whooped a greeting and one grabbed me around the waist and held his glass up in a toast.

"Hey chickee, here's to you. And bring us another round."

I laughed and tipped my head in recognition of the toast.

"Come on, fellas. How about keeping it down? The boss is getting upset."

The two seamen roared. Andy smiled quietly, his eyes on his glass cupped lovingly in ham-hock hands.

"What's he upset at?" one of them asked me.

"You're too loud. Knock it off."

"Tell him to come over here and have a drink with us. Come on. Tell him. We'll buy him a drink."

I shrugged and carried the message to the boss.

"I don't want a drink. Just get them out of here in two minutes."

I went back to the table.

"He doesn't want a drink, fellas. And he says you have to go."

"I'll be a son-of-a-bitch," one muttered. The other one brought his fist down on the table. "Goddamn," he said with bitterness. "What the hell kind of joint is this? What the hell?"

Andy still sat quietly. He raised his eyes at his companions and smiled a smile that told them not to be upset at what was going on. They reacted by breaking into smiles and beat their glasses on the table. "We want another drink," they chanted. "We want another drink."

I glanced over at the boss and he was boiling. I knew he'd call the police and that would have been terrible.

I decided to appeal to Andy.

"Hey, chief. Shut these guys up, will ya? Come on, you look like the captain. There's going to be trouble if you don't . . ."

Andy cut me off with a sharp turn of his head. He looked me right in the eye and said, "I'm not telling them to do anything. But I'll tell you something, little girl. *Bring us another round!*"

His friends beamed at their leader's strong request. I scowled. The nerve. I kept our eye contact and said in an even, deep voice, "Get your ass out of here, captain. And don't call me a little girl."

He started to get up out of his chair and I shoved against his shoulder, pushing him right back down into his chair.

"Out!"

Andy went into mild shock. He looked at his companions for support and all he got were curious looks for what he might do next.

He didn't seem to know what to do. But he had to do something if only to save face in front of his crew. He was well over six feet tall and must have weighed 240 pounds. He'd just been put down physically by a 95-pound shrimp of a girl.

He finally said, "Don't push," which is like saying "Your mother wears army boots," and other desperate things.

"Out!" I repeated.

His friends were now ready to do battle with the whole bar. Andy stood up, shrugged and cuffed one on the ear. "Come on. This is a dead dump. Let's go."

His friends grumpily followed him from the table and through the door. I walked right behind them like a warden. Andy stopped once they were all out and turned back to me.

"You're pretty tough for such a little girl. You get a little more meat on those bones and you might even look good."

I raised my fist in mock battle pose and he playfully threw his arms over his face in mock defense. I laughed and could hear him laughing with his friends as they went through the hotel lobby and out into the night. The bar boss came over and snarled, "Goddamn drunken drifters."

"I kind of liked them," I replied.

"You would, Lake, you would."

Andy returned at 2 a.m. He was alone, subdued. He entered the bar sheepishly and took a table in a far corner. I served him.

"Don't push," he said when I came to the table.

"You kiddin'? I wouldn't push my luck. You could snap me like a match."

I took a hard look at this man. He looked rugged but with a softness underneath. His hair was blond fringed with gray. Cornflower-blue eyes were steady and interesting. A handsome man, not pretty, but handsome as men should be.

"Where are your buddies?" I asked him.

"Raisin' hell in some other bar."

"What'll you have?"

"Is your boss going to let me stay?"

"Sure. I'll punch him around if he gives you any trouble."

"Tough little girl. Bourbon. With beer."

I served him and he nursed the order. I didn't talk to him again but we communicated. I perched at the end of the bar and munched on a ham and Swiss sandwich. We smiled at each other once or twice. We were the only ones in the bar with the exception of the boss who busied himself with preliminary checking out of the register.

Andy motioned me over at closing time.

"That sandwich looked good. I'm hungry."

"It was great."

"It'll put some meat on your bones, little girl."

"Yeh."

There was a long pause.

"How about something else to eat?" he asked with a certain charming awkwardness.

"Kitchen's closed." I knew what he meant but didn't want to be too quick to accept.

"No. I mean out of here. We'll go some place and get some food. I mean the two of us."

I waited an appropriate amount of time.

"O.K."

"Meet you outside."

"O.K."

We went to an all-night place and ate fried clams by the dozen and drank coffee and talked. I liked this man very much.

"What kind of a name is Elickson?" I asked him. We never got around to names until five in the morning.

"Norwegian."

"I'm a Dane."

"It doesn't sound it. Lake, I mean."

"That's not my real name. It used to be Ockleman. I had it changed."

"How come?"

"'cause I didn't like it. In fact, I had it changed to Keane. But I didn't like that either so now it's Lake."

"That sounds stupid, all that name changing."

"I guess it was."

"I mean really stupid. The only people I know who changed their names were people running from the law. You meet a lot of those in the merchant marines. You know what I mean?"

"Sure. I'm not running from the law. I do a lot of running but not from the law."

"I should have changed my name. Elickson is Norwegian and I'm from Stoton, Wisconsin, and that's in Dane County."

"That could be dangerous," I told him and we both laughed.

Conversation wasn't that easy between us. It didn't flow but was natural and relaxed in its own way. Sometimes we'd just look at each other and sometimes we'd each look at something else. It was pleasant.

"You always been a waitress?" he asked me once.

"Nope. I was a movie star."

"Come on. You could have been because you're pretty, but that's silly. You were no movie star."

"You never heard of Veronica Lake?"

It was obvious he hadn't. Bless him.

"Really, Andy. I was once a big movie star in Hollywood. Believe me."

"I knew a movie actress once. She went to bed with everybody. She said you had to do that."

"I never did."

"I guess you didn't."

"I wonder why you care if I did."

"I wouldn't care."

"I never did, Andy. Really."

"That's good."

Andy was married but separated for over five years.

I told him of my three marriages and their failures.

"Where is your wife, Andy?"

"In California, I think. I haven't heard from her in five years. It's dead. Nothing. Never was any good."

"Mine are dead, too. All three."

The sun came up and Andy walked me back to the hotel. The long night pulled down on his face and added more tired wisdom to an already wise face. His hair was crumpled and his suit seemed to hang more loosely from earlier in the evening.

"You're handsome, you know that, captain?"

"The hell I am."

"Really. Damned handsome. I bet all those little girls in Hong Kong and Marseilles just go mad when you come in to port."

"Sure. They know where the money is. Anyway, you're pretty."

"You bet I am."

"A little skinny."

"It's all there where it should be."

"That's where the money is, huh?"

"What the hell do you mean by that, captain?"

"All ladies have gold built in. You know what I mean."

"Yeh. I understand."

"Is that what you want?"

"Wait a minute." I stopped our walk and chewed my cheek as I looked deeply into my friend's face. "If you think I'm a hooker, you're all screwed up, fella. I've sold myself many times but never what's between my legs. And don't you forget it."

He looked relieved, enough so to justify having brought up the subject and causing me to react.

"Hell, we all sell ourselves," I said.

Andy's face broke into a broad grin. "Not me. What the hell do I have to sell?"

"You'd be surprised." I hauled off and punched him square in the chest. I had no reason. I just wanted to hit the big guy standing there on an empty Manhattan street. I hit him a good shot but he never flinched. He just reached out and grabbed my nose between his index and middle fingers.

"Got your nose, little girl."

"Keep it, captain. Give it back another time."

"I will."

Without another word, Andy Elickson turned on his heels and walked away from me. It took me by surprise and I yelled after him, "Hey, when do I get my nose back?"

"Tomorrow night." He never looked back.

Andy came back to the bar as promised, gave me my nose and got drunk. I secretly joined him right there on the job, nipping behind the bar until the boss caught me. It wasn't the first time.

"Either you work here or you're a customer. Make up your mind, Lake," the manager snarled. That was in early February 1962. I made up my mind in April to be a customer. I quit the job and spent every possible moment with Andy. He was in New York on a long lay-over between trips and we quietly tore up the town. We presented the odd couple, I suppose, tiny me, the aging movie star, and the big sea captain who never heard of the aging movie actress and just liked being with me. I fell in love with Andy Elickson. I fell early in the game. It was like being a child with the biggest Teddy Bear in the world. All I wanted to do was touch my Teddy Bear whenever I could and hold it and find comfort in its size and strength, to fall asleep in its warmth and protective cover.

Andy was a man, so much a man, proportionately large in all things, rough within bounds, serious when making love and playful after we'd spent each other. He expected me to please and wanted to please in return.

I performed whorish rituals but never felt the whore. Our bed was sacred, the business of no one else, two bodies in the dark put to work by two minds in each other's interest. I loved Andy's large, coarse body, his manhood, his function. I treated him with respect and worked to make him happy. I was his geisha and proudly served him in sex. And when it was time, I welcomed him over me, in me, his entrance, his throbbing moment of release, and I stated my pleasure in a tight whine as we so often achieved a miraculous and simultaneous climax—mutual detonation.

"I love you, Andy." He'd cradle me and kiss my hair and touch me, cup me, knead me and fall asleep, his hand large and warm on my body.

Once he asked if I'd ever lived in Seattle.

"I lived there for a while, Andy."

"You'd never know it," he said, kissing my knee. "Girls in Seattle have big legs, lots of muscles. It's all those hills. You have skinny legs."

Andy loved my skinny legs, unlike people in Hollywood who never issued pictures of me in which my legs were prominent. Just eight-ten glossies of hair and breasts.

"You're the one with the hair, aren't you?" he asked me one night. "I was talking to someone about you today and he said he'd seen a lot of your movies. You were a big star."

"I guess I was, honey."

"That must have been fun."

"It stunk."

"My friend said you used to sleep with Alan Ladd."

"Oh my God, you great big dope, Andy Elickson. I love you and I never slept with Alan Ladd or Sonny Tufts either."

"Who?"

"Come here."

He took me again with a gentle vengeance and later we lay there together smoking, the ashtray perched on my naked belly.

"Don't miss," I said as he put his cigarette out in the ashtray. "And give it to me again because I won't see you for a long time."

I watched him dress the next morning, put things in his pockets, comb his hair and make ready to leave me. He came to the bed and kissed me on the nose.

"Be back in a couple of months, little girl."

"Will you bring me something from India, Andy?"

"Sure will."

"Andy."

"What?"

"Do you love me? I love you."

"I love something lately. Maybe it's you."

"I don't care, Andy. I really don't. You never have to say it. Bring me something nice from India."

"I will."

He left the room. I didn't feel sad. I felt happy.

* * *

I needed money. I needed work, both for the money and to keep busy until Andy returned. Jeff Sparks, a friend of mine at the U.N., must have been on my wavelength. He came to me with an idea. It had to do with an opening at WJZ-TV in Baltimore for a hostess to introduce and chat about films on the Station's Saturday night film feature program.

"It's called the Festival of Stars, Connie, and I think you'd be perfect. Old movies, Hollywood chit-chat and the like. I'd like to suggest you to them for the job."

Jeff did suggest me and they bought. I began my hosting duties each Saturday and loved every minute of it. The money was very good and enabled me to take a rather plush apartment in New York. I commuted to Baltimore.

WJZ-TV owned the rights to only one Veronica Lake film, *I Married a Witch*. It was programed during my fourth week as hostess and I had a marvelous time talking of the filming of the movie and the people with whom I was involved. We received a great deal of mail after that particular show and I was surprised to read that one of my off-mike comments had actually been broadcast. I'd just listed the cast and mentioned my name last. I assumed my mike was cut and followed my name with, "What ever happened to that broad?" Many viewers wrote to let me know what happened to her.

It was during this period that I entered the world of high finance, certain that between the TV show and this new-found Wall Street activity I'd become rich and fat. As it turned out, I was lucky to escape jail.

I was approached by a group of businessmen to lend my name to a firm they'd created, World-Wide Restaurants, Inc. I was to be president and share handsomely in the profits. I was flattered and pleased at this opportunity to maybe become involved in a business venture that would reap rewards for the future. I accepted their proposition.

World-Wide Restaurants was conceived to buy up hotels, motels and resorts and turn them into profitable operations. I gladly was present at numerous meetings during which the four men behind the corporation talked with potential investors. I remember my first such meeting. Obviously, the gentleman considering investing in World-Wide was pleased at meeting Veronica Lake, former movie actress and now president of an ambitious Wall Street firm. After pleasant preliminaries, my partners got down to business.

"We've bought an option on Plum Point, the hotel and country club on the Hudson River in Dutchess County. We've paid $10,000 for the option and are now raising $450,000 to make the purchase."

The meetings were always casual and without pressure. Generally, the potential investor would say he'd consider the opportunity and get back to us. He'd be given our prospectus which outlined the venture. Then, he'd leave. I should mention that our prospectus also stated that World-Wide Restaurants, Inc., had entered the trading stamp business. It boasted of our having closed trading stamp deals, amounting to $1,456,520-worth of stamps. It was all very impressive and solid-sounding.

I've never had a head for business. I never was able to understand a great deal about the workings of business, the complex world of high finance, options, security markets and such. But I did rapidly develop a definite feeling that all was not as it was represented by the firm for whom I so readily served as president. Maybe I was in over my head. At any rate, I decided to get out.

It proved to be a good decision on my part. It wasn't long after my resignation that New York State Attorney General Louis Lefkowitz went to the state Supreme Court and obtained an order requiring World-Wide's officers to show cause why they should not be barred from the securities business in New York State. According to Lefkowitz and his investigators, World-Wide used what money they raised on the basis of already having purchased the option on Plum Point to actually buy the option. And, it was alleged, that the option ran out on Plum Point but the World-Wide continued to raise investor money, over $20,000.

The trading stamp deal also came under Mr. Lefkowitz's astute examination. Rather than have closed $1,456,520-worth of stamp deals, the firm was accused of having made tentative deals amounting to only $5,760. Quite a difference.

I never made a dime from my brief turn as president of World-Wide Restaurants, Inc. But I must thank Mr. Lefkowitz for making such a point in telling the news media that I was only a dupe in the deal and held no responsibility for any criminal acts arising from the deal. I'm quite certain there are a number of people around who curse me to this day for being party to their losses. I can only say I'm sorry.

Andy came back and it was good. We settled into a comfortable pattern of togetherness, devoid of pressure to love and please, rich with the contentment of mutual satisfaction. Some periods were platonic; others desperate in their passion. But there was definitely a leveling-off of emotions and a smooth relationship.

Andy kept his promise about bringing a gift from India. He handed me the box and I hurriedly opened it. Nestled in the box was a tiny piece of formless matter, obviously part of some living thing but unrecognizable.

"What is it, Andy?" I tried to look pleased.

"A cobra brain."

I suffered immediate paralysis of my arms and dropped the box to the ground.

"Why in the hell did you bring me a cobra's brain?"

He gingerly scooped up the box and its contents as he answered me.

"It's a damned valuable thing, a cobra brain, in India. Damned valuable."

"Well, I love it, Andy," I said with great conviction. "I love it."

He seemed pleased. He reached into his pocket and brought out another small package.

"Here, Connie. Here's something else."

It was too small to contain the real cobra so I opened it. It was a root. A dried-up little root.

"That's what the Indians rub over a cobra bite. It cures it." Andy looked for the reaction. I smiled approval and that pleased him.

"There's one other thing, Connie. Here."

Andy handed me his ring, a huge onyx in its gold setting, too large to even fit on my thumb and stay secure. I was very touched and perhaps read too much into the gift of the ring. I filled up and threw my arms around Andy's neck.

"You're happy, Connie?"

"God, yes. I feel like an honest woman."

"That's good."

My collection of things from or to do with Andy grew, the result of meeting Johnny, Andy's fourteen-year-old nephew. Johnny worshipped the ground under Andy's feet. The sea and its tales were part of the fascination, but I believe it was more to do with Andy's stature, his calm vision of everything, worldly, manly, someone for a young boy to view in vicarious fantasy.

Johnny and I got along beautifully. And he floored me one day while visiting his uncle by handing me a lovely Danish silver cross.

"I just want you to have it, Miss Lake, because I know my uncle Andy likes you very much. And I do too."

I've treasured the cross along with the ring and even the cobra brain and healing root. In fact, I kept them all together in the cobra brain's box. I only misplaced them once and that was during the run of *Goodbye Charlie* in Miami. It threw me into a panic and I frantically searched through everything I owned. I was staying with my friend Yanka at the time and asked her to help me look. She did and came up with the missing box.

"Where was it?" I asked her.

"In with all the ammonia boxes."

"Christ, Yanka, how many ammonia boxes do you have?"

"A couple dozen. You never know when you'll need one, you know."

Johnny told me once that of all the things in the world he wanted, it was Andy's watch, one of those over-sized instruments with many hands and dials capable of telling time all over the world, tides, the date, depths and maybe even menstrual cycles for all I know. Johnny loved that watch.

"Why don't you give Johnny your watch, Andy?" I told him of his nephew's comment to me.

Andy acted tough about it, but I knew he was debating the situation.

"When he graduates from college. That kid ought to go to college. He's smart as hell and he ought to go to college. Don't you agree, Connie?"

"That's a good idea. Can I tell him?"

"Sure. Tell him for me."

Naturally, Johnny was disappointed. College, even if he'd considered it, seemed three light years away. But at least Andy hadn't said "no."

I sailed with Andy once. I was determined to do that; my love for the sea and ships and my natural curiosity about working a merchant freighter were insatiable. It was only a one-day trip, from Tampa to Port Arthur. I flew down to Tampa and joined Andy on board.

"I'm coming along," I told him.

"Like hell. They find you and there goes my card."

"Who'll find me, for Christ sake? Come on. Take me along."

Andy wanted no part of my scheme, but he gave in just before sailing time.

"Goddamn it, Connie, keep the hell out of the way and out of sight. The Guard will inspect and you'd better disappear one way or the other."

The Coast Guard inspected us twice, once in Tampa before sailing and again at Port Arthur on arrival. I hid under a bed in the three-bed hospital room. They never even entered the room, although they did stop outside in the hall and I felt my heart pound and my mouth go dry.

"Never again," Andy muttered when we'd left the ship in Port Arthur and settled into a waterfront bar.

"No sweat, sailor. I think I'll come with you all the time."

"Yeh? Next time I'll kick your pretty ass overboard for the fish."

"Big man, huh? Remember the Marth Washington. I took care of you then and I can do it now,"

We settled the argument with ten or more games of 8-ball on the bar's pool table and a bottle of rye. And then we sneaked back on the ship and made love in Andy's quarters. When we were through, Andy looked at me and said, "You make me feel good, Connie."

"See, you big dope? Take me along and you'll always feel good."

"Not on your life. Goddamn it, little girl, you bring that up again and I'll . . ."

I never did ship out again with Andy. But I did apply for and receive my Merchant Marine Z-Card, the working card for merchant seamen. I studied the manual, took the test during another brief stay in Port Arthur and had my application signed by Andy and a few of his cronies. I still have the card and some day will use it and work my way to some place. That's a pleasure I've promised myself.

I saw a lot of Andy, especially in light of his job that took him away so often. I'd always manage to scrape up enough money to fly to meet him at a destination and we'd spend every possible minute together until he had to ship off again. Actually, I didn't consider myself living any longer, not a day-to-day living. I existed simply to meet Andy. By blotting out most of the day-to-day trivia of living, the times between our meetings were compressed. It worked well.

I was content with my life and secure from interruption until the phone rang one morning. It was theatre producer Arthur Whitlow.

"Veronica?"

"I guess so. I'd sort of forgotten about her."

"This is Arthur Whitlow. I'm producing a revival of *Best Foot Forward* at Stage 73. I thought you might be interested in discussing one of the lead roles with me."

I told Mr. Whitlow I hadn't been thinking of doing any stage work but would certainly be willing to discuss the possibility. We met and I found myself developing a semblance of enthusiasm for the idea.

"Might be fun," I told Mr. Whitlow. "I'd like to give it a try."

I didn't join the original cast of the revival. Paula Wayne played the role of Gale Joy, the fading movie queen who takes a last fling for the sake of publicity and, hopefully, a come-back. Paula left the show and I stepped in. The role of Gale Joy was close enough at times to my real-life situation to make me wince, but my primary reaction was to feel I was spoofing myself and all others like me in the business, a sort of theatrical do-it-yourself-kit in psychiatry.

I opened in *Best Foot Forward* on August 29, 1963. It was an incredible feeling of adulation I received from my opening-night audience. They stood and applauded for minutes on end on my entrance and I cried like a baby, not professional conduct but simply a necessary reaction on my part. It was wonderful.

The rest of the cast had also been warm and welcoming. They strung a large sign across the rehearsal stage which said, "This is our new mother. Wow!" Gale Joy is, in the show, a devoted mother as well as ex-movie queen. The critics said nice things about my performance and, all in all, the experience was a rewarding and satisfying one for me. It also put some money in my bank account for plane fares to Andy. I wish he could have seen the show. I think he would have been pleased.

I received a cable from Andy in April 1965. He was in San Francisco preparing for a trip to Vietnam and wanted me to join him on the coast. I was on my way the same night and in his arms by eleven o'clock.

I enjoyed being in San Francisco with Andy. We took long leisurely walks, stopping for sidewalk crab snacks on Fisherman's Wharf, a belt or two at bad-looking bars or just sitting on the piers wondering about our own personal destinies. We never intruded on each other. There was always a listener but never one offering pennies for thoughts. Once, as we sat together holding hands on the beach, I saw tears come and go in Andy's eyes as he looked out over the nothingness of the Pacific.

I wish he'd cried that once. He was a man enough to cry but he never did. Never. Not even at the end.

We stayed together on his ship in San Francisco, a converted T-3—a tub. I shared Andy's quarters there, in San Francisco, and the gentle swell of the dockside water would rock us to sleep, holding each other, me feeling so small in the comfort of his size, large hands resting on familiar places, beard stubble pleasantly uncomfortable on my cheek or breasts. Andy snored, and I'd lie there trying to put together the rhythm of his snoring and the lap of water against the ship. Hum myself to sleep.

Andy's departure to Saigon was delayed because the Coast Guard refused to pass his ship as safe for ocean navigation. They were right, I'm sure. This country's merchant fleet has to rank on the bottom of the international list. Buckets of rust getting worse and probably all beyond repair. But facing a long voyage with a lousy ship didn't phase Andy in the least. He wanted only to clear with the officials and get on with the trip. He used me to reach that end.

I dressed up and went with Andy to Coast Guard headquarters where the sailing permit was being withheld. He marched me in proudly to the local commander and announced, "Sir, this is Miss Veronica Lake, the great movie star."

I blushed. The commander smiled, invited us to have seats and we launched into a terribly long and boring re-hash of all my films; he'd seen every one.

He must have been impressed with something because he released Andy's ship for duty.

"I'll be damned," Andy said when we were back on the street. "You really were a big deal weren't you?"

"Let's have a little more respect in the future, captain."

"Yes, ma'm. How about a respectful drink to celebrate things?"

"Celebrate what, you jerk? I just arranged for you to leave me."

"That'll make you appreciate me more when I get back. Come on. Time for a little sauce."

We got gooned together and rolled back on the ship at dawn. We pulled off our clothes and stood there naked, weaving back and forth trying to decide what to do next.

"You know what, you big bastard captain you? I'm gonna drain you dry all night long so that you don't have anything left for all those Viet bitches."

"The hell you, little girl. I'm gonna show you what a real man is like."

We lunged at each other, fell into each other's arms and collapsed across the bed. We woke up at noon.

Andy left San Francisco for Saigon and I returned to New York. The memory of Andy, all 240 pounds of him, filled me with hope and pleasure. He would come back to me soon—three months he'd said. And someday soon he'd say he loved me. I knew he did love me. All I wanted was to hear it said once, just once. And maybe he'd even cry when he told me.

Alan Ladd died while Andy was away. To me, it was like losing a piece of jewelry you never wore but enjoyed every time you open the jewel case. There was a bond between Alan and me, an intangible one that would quiver long after it had snapped in two.

I continued my hostess chores in Baltimore and patiently, at first, and later impatiently, awaited Andy's return. What was to have been a three-month absence soon stretched into six months. And eight.

Andy returned one year later. He came into Galveston and I went there to meet him. Suffice it to say that the year without Andy proved to be excruciating. But it was over. He was home and we'd be together again.

I can't say I didn't recognize him. I would always recognize Andy no matter what forces changed his appearance. But when I first saw him in Galveston, my recognition was a shocked one, a gasp engulfed in gray confusion. His large frame, once so admirably supporting 240 pounds, now provided nothing more than a series of hangers for loose, pale skin, no more than 160 pounds the total package.

We hugged each other and I could feel the loss, his lack of strength. He spoke so slowly.

"Well, little girl, what do you think of your skinny old man?"

I forced a smile. "Great. You always were too fat."

His smile was equally forced.

"Did you try and lose the weight, Andy?"

"I guess not really. Just sort of came off."

We walked away from the dock together. His steps were deliberate but with his usual firmness. He was working hard at it.

Andy was drinking heavier than ever. He seemed determined to maintain a level of detachment from the reality of living. He started each day consuming as much alcohol as necessary to quickly bring him around to the desired level of inebriation. And he kept drinking to stay there. Andy never became drunk in the classic sense of the term. He was never sloppy, never lost control of his speech or movement. But his drinking lifted him from the day-to-day flow of things and allowed him to shuffle his problems into more convenient order, ignoring the most pressing and bringing to the front those which he felt were more easily handled.

I understood. I'd been there myself. I joined him in his escape and tried to share with him his thoughts and agony. It was a difficult chase after the inner Andy. His drinking heightened what was already a basically uncommunicative person.

"Why, Andy?" I asked him so often in the tiny room we shared. We would lie together on the bed, both drunk, and I would ask him why. He never answered the question and it really didn't make any difference. I wouldn't have known what to do with the answer. I did know that the physical wrongs within him had to have something to do with his drinking. Cause or effect. Probably the proverbial vicious circle of cause effecting and effects causing. Alcohol rot demanding more decay.

I think Andy surrendered to life and its demands. At first, it presented to me an incongruity. This rough and tumble seaman, his entire existence fed by a simple love of life. Withdrawing from life seemed to me an intellectual decision made by the weak. Andy typified strength to me. Even his physical deterioration could never bring him to his knees and drive him to surrender.

"Andy, let's go away together. We'll go anywhere you want and we'll get married and toss away the bottles. Huh?"

"I am married."

"I know and you can get a divorce and we'll make it. It'll work. I know it will."

Andy always escaped these thoughts of mine by drinking more. And while I found it easy to simply join him at first, fright and concern eventually crept into my thinking. I took to watching him as he slipped away from me and the life we shared. It worked on me until I, too, no longer wanted contact with what was really happening.

Andy took his ship out on a short trip early in April.

I watched him leave with proud pity and retreated to the seclusion of a cheap hotel room and my hugging bottle.

There is little more disgusting than a shriveled, drunken woman slouched over the bar in a cheap joint.

I can feel the disgust in retrospect. I never gave it a thought in April of 1965 while I sipped the cheapest booze at a waterfront joint and watched the hazy television picture above the bar. Andy and I were known at the bar and my credit was in good order.

"Andy'll be back and pay all this," I'd slur each night at the bartender.

"Sure. He told me to take good care of his little girl."

"You know what?"

The bartender was an agreeable soul.

"What?"

"That big son-of-bitch is gonna die soon. Whatta you think of *that*?"

"He'd better pay his tab first," the bartender would humor me.

"Pay his tab. He paid his tab plenty 'a times. You know that, too, don'tcha?"

"You want some coffee?"

"I don't want any goddamn coffee. I want him back. You know?"

"Sure. He'll be back. He'll take care of you."

"He can't even take care of himself, the big dope."

"Andy can take care of himself. So don't worry about that."

"The shit he can. He's gonna kill himself."

"Yeh. You, too, if you don't knock off all the booze. I'll give you some coffee."

I'm a gentle drunk, but I threw my hand across the bar knocking glasses and a bottle to the floor.

"You knock that shit off." The bartender wasn't kidding.

"Yeh, knock it off. And whatta you gonna do when he kills himself? Huh? Pay your own goddamn tab, huh?"

He tried to take me from the bar stool and gently help me out of the bar. My hotel was only two doors away.

"Come on, sweetie. I'll take you home. Like Andy said, I'll take care of you."

"I don't wanna go home. And I'm sorry as hell I knocked all the stuff off. I'll be good and I won't say another word."

The bartender let me stay and I continued to drink, my slouch over the bar more pronounced, my speech one long slur, the TV screen nothing more than a gray light through smoke. But then his face came on the screen and I could see it so clearly and every word he said was crystal clear and I started nodding at everything he said and I was crying, sobbing so my ribs hurt and I could see so plainly his black suit and white collar and God will save us.

"Oh God, oh God, oh God," I yelled at no one.

I stumbled from the bar and up the street. I remember hearing the bartender yell from the door but I never turned around. I just ran, around corners, up alleys, anywhere.

I have no idea how long I ran and tripped; hours or minutes. It seemed seconds to me and there it stood, so majestic, ringed with a prismatic nimbus as light was captured by the fog and backlit the steeple and the whole church itself. I could picture inside, cool and empty, a candle, a presence of something everywhere.

I tried the door. It was locked. I pulled and yanked and kicked the door and cursed its reluctance to allow me inside.

"Please Momma, please." It stood firm against me.

And then I was in back of the church, windows sealed so tight and so dark. There was a light. It came from the tiny house attached to the main structure of the church. I went to the door of the smaller building and beat my fists against it.

"Momma, Momma. Oh Momma of God."

The sobbing came again and I slumped down on the brick stoop and leaned against the door and just let it come, tears, mumbled curses, vomit.

Maybe I died that night. Is that possible? To die standing up and crying. I think it is possible. I think I did. And I was snapped back to life by the policeman who just seemed to appear over me.

"Come on, lady. Let's get up and go."

"I want to see the father."

"You'll see him. Tomorrow. When you sober up."

I went away peacefully with the policeman, looking back only once at the sound of the front door being opened. The priest looked out and quickly closed the door. I never did mean to frighten him.

I spent the night in jail and they fined me twenty-five dollars. I deserved it, I guess. We all deserve what we get and there's no getting around it.

* * *

In June of that same year, 1965, Andy returned from his trip. He returned in time to be idled by a nationwide maritime strike that lasted until August 29. It was one of the most enjoyable times of my life.

Andy had been assigned to the S.S. *Baltimore*, a converted T-3, just before the strike hit. It sat in the harbor just outside of Galveston and would sit there for the entire strike.

In effect, the S.S. *Baltimore* was the first and last home Andy and I would have in our romance. I mean a real home. There were always the rooming houses and the cheap merchantmen hotels and even the tiny apartment we shared in New York just before the end. But the ship represented some solidarity for us. Perhaps it was the familiarity with which Andy viewed any quarters that floated on water. An apartment, based on concrete, never seemed to give Andy a feeling of security; it had to sway a little to be good.

What a marvelous couple of months that was. I had a daily job, that of putting up the kerosene lamp each evening at dusk. I felt so proud doing my task and did it with great and loving care. There were four other crew members on board with us and they accepted me as an integral part of the crew. We had the damnedest card games, sometimes inviting crew members of other ships moored near the *Baltimore*. We had the *Savannah* on one side, but I don't remember our other next-door neighbor. At any rate, it was one big happy family of out-of-work seamen and yours truly. Andy never could get our radio to work and we'd go over and use the *Savannah*'s. That was a great ship, a truly great one.

Unfortunately for me, the strike came to an end. Andy shipped out and I went to Florida. I decided I didn't want New York any more. I wanted the sun and easy life. Andy came in to Tampa once and he looked better to me. I don't think he was any better physically, but he looked better and that was enough for the moment. We spent a week together in Florida and then Andy left again. It was in December 1965, and we planned to meet again in New York in March. As it happened, we met sooner.

Andy called me from New York in early February.

"Andy! Where are you?"

"New York. Can you come up?"

"Well, sure. But I thought you wouldn't be getting in until March."

"I haven't been feelin' too good, Connie, and they thought I'd better get to see a few New York docs. I'm feelin' better now, though."

"I'll come up as soon as I can. Maybe even in a couple of days."

"That'll be swell, Connie. You come on up as soon as you can."

I didn't waste any time. For Andy to admit not feeling well meant he felt terrible. I flew into New York and went to the address he gave me on the phone. It was a small apartment in a respectable but run-down building on New York's east side.

"Andy?" I yelled through the door.

I heard some shuffling inside and waited for what seemed an eternity. Finally, Andy opened the door. He was thinner but not ghastly so. He smiled and so did I. He grabbed me and held me in an almost desperate embrace. It wasn't until we walked across the room to the couch that I noticed his legs. He sort of pulled them behind as he went and once we sat down, their increased size was apparent. They were bloated and stiff.

"Your legs, Andy. What's the matter?"

"Ah, nothing at all. Just some damned thing I picked up overseas I guess. Be good as new in no time soon as I stay off them awhile."

I spent the next eight months watching Andy die. We shared those months together and I never intruded into Andy's mind. He didn't know he was dying.

"It'll be good to get over this damn bug and get back to sea, Connie. Damned good. I'd like to get a command over to Scandinavia this time. Be good to see that land again."

"If you don't do what the doctor says, you'll go nowhere," I'd snap at him. It was true. Andy was being cared for at the Merchant Marine Hospital on Staten Island. His doctors had put him on a very strict diet which did not include alcoholic beverages of any kind. Andy never followed any of the rules. He drank, ate all the wrong things and in general abused himself. At least when I wasn't looking. I'd cook him special things and he'd eat them despite the blandness of the diet. And he'd catch a nip or two of Scotch when he thought I was looking the other way. It became evident that the only way to get through to him was to yell at the top of my lungs.

I started doing that and that's how I met Bill Roos and Dick Toman. They lived in the apartment below us and the air shaft was like a microphone. Bill inquired one day whether he could help in any way and we all became fast friends.

Andy became weaker but still maintained a front of enthusiastic optimism. He insisted we take walks around the neighborhood. They each took an eternity and I know they were agonizing for him.

But he insisted and I'm sure they did do some good for him. His spirit was so large, so positive. It had to be fed and exercised.

Andy received a note one day informing him of the wedding of a shipmate of his.

"I sure would love to be there when that guy gets himself all tied up."

"Why don't you go?"

Andy thought a minute and finally said, "I don't have a suit that looks any good." I knew he really didn't want his friend to see him in his physical condition and was using the suit as an excuse. I decided that going to the wedding would be beneficial for Andy and I prodded him into buying a new suit.

"Hell, no," he'd mumble. "They wouldn't fit me too good any more."

"Nonsense, Andy. What the hell do you think tailors are for? Come on. I'll go with you."

"No. I'll go by myself."

Andy went to a men's store.

"What kind did you buy?" I asked him on his return.

"A blue one."

"That's perfect for a wedding." It was also amazing because Andy was a total nut for anything brown. He didn't own a thing that wasn't some shade of brown.

His suit arrived and I made him try it on immediately. It looked good on him. But it was brown.

"I thought you said you bought a blue suit."

"I did. This is blue."

"It's brown, Andy."

"You're color-blind, little girl."

I didn't argue any further.

By August, it was evident that any hopes of recovery for Andy were slim. Even with that knowledge, you never stop thinking the best. And of course Andy had no inkling just how seriously ill he was.

I finally got to speak with one of his doctors on Staten Island.

"Andy is a very sick man, Miss Lake," he told me. "There's a great deal wrong with him. Unfortunately, the failing of one bodily function causes damage to others. With Andy, it's a combination of his liver, his spleen, kidneys and bladder. That's a lot to have wrong with you. Frankly, the only chance he has is if we go in and re-tube everything to try and by-pass the worst trouble spots."

I brought up the subject of surgery to Andy in as subtle a way as possible. His reaction was violent. Obviously, he'd been told many times before by his doctors and had given it a great deal of thought.

"Nobody's going inside of me and taking me apart. Nobody's putting plastic tubes in me."

And that was that.

Andy slid further downhill despite any efforts to halt the slide. I kept him on his diet, kept whisky away whenever possible and tried to keep him comfortable. The nights became especially bad for him and we'd sit up until dawn talking of anything and everything. Usually, Andy talked of the future, the tangible future. He was certain he'd soon assume another command and looked forward with relish to that day.

But, occasionally, he'd slip into more of a fantasy train of thought, never for long and always abruptly ending with more visions of sailing again.

"Do you ever think about the green valley, Connie?"

Of course I did. Any child with any Nordic links hears of the green valley, that peaceful place where the dead gather to begin a new life.

"Sure I have. When I was a kid my father used to tell me about it. He told me about it when a cat I picked up died."

"I think when I get there I'm going to build a house and settle down. That'll be the time to do it, I guess."

"That's a long way off, honey."

"I know it. I've got a lot of sailing to do first."

"You know, Andy, that surgery the doctors talk about might get you back on a ship a lot faster."

"And I said no cutting up. No tubes. Besides, this damn diet you feed me would make anybody better. Christ, there's no taste to anything. Baby food."

"For my baby."

"Let's have a drink."

"No sir."

"Oh Christ, come on. What the hell is this?"

"No drink because the doctor said no drink. The end."

He'd fume a little but drop the subject. And I'd feel like a king-sized rat for slipping into the kitchen and downing a fast water glass of the stuff. And then a mouthful of Clorets. But he knew. And he was doing the same thing. What the hell?

He became thinner and thinner. Soon, his upper body was that of a skinny man. And his legs became more bloated as he retained more fluid. And still he wanted to take walks with me. And more and more alone.

"I think I'll get out of this dump and buy us some food," he'd say. "No, you stay here. I'll be back soon."

He'd leave and I'd wait anxiously to hear him drag himself up the one flight of stairs. One day, even the one flight was too much.

"Connie," I heard him yell from the street. I looked down and saw him standing there, a bag of groceries in his arms, a look of frustration on his proud face. "I need a hand." It hurt him so to say that.

I went down and took the groceries. I tried to take his arm on the stairs but he shook me off and made it himself.

"Don't do that any more, Connie," he scolded me when we reached the apartment. "I don't need a little gal like you helping me up stairs."

It was a moot point. Andy didn't venture out onto the street any more. He knew he couldn't make it. It took too much from what was left of him.

Soon, Andy didn't leave his bed. He was in pain and even to sleep beside him caused suffering. I began laying a blanket on the floor next to the bed and I'd sleep there when he slept. I'd lie there and hear him breathe with increasing difficulty and moan with him. *I love you Andy and you're going away from me. I love you and you mustn't leave me. Cry if you must but stay here. Say you love me Andy. Say it and it will all go away.*

Early September left little doubt that time was short for Andy. His weakness was total, so total that I called his mother in Wisconsin and suggested she come to be with her son. She came immediately; so did Andy's sister.

The last few days were brutal on everyone. Andy slipped away before our eyes and we could do nothing but vent our own wounded emotions on one another. It never fails, does it, that a dying loved one brings out the worst in those who grieve most bitterly? His mother and sister would sit there and stare at him. It was so natural and yet so maddening. I'd end up in the kitchen with his mother or sister and blow my stack at them, which never did a thing to endear me to their hearts. It was the same when I screamed at Andy to do this or that because I knew he had to do those things.

"You don't have to talk to him that way," I'd be told, again in the kitchen.

"Yes I do," I'd fight back. And we'd all cry a little knowing we each had our own madness at the moment.

On the morning of September 18, I called Andy's doctor and told him his patient's condition was at its lowest.

"He should be in a hospital, Miss Lake," the doctor said. He'd said it often during the previous two weeks but Andy would not hear of it. Now, I wouldn't hear of his not being there. But his mother was not in agreement.

"He'll die in there," she rasped at me when I told her of my phone call.

"He'll die here faster."

"How could you do this to him? He doesn't want to go to the hospital."

I didn't even try to answer her. I just waited for the ambulance. Surprisingly enough, Andy's reaction when I told him it was coming was mild, mostly due to his weakness but partly due to resignation. He knew.

"Come with me, Connie."

"I will Andy."

Andy hadn't been out of bed in a week but he insisted on dressing himself. How he managed I'll never know. I tied his shoes; his legs were so bloated he couldn't even lift them. And then the ambulance came.

"I won't go down on that thing," Andy told the attendants who arrived with a stretcher. "I'll walk down."

He did walk down the stairs and shunned the rear of the vehicle for a seat up front. I climbed in back and we raced off for Staten Island. The doctors got him into bed and suggested I go back home.

"We'll call you if there's any change, Miss Lake."

I kissed Andy on the forehead and squeezed his hand before I left. He looked straight into my eyes and smiled. "You're a good mate, little girl. Damned good. We'll sail together again."

His mother and sister stayed at the hospital and I returned to the apartment. I felt a certain feeling of well-being with Andy in the hospital. There, he would receive the right medicine and care. They could alleviate his pain. They could make him better.

Andy died the next day. I didn't know he died. No one called me until the following day when the doctor phoned to offer his condolences.

"He died?" I screamed.

"Yes. Yesterday. I assumed his family told you. They were there."

Andy's mother and sister had left immediately for Wisconsin. Whether they ignored telling me in their rush or as a conscious act is irrelevant. I just wish they had. I knew, of course, the scorn in which they held me and my relationship with their son and brother. They never tried very hard to hide it. But they should have told me he was dead. I deserved to know.

I called Wisconsin to find out about funeral arrangements. They told me the date of the burial and I brought up the question of Andy's wishes.

"He wanted to be buried at sea, you know," I said.

"He'll be buried here," they said.

His family had turned down the doctor's request for an autopsy. That's something else I knew Andy would have wanted. But what difference did it make? None, really.

I sent one white rose and asked that it be placed in Andy's casket. I received a note from the florist informing me that the flower arrived one day late. It was delivered on the date I'd been given for his funeral. But he was buried the day before. He took nothing of mine with him. Nothing.

25

ANDY's death struck me with a force I'd never felt before. He had disappeared on me, taken leave without permission and despite great protestations. Death is the master, I'm afraid, of finality. Other losses happen with the hope of recovery. There is no such hope with death. There is no after-life. Of this I'm certain. There is no feathery meeting-place to get together again. No soft music and understanding. No permanent tranquility in the sky. Just reality of the earth and its yearly transition from brittle, hard-packed frozenness to the mud of springtime. The decay of death unfelt by the dead. No heaven.

I felt so alone. My tears went with Andy, leaving me with dry wells. Even the ache was distant. I seemed to walk through some vast and all-encompassing void, a living limbo all people must sink into when something important is taken from their grasp.

But, with a curious mixture of blessedness and cruelty, reality fills in the void and you begin to feel things again, reach out and touch substance, and experience the need to cope with the world. And all the whisky in the world won't help you.

There is usually luck that arrives after a tragic loss. Maybe it just seems lucky after going through trouble. At any rate, I was pleased when Terry Darling, a Florida producer, invited me to Miami to appear in his production of *Goodbye Charlie*. Darling had taken over a Miami nite spot and converted it into a theatre and supper club, a popular thing these days in more and more cities. He named the place "The Gallery," and *Goodbye Charlie* was to be his opener. I always enjoyed the play. It was written by George Axelrod, and although I found it necessary to rewrite many of the lines to suit my own particular fancy, I loved the way the play was written. I played Charlie, the ghost.

Also appearing in the show was an actor named Bill Mayer and an actress named Yanka Mann. Yanka and I became very good friends and I ended up living with her. Together, we ran a cat house, the classiest one in Miami. I'll get to that.

Doing the show was a ball. If only Mr. Darling had paid me. Eventually, he owed me $3,000. He's broke, of course, and now works as a bartender in Key West. According to the court order, he cannot own property or invest in Florida until the judgment is satisfied. The Gallery went under and is now a restaurant called The Chateau. When I told Yanka I was instituting the suit, she commented, "Honey, you got screwed without even getting kissed." I think she was right.

I should mention, to satisfy those in Miami who feel my victory in the suit against Terry Darling was suspect, that the judge, Red Lake, is in no way related, friendly or connected with me. Honest.

Yanka Mann is one of my "nut" friends. You know what I mean. You can depend on nut friends to react differently. You can depend on them to come up with the unusual when all the usual is getting you down. I treasured my nut friends above all others. Maybe it's because they're more likely to accept you for what you are. After all, you've done the same for them.

Yanka is a terribly talented woman, misdirected in her talent and what she does with it. But it's there. And so is the cat house.

Yanka and I are cat lovers. I mean *really* cat lovers. Animal lovers in general. Cats in particular. I own one cat at the present, a calico cat named Shadow who thinks she's a dog. Maybe even a male dog.

I named her Shadow because she has what looks like a five o'clock shadow under her chin. I found her in Texas—in an alley. She's therefore pure alley cat, part Persian and part Angora. It cost me seventy-six dollars to get her from Texas to New York and then down to Florida. You bet I love her.

The problem with Yanka is that she loves too many cats too much. Twenty-nine of them when I was living with her. And there was no official cat house at that time. Yanka's house was the cat house. The humans were also allowed to live there.

You needed a gas mask when you walked in the door. All the furniture was torn to shreds and none of the cats had been toilet-trained. It didn't bother me as much as it bothered Yanka's teenage son.

"I hate to bring friends home, Mom," he told her one afternoon.

"Why?" she asked.

"'cause 'a the smell."

He had a point. Yanka considered it and decided we needed a special dwelling for the cats.

"Who's going to build it?" I asked her.

"We'll hire a contractor."

"That'll cost a lot of money, Yanka."

"So? Do you want me to turn the cats out on the street?"

"Of course not."

"Then we'd better build a cat house in the back."

Next to Hungarians, Bulgarians are the second most stubborn and illogical. Yanka is Bulgarian.

The cat house was built. It was beautiful. It had a door with a lock and gray shingles and aluminium screening all the way around so that the cats shouldn't be bothered by flies. It's a two story cat house and has vents in the roof and plenty of room for all the cats to run around and play without disturbing those napping.

We did make one mistake in building the house. We discovered it the night a flash storm hit the area and flooded the house. We ran outside and there were the cats floating around and screeching like the devil. We bailed them out and had the house raised off the ground at considerable expense. It has paid off in dry cats, however. I assume they appreciate it.

Yanka's son started having friends in once the house aired out. And that meant I couldn't have friends in. Her son is a rock-and-roll lover, complete with ear-shattering amplifiers, guitars, electric organs and the like. You can hear the boys practicing five blocks away. And don't think the cats aren't affected.

"Those cats will all have breakdowns, Yanka," I told her one day between aspirins.

"Why?"

"The music. The noise. Have you ever noticed how they go a little nutty back there when the music starts?"

"Sure I have, Connie. But they're enjoying it. Honest. They have a ball when the music starts."

Never argue with a Bulgarian.

I truly love Yanka. She was very good to me when I came back to Florida, and we remain good friends. She's dark, radiant and full of the unusual, the unexpected.

I attended one ballet class with her and almost died from the exercise. Yanka attended because she wanted to put together a nightclub act. She's been working on it for what seems forever. It might be a smash. I can see the billing now on the Ed Sullivan Show:

"And now, ladies and gentlemen, a really big act. Yanka Mann and her cat-house chorus singing *Pussy Cat, Pussy Cat, Where Have You Been? I've Been to a Gay Bar and Married The Queen.*"

I don't want you to think I simply sponged off Yanka. What money I did have was put to good use. I can't remember how many cats I had spayed. Oh how many vet bills I paid. Doctor Dolittle would have been proud.

I was even kind and generous to Tomasina, Yanka's queer male cat. He loves boys and won't have it any other way.

I belong in Miami, at least as a home base. I love New York, but I find living there a wearying experience. Cape Cod and its summer theatres is delightful, something I always look forward to during Miami's hot summer.

But Miami is my home now, just as it was long ago. I've settled in my new apartment, a small one but castle-size to me. It's been so long since I've had my own place, my own solitude, my own life. I'm also able to pay for it, now, and that provides untold comfort to me.

My landlady, Peg Wessel, had become one of my very best friends. She's a character and a good person. We met at a Christmas party in 1966. It was held at a friend's apartment and I was designated cook-in-residence for the bash. I love to cook. Some day I'm going to write the Veronica Lake Cookbook. And with a glutted, totally confused cookbook market these days, my book will be a welcome addition. It will not be exotic. It will not be ethnic. It will not specialize in 1,000 chocolate chip recipes or what to do with leftover potato chips. It will be simple and fraught with easy dishes to whip up when you're drunk or tired or both.

I cooked a turkey at the Christmas party. And I got in a fight with Peg Wessel. I'd had too much to drink and, according to Peg, was obnoxious, something I find difficult to believe. We ended up having words and she called me a drunken mess and I told her where she could go with her opinions.

I was so upset I burned my arm on the oven wall as I tried to extract the turkey. That did it. I left the party, retired to a nearby bar and quietly tied one on without benefit of anyone.

They tell me the turkey was delicious. That pleases me. I m also pleased that I again met Peg and we got along famously. It was a stroke of good fortune to meet Peg. She owns the small apartment building in which I now live. A better landlady and friend is not to be found anywhere, north or south.

There's nothing luxurious about my apartment. The luxury is provided by me and my enjoyment of the place. I went out recently and bought the biggest, most complex color television, stereo, AM-FM radio in captivity. It takes up one whole wall and, as the advertisements say, is my home entertainment center. I'm nuts about westerns and watch every one I can. "Bonanza" is great and Marshal Dillon really turns me on.

Those people fortunate enough to have heard me sing (have I taken a shower with anyone lately?) will attest to the fact that I have no ability whatsoever. I do love music, though, not today's noise but pretty things. And Peggy Lee and Sarah Vaughn to me are superb artists. I'm a Scrabble player and always do better when I have those singers on the stereo.

I lead a quiet life in Miami. I do it by design. I'm away from it enough doing theatre work that I look forward to relaxation when I return home. I suppose all my life has been spent in the pursuit of peace, personal peace. All people reach a point in their lives when they realize that peace is the most desired and least obtainable goal they can go after. For the first time I seem to have found peace. It's interrupted, of course, from time to time. I resent the interruptions but they're unavoidable, I guess. The whole trick is to keep them to a minimum.

I came to realize just how quietly I do live in Miami when my telephone was out of order. I called the phone company and they promised to send a serviceman right away. He never showed up. I called again the next day and again received a promise. Still no serviceman. I was furious at this point and ranted and raved at the telephone company. I needed my telephone. I needed it and wanted it right away.

Finally, three fitful days later, the serviceman arrived. He was a nice young fellow and we chatted as he straightened out the difficulty.

He left and I let out a big sigh of relief and pleasure at having my precious telephone back in use. And then I sat down and tried to think of someone to call. I couldn't think of anyone. Not a soul. I ended up calling Peg who lives directly upstairs.

"Peg?"

"Yeah."

"This is Connie."

"Hi, Connie. Where are you calling from?"

"Downstairs."

"Why are you calling from downstairs? Come on up."

"I don't want to see you. I just wanted to call you."

"Why?"

"Because the phone is fixed."

We hung up and I turned on an old movie on TV. The next time the phone was used was two days later when I received a call from the Priscilla Beach Theatre in Plymouth, Massachusetts.

"Miss Lake?"

"Yes."

"This is the Plymouth Playhouse in Massachusetts. I'm Vincent Curcio. I'd like to talk to you about doing *Goodbye Charlie* this September."

We talked awhile and finally got around to money. "Well, my price is $1,250 a week. Plus rehearsal fees."

"That would be too much for us, Miss Lake. Our theatre has only 250 seats. We could pay you $750 for the week. And room and board, of course."

I mulled it over for a second.

"Tell you what," I told him. "Let's split the difference. Make it $800 and it's a deal."

I think Mr. Curcio was confused over my arithmetic but did know it made sense for him. We made the deal and I spent the first two weeks in September 1967 in Plymouth. It was a good show with a fine house every night. My trouble started after we closed the play.

I'd been invited to spend a week with a very dear friend in New Hampshire. I took her up on the invitation and spent the first few days lolling around and soaking up that good New Hampshire air. It was the third morning when they arrived.

"Are you sure you're with the F.B.I.?" I asked with a doubtful look on my face.

They showed the proper credentials, which really weren't necessary. They looked the part from shoes to haircut.

"So, you're the F.B.I. What do you want?" By this time my hostess and other friends who were staying the week had joined me at the front door. I could feel the embarrassment setting in: what had Michael done now? Why did they have to come here, to the home of my friends?

"It's Michael, isn't it?" I asked flatly.

"Michael?"

"Yes, Michael. My son."

"I'm sorry, Miss Lake, but we don't know any Michael." I don't know why, but they seemed over-anxious to prove they didn't know Mike.

"Well, what do you want then?"

"Well, it's you, Miss Lake. May we come inside and talk privately with you?"

Everyone in the house shuffled away, some coughing nervously, some hanging back to pick up the next words.

I just wanted to slide under the rug.

I led the two F.B.I. men into the house and we settled in a corner of the living-room. They came right to the point.

"Miss Lake, we've been informed that you are in the possession of illegal drugs and have them with you at this house."

"Drugs? You gotta be kidding. I've been accused of being a drunk but never a hophead. Come on, fellas."

"I'm sorry, Miss Lake," the leader continued, "but I'm afraid we're going to have to search the premises."

"Like hell you will," I said with a bit of a snarl. I had nothing to hide but a great deal of pride to salvage with my hostess and her friends. The F.B.I. men sat passively, their eyes steady and without movement. I guess I did all the usual hand-wringing and shoulder shrugging and finally realized there was no sense in telling them they couldn't do what they wanted.

They searched. Naturally, they found nothing. They apologized professionally and left the house. I didn't beat around the bush with my hostess. I told her exactly what they wanted.

"I'm surprised they knew you were here," she commented.

And then *I* became surprised. I hadn't thought of that. I'd taken every precaution to not tell anyone where I'd be spending this week. I told no one at the Plymouth Theatre, no one in Miami, no one.

I very seldom see Michael any more. I never know where he is or what he's doing. He just seems to show up occasionally in Miami, stays a few days and leaves again for points unknown. I must admit I don't look forward to his unannounced visits. Mike upsets me. I suppose I upset him. There is, of course, some trace of a mother-son feeling between us. But very little.

I try never to dwell on Michael. I certainly don't want to dwell on him here, in this book. Every time my thoughts do come to rest on Mike, I become depressed and prone to giving in to my weaknesses. Michael worries me because he seems to be blowing his life at times. In effect, he seems to be out to prove he'll end up inferior to others. But his failings are the result of my failings, his father's failings, our combined failings. Michael is bright and good looking. I only hope he'll direct what he has to some good for himself. And as guilty as I may be in his upbringing, I do wish he'd throw away the crutch.

I seldom see any of my children. Elaine is happily married to a New York advertising man named Maynard Berger. They have three children and I suppose live the good life. They have embraced a religion called Subud, one of these deep-thinking routines where you sit on the floor and meditate. Maynard sent me a book once about Subud and I read it twice I didn't understand a word, but that doesn't prove anything. I think Elaine is called Ruth now because Subud changes everyone's name for reasons of its own.

Diana, the baby, works as a secretary for the American Embassy in Rome. She's doing very well.

I suppose my life in Miami does fall into a routine of its own. I like it that way. I'm not looking for the fast life, the mad mod folk, the laugh-a-minute life. I'm content with my routine and outraged when it's interrupted by uninvited people or events. Such interruptions can upset me terribly, even send me back to heavy drinking. Like when Mike called me in the summer of 1967.

"Ma?"

"Yes."

"It's me, Mike."

"I know."

"I'm in jail."

I bailed him out. The Miami police had picked him up on a drunk and disorderly charge. His face was a mass of cuts and bruises, the result of a brawl here or there. He's always cut up, it seems. I got a lawyer for him and, all in all, it cost me $750, a big sum of money for me these days. Naturally, as soon as everything was settled, Mike was gone. I know not where. His call was upsetting and I did go on a brief binge, much to my dismay. I wasn't to see him again until a few months later when he arrived one morning with a very lovely girl, collegiate-looking and sweet.

I could hear the banging on my window and then his voice.

"Ma?"

I sleepily opened the door for him.

"Ma, this is Nancy. This is my ma, Nancy."

"I'm very pleased to meet you, Mrs. Lake," she said with some sincerity.

"We're married, Ma," Mike said proudly.

Nancy blushed appropriately.

I was thunderstruck. And pleased. Could it be that this son of mine with all his hang-ups actually found and married this nice girl? I became more pleased as I more fully awoke.

"That's nice," I told them. "Wonderful. I'm very happy."

Mike and his bride stayed four days. I gave them my apartment and moved upstairs with Peg. At night, I could hear them giggling downstairs, robust laughter indicating the beginnings of the young husband chasing his wife. And then it would become quiet with only the smooth regularity of my bed springs to break the silence.

And then more laughter and the toilet being flushed. And sometimes I'd wake up in the middle of the night and hear it again and live it vicariously.

Mike and Nancy left four days later. I couldn't get over my pleasure at his being married to such a lovely girl. She was a Marymount graduate, Mike told me, and a bright girl.

My pleasure lasted until I received a note in the mail from Mike's bride.

Dear Mrs. Lake:

Mike and I are not married. We just sleep together sometimes. I'm sorry we took advantage of you like that.

Nancy

At least she had the decency to write that note.

Mike's visits are becoming scarcer lately and that's fine with me. We seem to fail each other at every turn and the best thing is to just stay away. Still, there are times when I miss Mike. There are times when I find myself wishing it all could have been different. It depresses me to think of Hedy Lamarr and her book, *Ecstasy and Me*, that caused such a sensation recently with its explicit recountings of Hedy's sexual life. What got to me, I guess, was her dedicating the book to her children. I understand her children are quite devoted to their mother, regardless of what she told in the book. Compared to Hedy, my life has been dull and routine.

I believed in my marriages. I only wanted a home with my husband and children. Yes, I contributed mightily to ruining things when I had an honest shot at achieving my professed goals. And evidently Mike and his actions will never allow me the peace of living the mistakes down.

Interruptions aside, Miami is good for me. It's warm and near the sea. More and more, the sea takes on an urgent position in my life. I often sit on the beach and allow the sea's sound to take over all others. It seems to be limitless, the sea, without apparent end, the elusive perpetual motion, perpetual peace. I feel in perspective in relation to such size. People generally experience that feeling with the universe. The universe doesn't awe me that way. Too often

I feel I can take one giant step and walk over the stars. But I'm not about to walk on water. No one ever has.

26

SOME day soon, perhaps on your local television station during their daily horror film show, you'll be able to see my two latest films. Fortunately, I did not have to return to Hollywood to make these films. They were produced in Canada and Florida and, in vogue with today's trend of putting older stars in horror movies, both these efforts are designed to turn your knuckles white, set your heart pounding and cause your girl friend to cuddle up close in sheer terror.

The first one was the Canadian epic. It was titled *Footsteps in the Snow* and deals with dope traffic and ski bums and other goodies. They paid me $10,000 for this, plus expenses. I left immediately after shooting was concluded and still have not seen an edited version. All I know is it was cold in Canada and I was happy to return to Florida.

The other film must rank as one of the great Chinese productions of all time. Its tentative title is *Time Is Terror.*

Not only do I star in this film, I am also the titular producer and director. It came about because of Yanka Mann, my partner in the cat house. Yanka does get around Miami, and in her travels she came across a local Miami production house. They told her they always wanted to produce a feature film and she suggested they get together with me. That they did and we concocted *Time Is Terror.*

The film's premise is a simple one. Adolf Hitler is alive and living in South America. He wants to return to Germany and those he loved. But everyone will recognize him.

So, he consults with a noted but mad doctor who has perfected a way to change the facial features of anyone. What this mad doctor does is let maggots eat away at your face until they've accomplished enough eating to make you look different. It made for a great scene in the film.

Making movies, even low-budget ones, is an expensive and demanding chore. You'd better know what you're doing or your low-budget job will blossom into a bankrupting one. That pretty much is what happened with *Time Is Terror.*

There's a great basic rule in directing that dictates you always get your master shot before going after close-ups, cut-aways and inserts. A master shot is just what it sounds like—one continuous shot of all the action, usually from as distant a point as necessary to include all the action. Once you've got that master shot, you're safe. If nothing else turns out, you can at least use that shot, as dull as one long shot like that might be. All the detailed close-ups, reactions and business insertions add greatly but *can* be done away with.

Time Is Terror still can't be edited simply because the film's working director would not shoot master shots. He's quite talented and has a good eye for framing close shots and effects. Master shots to him were a bore. But without a master, you have nothing to cut away from, nothing in which to insert reactions or prop business.

Over 130 thousand feet of 35-millimeter color film was used up filming the movie. That represents an outlay of about $20,000 just for the raw film and basic processing to see what you got. And it can't be edited. It sits there in the can, some of the footage very good and imaginative, and will continue to sit there until the production company comes up with more money with which to go back and re-shoot master shots.

The film stars, along with me, included a local unknown named Phil Philburn. Phil's a nice boy and we had a lot of fun shooting the movie. There were the inevitable flubs, some funny and some just plain dumb. But one, a flub of mine, has made some sort of fame among the Florida film people.

I blew a line as we all will do now and then. For some unexplained reason, I turned and looked at the camera and said, "Oh, shit on a bicycle." The line means nothing. I can't even explain it. It just came out. But that piece of "out" film is in great demand. Some day I'll sit down with people and figure it all out.

Throughout the filming, Peg Wessel proved to be a constant source of encouragement and joy. She'd laugh along with me while everyone else seemed to be taking everything so deadly serious.

Peg is a character. She's been in Florida since 1926 after leaving Michigan and a promising career as a football quarterback. She was always an unofficial member of her high school team; girls weren't allowed. But when the big game was near, the coach asked permission of the conference and Peg's parents. Permission was granted and Peg played a magnificent game. We're good buddies and find a great deal to laugh about.

I've reached a point in my life where it's the little things that count. I'm no longer interested in doing what's expected of me. I've had enough of that. Of course, I never did play the game. I was always a rebel and probably would have got much further had I changed my attitude. But when you think about it, I got pretty far without changing attitudes. I'm happier with that.

I love my little jewel box of an apartment. The walls are exactly the shade of white I like. In fact, I had the painter smear eleven shades of white on the wall before I decided on one. I recently had avocado wall-to-wall carpeting installed and that pleases my bare-foot nature perfectly. I eat what I want and drink what I want. For breakfast I love Coke mixed with milk. Or maybe even a glass of Busch Bavarian beer and a pound of grapes. And left-over pizza from the refrigerator.

I seldom answer letters and never return phone calls unless they have to do with business. There was a time when business calls never came. I wasn't at all in demand, and when the phone rang I could pretty much count on it being an irate bill collector from a department store.

But ain't life great? Lately, I find more and more offers coming through to me. I seem to be coming around full circle to the point where Veronica Lake is almost in vogue again. That is not to say I was invited to Truman Capote's party. I wasn't even listed in *Esquire* as one of those who wasn't invited but should have been. But I am working again, working good and worthwhile things, not horror films but good theatre, substantial shows, meaty scripts and warm audiences.

Perhaps the best example of this came on October 28, 1967, in Boston's Hancock Auditorium. It was on that evening that I read *The World of Carl Sandburg* to a small but enthusiastic audience. I was as appalled at the thought of doing it as you probably are at the idea of hearing it.

27

"I HATE Sandburg," I told the producers when they called me in Miami. It was true. I'd met the great poet in an elevator of a New York high-rise building back in the 50's. We both got on the elevator on the thirty-third floor and rode down together. I forgot what the elevator operator said to Sandburg, but it started him off on a tantrum of abuse towards the operator, a sweet little guy minding his own business and doing his job. God, how Sandburg treated that fellow. It got so bad that I had to say something.

"Why don't you shut up, Mr. Sandburg?"

He glared at me, his bushy eyebrows at attention, his eyes boring through me. I must admit he frightened me. Just a little. Just enough to cause me to tense against what I was sure would be a violent outburst. But it never came. He did shut up. He rode the rest of the way in silence, an obvious relief to the elevator operator.

"I hate Sandburg," I repeated on the phone.

"Why?" my caller asked.

I told her the story. She was unimpressed. After much dialogue about many things, I agreed to do the reading. It was after I hung up that I realized it wasn't hatred for Sandburg that caused me to hesitate. I really didn't believe I could effectively read poetry before an audience especially an intellectual Boston audience filled with college students and literature teachers.

I came to New York early in October to see friends and take care of some business. Naturally, I spent a great deal of time with Nat Perlow. His first question upon hearing of the Sandburg thing was, "How much are they paying you?"

"Nothing," I admitted. "It's a benefit for The Hub Theatre Center, Nat. I'm just scared to death I'll fall flat on my face up there."

Nat agreed there was that possibility. But Nat also shrugged it off as he's so capable of doing.

"So fall on your face, Connie. I still think it would be better if they paid you to fall on your face." He lighted a cigar.

"I'm going to need help with this, Nat. Will you help me?"

He took a few puffs and looked me straight in the eye. "What do I know from Sandburg and poetry, Connie? We'll find you some artistic type."

That somebody was Bill Roos, my downstairs neighbor of a few years back. Bill had since moved into a lovely penthouse apartment on Park Avenue, the perfect setting of tranquility for someone trying to make sense out of a poetry reading. And Bill was willing to help me in whatever way I wanted.

The first thing we did was thread a reel of tape on his tape recorder so I could hear myself back. At first, that proved to be the most depressing move I'd ever made. I was awful. To compound it, I couldn't shake the thought that Bette Davis had done the definitive reading of the work, along with Gary Merrill. I remember Miriam Hopkins telling me, "Never work with Bette Davis, Veronica. She's evil, evil."

And then Bette went and said in her own autobiography that one of the most beautiful women she's ever seen was Veronica Lake. I had mixed emotions that were overridden by respect for Bette and her acting. She's so superb, and I felt I would pale in her shadow. But even more upsetting was knowing what a parrot I could be. I found myself giving lines into the recorder with a definite Davis touch; even my hand would swish at times.

Bill proved to be taskmaster. He was sympathetic when indicated, and certainly encouraging. But when I'd throw up my hands in despair, he'd tear into me with just the proper cutting edge to bring me around to a more sensible attitude.

It gradually took shape. The more I worked, the better it seemed to sound. I heard less of Bette Davis and more of Veronica Lake. I was almost pleased.

But any confident pleasure I did muster soon slipped away when I arrived in Boston for the week of rehearsing prior to the one-night performance.

I can't really blame anyone else. The minute the plane touched down at Logan Field, I felt out of my element. Boston, its lofty reputation for academic excellence and literary understanding, settled over me in a stifling cloud of negativism. And I could sense a controlled scepticism on the part of the Hub Theatre people connected with this charitable undertaking. It was understandable, I suppose, for them to accept me with reservations. My name was of value. Of that they were certain. It would bring people to the hall and that's always important. But I had little doubt that each of them watched me perform with the thought and knowledge that they knew a young, budding actress, maybe from acting class of summer stock, who was charged with all the necessary emotions, programed inflection and youthful enthusiasm for the role the work demanded. I don't blame them. But it was discouraging, especially in view of the difficulty I had in coming up with anything near an acceptable rehearsal performance.

The week ground on, day to day, late evening rehearsals piled on top of strenuous daytime work. And nerves stretched into the soprano range and nasty tempers surfaced until it was the night before the performance and all was not well.

That final night was spent rehearsing at the home of a local Jewish couple, lovely people, who, I'm sure, were aghast at the goings-on. As I've mentioned before, there is no fouler mouth than the theatrical mouth. Not that I object. I take no back seat to Norman Mailer. I can gutter talk with the best and have done so on what is probably too many occasions. Filthy talk is accepted in the theatre. It's phoney, really, like all filthy talk is. And funny. "Filthy words do not a dirty book make," is my motto. But it is shocking and, I'm sure, distasteful to people not accustomed to such talk.

My leading man, the only other person in the show except for the guitarist, was a very talented young actor named James Lonigro. His career had been a full and impressive one, including extensive poetry readings as a one-man show touring the nation. Great talent, indeed. And scorn for a former motion-picture actress, born of Hollywood's star-system parents and rocketed to world-wide fame by publicity and more publicity. Because of these feelings, it was hard for Jimmy to act with me. And it was impossible for him to take any criticism from such an inferior and suspect performer.

He was constantly on my back. Finally, about midnight, I snapped. I let loose a stream of invective in a voice loud enough to awaken the swans on Boston's Common. My performance piqued Jimmy to new heights.

"You amateur Hollywood has-been," he screamed as he rushed towards me. He stopped just inches from my face. "You washed-up, petty bitch."

The Jewish couple were peeking around the corner of the doorway. The other members of the troupe stood silently, their expressionless faces masking inner glee at this spicy bit of back-stage banter.

I yelled louder than he did.

"What would you know about *that*?" I shrilled. "You read this play like a fag with a hernia."

We continued this screaming until finally, in one magnificent sweep of my hand, I demanded a cab be called. Rosann Weeks, the director, stepped in between us and managed to cool everything down, the director's true value. The rehearsal was over. Whether there could be a performance remained to be seen.

We rehearsed all Saturday afternoon in Hancock Hall. Things were definitely getting worse, not between Jim Lonigro and me, but in my ability to perform my role. I couldn't remember a line, I dropped every cue I had and struggled to gain voice level needed in the large auditorium. At five, the time we had to vacate the hall, I was a miserable wreck of an actress. A deathly silence had pervaded the hall, a silence that reeked of disaster.

The show was at eight-thirty. If I ever wanted a swallow of Scotch it was then. But that was not the answer. It never is. I contented myself with deep breathing and knuckle cracking as David Bernard performed magic on my hair. He had me looking almost like my early star days, with the hair length modified, of course. I looked better so I felt better. Jim and I had no communication since the blow-up the night before. I was certain it showed on stage. It ran through my mind that the worse thing that could happen to me was if Jim in any way displayed nastiness or scorn for me during the performance. I dwelled on that thought until I was able to displace it with the confidence that he was a professional actor, far above that kind of petty action.

My mind swung back to the dress rehearsal that had just been concluded. The pace of the show was bad, most of it my fault. What was it Rosann had said? "The first act is a half-hour too long, Ronnie. Pick it up. Pick it up." I wanted to just walk away from it, go back to Miami and my jewel box and my Philco TV and its cowboy movies. But I'm a pro, too. I'm above the disappearing act. I'll be there. Just let me be good.

The size of the audience was disappointing. But we had formidable competition. Harvard was in the midst of its homecoming week-end and Ravi Shankar, the hippie's sitar player supreme, was performing to crowds that formed lines two blocks long. I knew some of my friends from New York, led by Nat Perlow, had planned to attend the show. I viewed that with mixed emotions. It was flattering to have them there but disconcerting in the thought of failing their faith.

"How's the house?" I asked one of the backstage people.

"Tiny," she responded. "Maybe fifty at best."

Quite a comedown, I thought, as I recalled the time when I couldn't show my face anywhere without attracting a crowd. Boston was no exception. One example came to mind that occurred during the mid-fifties. I was shopping in the famous Filene's basement store. I've always been a compulsive bargain hunter and there is no greater bargain haven than Filene's. I was with a Swedish friend of mine and we both were dressed very plainly. I wore no make-up, had a kerchief over my head and a coat with the collar turned up. We were doing fine. No one recognized me. Well, no one until I heard a young woman say to her shopping companion, "That's Veronica Lake." That did it. The word got around and people began coming up to me and starting conversations. We left very quickly.

People who haven't experienced fame tend to think of it as wonderful. They secretly wish they would be recognized wherever they go. It's human and no one is immune from this kind of wishing.

But it becomes terribly old after you've gone through it for a while. You find yourself dreading a shopping trip or dining out. It's all so flattering in the beginning but so dreadful and bothersome in the end. The problem is it's so hard to convince someone that feeling that way is not dishonorable and high-hatted. A public adopts you as communal property. I don't buy that. I fulfil my obligation to my public by performing as best I know how. After that, I belong to me and those I choose to share me with.

But strangely enough, once you've experienced fame and the annoyance of public recognition, you can find yourself craving it after a long hiatus from it. Some former stars suffer worse than others in this regard. I happen to fall victim to only minor and brief cravings. One of those times was at Hancock Hall where a theatre full of admirers would have been welcomed with open arms.

"That's a shame," I answered the girl with the news of the very light house.

"Maybe it's just as well," she muttered and walked away. There were many ways to take that remark but I took it personally. And maybe she was right.

I again come to a point in this book where the autobiographical nature of the work proves inhibiting. How can I relate the success of my performance without revealing a picture of the egotistical woman? I can't. So I'll present that picture and beg understanding.

I walked out onto that stage and was met with the warmest applause of my life. Its quality made up for any lack of quantity. And it continued. It was like an intravenous feeding of joy juice, an overdose of happy pills and whole blood. And there's nothing a performer reacts better to than acceptance and applause.

Jim Lonigro was marvelous. Our interplay was warm and spontaneous. There were times when it seemed appropriate to comment off-the-cuff. Everything worked. Yes, there were flubs and rough moments. But even these were glossed over by Jim or me. It was one of the finest moments of my life. I cried a few times on stage, initially to do with the audience reception, later during one of Sandburg's more poignant pieces. It's titled *Out of Windows Look Mother Faces*. It ends with . . .

> . . . Out of windows look mother faces
> Knowing love is a deep well
> And a mirror of shadow-changes:

Here looms water for a deep thirst,
Here gleams a looking-glass too dark
To print a face and foretell a fate
And bring a moan:

Poor Michael.

And what of Elizabeth Umpsteadt of whom Sandburg wrote
with such understanding and fondness? Indiana was Elizabeth's
Hollywood. She's all of us.

I am Elizabeth Umpsteadt, dead at seventy-five years of age,
and they are taking me in a polished and silver-plated box
today, and an undertaker, assured of cash for his work, will
supply straps to let the box down the lean dirt walls, while
a quartet of singers—assured of cash for their work, sings
"Nearer My God To Thee," and a clergyman, also assured
of cash for his services—will pronounce the words: "Dust to
dust and ashes to ashes."

I am gone from among the two-legged moving figures on
top the earth now, and nobody will say my heart is some-
way wrong when I assert, I was the most beautiful nigger
girl in Northern Indiana; and men wanted my beauty, white
men and black men—they wanted to take it and crush it and
taste it—and I learned what they wanted and I traded on it;
I schemed and haggled to get all I could for it—and so I am
one nigger girl who today has a grand funeral with all the
servitors paid in spot cash.

I learned early, away back in short dresses, when a lawyer
took me and used me the same as a brass cuspidor or a new
horse and buggy or a swivel chair or anything that gives
more life-ease for spot cash. He paid $600 cash to me for
the keep of the child of my womb and his loins. And then he
went to a revival, sang "Jesus Knows All About Our Trou-
bles," moaned he was a sinner and wanted Jesus to wash
his sins away. He joined the church and stood up one night
before hundreds of people and blabbed to them how he used
me, had a child by me, and paid me $600 cash. And I waited

till one night I saw him in the public square; and I slashed his face with a leather horsewhip, calling him all the wild crazy names that came to my tongue to damn him and damn him and damn him, for a sneak in the face of God and man. Well . . . they put me in a grave today, and I leave behind one child fathered by a white man lawyer, thousands of dollars in the bank, eight houses I owned as property in the same way my mother was owned as property by white men in Tennessee. All these I leave behind me—I, who was the most beautiful nigger girl in northern Indiana.

The curtain fell. We took many bows. I cried. Jim was sweet and praised me with sincerity. And then I raced for my dressing-room, opened a bottle of Scotch and filled a water glass. It went down so nicely, penetrating my nerve ends and putting them to rest. I relaxed for the first time in a week. And people started coming back to see me, wish me well, tell me how well I'd done on stage. There was Nat Perlow, Courtney Wright, Joe Garri, a long-time fan, Warren Rideout who's collected so much on me over the years, and a very special fan, one whom I'd never met but whose story came back to me the instant he brought up the incident. When this man was a small boy, he was afflicted with some sort of disease that left him partially incapacitated. The family doctor suggested his taking up a quiet but interesting hobby to help him pass the time and fill the void his illness created. He chose, of all things, to collect and save pictures and stories about Veronica Lake. It was during my active Hollywood days. He sent me various photographs and I auto-graphed them. He told me in letters of his illness and I felt terribly close to him. We never met, until that night in the dressing-room. I was sitting at my dressing-table, Scotch in hand, loose robe thrown over the underthings. People were milling about and we were all laughing, too loud and sometimes forced, at comments and jokes about the performance. My visitor, now grown into manhood, stood quietly just inside the dressing-room door. Finally, he came over and started to talk. He mentioned those letters and photographs and I remembered immediately. And for some reason, I felt uneasy, embarrassed at the drink, my let-down hair, my loud laughter and four-letter-word vocabulary.

He didn't stay long. When he left, I wanted to run after him, hold on to him and let him take me back to those days when I truly meant something to someone. The whole thing, as brief as it was, touched me deeply. But it was also frightening, that momentary slip backwards, too dangerous to dwell on.

One of the Hub Theatre people, Harron Ellinson, threw a very last-minute and informal party after the show. It took everyone hours to find her apartment and even longer to rustle up extra chairs and booze. I was a little loaded from the dressing-room drinking and felt high as a kite. I wore my West Point gray athletic T-shirt, dirty slacks and slippers. I was definitely the most under-dressed person at the party, but I was entitled, I figured. There were a lot of people I'd never seen before and everyone soon settled into a comfortable and happy party mood. I was having a long conversation with a lovely Irish girl, Fran Richer, who was there with her husband. I admired the dress she was wearing.

"I love your dress. Where did you get it?"

"My favorite bargain spot," she answered. "Filene's basement. Ever been there?" There was a glint in her eyes that indicated she already knew the answer to that question.

I started to tell her about my one and only trip to Filene's when she laughed and interrupted me.

"I know all about it. I was the gal who spotted you and sent you running."

That's the problem with growing older. Those vicious, concentric circles that give meaning to the small world adage get tighter and tighter and swirl closer and more often to your life. And pretty soon they wrap around you and get rid of you.

There is talk of my doing a national tour of *The World Of Carl Sandburg*. I'd like that, I think. My uncertainty stems from fear of moving out and away for too long a period of time. My new-found peace is at stake; I wish no more of the world's deals. I want to work. I know I will more and more. But spare me the high pressure of success. I've been there.

What is it like, this business of being an ex-star living the middle-class life in Miami?

It's delightful. Truly it is. After living a life that seems to have been one great big game of blind-man's-buff, I've found my groove, settled into it and I fit fine. They pamper me in Miami, this aging movie star, and I react to the pampering like a hungry pussy cat. The more they stroke, the more I purrrrrrrr, belly sated with milk and Coke, bare feet massaged by carpet, a working telephone. And some friends.

I have a lot of gay friends in Miami. Miami has a lot of gay people with whom to make friends. I really have no desire to go into a discourse on why heterosexual people should buddy around with homosexual people. I simply do and enjoy every gay minute of it. My "Nellie" friends have crowned me unofficial champion of the pool table, a little skill I learned in Texas. I'm really not very proficient with a cue stick, but they've been kind enough to honor me with this title. There was a time long ago when a homosexual revolted me. So did a lot of other types of human beings. I've changed. Don't hurt me, allow me a mis-cue now and then and I'll accept you. Who the hell am I not to accept anybody?

As they say, I've learned to cool it. I fish and enjoy that pleasant activity. I enjoy riding past where Robert Frost lived and sometimes I sail with friends, and other times I don't do anything. That's probably the most fun of all. It's very difficult to fail at doing nothing and everyone could benefit from occasional success, no matter how small the challenge.

I will continue to work at my trade. I both need and want to work as an actress. And to live. The world looks very different through *both* eyes. It takes on dimension. It's safe.

Long live short hair.

VERONICA LAKE
(1922-1973)

Made in the USA
Monee, IL
22 June 2021

71945072R00125